D0910029

Twayne's Theatrical Arts Series

Warren French
EDITOR

Alain Resnais

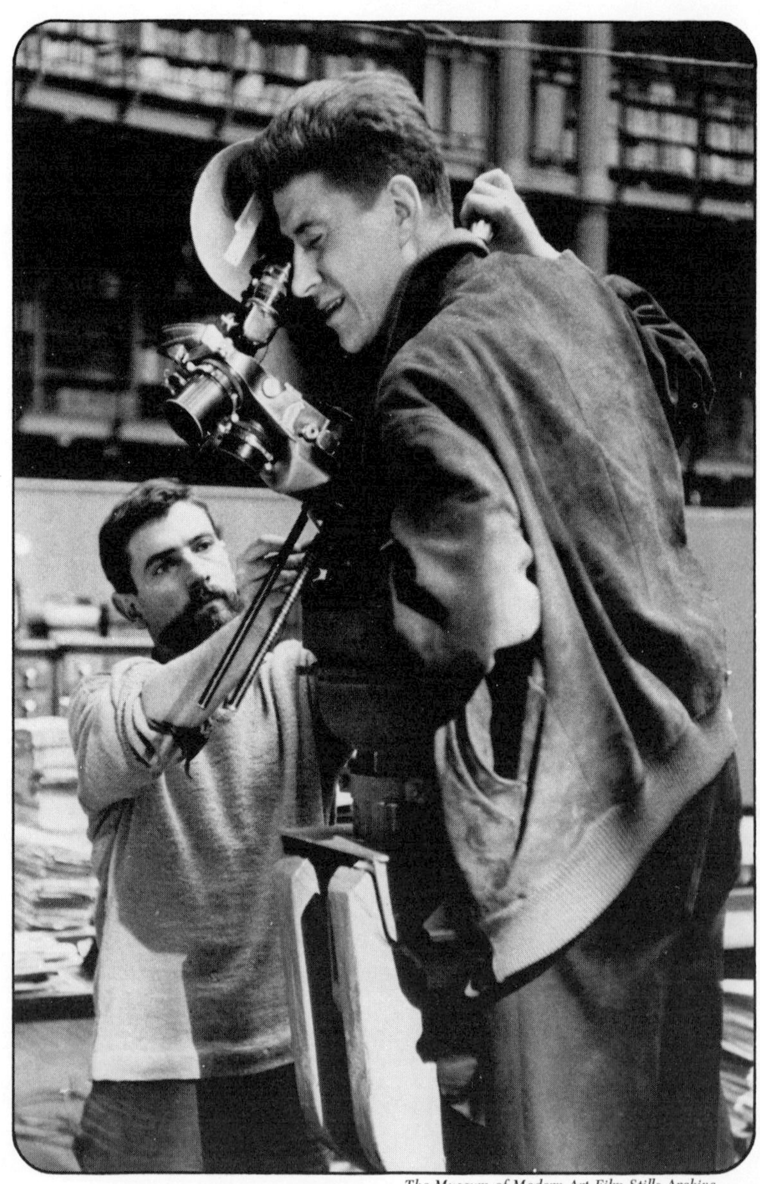

The Museum of Modern Art Film Stills Archive

Alain Resnais

Alain Resnais

JOHN FRANCIS KREIDL

BOSTON

Twayne Publishers

1977

Alain Resnais
is first published in 1978 by Twayne Publishers,
A Division of G. K. Hall & Co.

Printed on permanent/durable acid-free paper and bound
in the United States of America

First Printing, October 1978

Library of Congress Cataloging in Publication Data

Kreidl, John Francis
Alain Resnais.

(Twayne's theatrical arts series)
Bibliography: P. 237 - 42
Filmography: p. 243 - 47
Includes index.
1. Resnais, Alain, 1922 -
PN1998.A3R4815 1978 791.43'023'0924 78-12462
ISBN 0-8057-9256-2

Contents

About the Author

John Francis Kreidl's involvement with film dates from childhood and the film club founded by his father, Dr. Norbert Kreidl, who developed the glass used for the CinemaScope lens. Mr. Kreidl attended Swarthmore College and the University of Rochester. He has also been associated with Harvard University's Carpenter Center for Visual Arts.

Mr. Kreidl has been active as a film scholar and filmmaker since 1963. His publications include articles and reviews in popular and scholarly media and the recently published study, *Nicholas Ray*, in Twayne's Theatrical Arts Series.

Editor's Foreword

Because Alain Resnais began to make strikingly original feature films at the same time at the end of the 1950's as François Truffaut and Jean-Luc Godard, he is often linked with them as one of the founders of the "New Wave" that has exercised unique influence upon international filmmaking. Most film historians dispute this bracketing, however, arguing that Resnais was not one of the group who moved from outraged criticism—principally in André Bazin's *Cahiers du Cinema*—of conventional French directors to bringing their personal visions to life on the screen, providing along the way the since controversial theory of auteurist criticism and some of the important evidence in support of it. Resnais was rather an independent individual—an isolated figure like many of his fellow Bretons—who moved to film from the stage.

As John Kreidl points out in this study, although Resnais has many associations with the "New Wave," he differs from Truffaut and Godard, Rivette and Chabrol in the emphasis that he places upon the writer of the screenplay. Like many theatrical directors, Resnais sees himself primarily as an interpreter of a text. He has collaborated in his most highly regarded films with such creators of the "New Novel" as Marguerite Duras and Alain Robbe-Grillet, who have subsequently directed their own films. As Kreidl demonstrates, Resnais' success has been directly proportionate to the strength of the scripts that he has translated into films. Provided with excellent material as for *Last Year at Marienbad* and *Muriel,* he has produced innovative classics; from mediocre material, he has produced his least successful film, *Je T'Aime, Je T'Aime.*

Kreidl also argues that Resnais may prove at last the most important creative force in giving the cinema new direction in the second half of the twentieth century. Resnais' later films have not enjoyed the popular success or critical acclaim of "Night and Fog," *Hiroshima, Mon Amour,* or *Last Year at Marienbad;* yet *Muriel* is arguably his greatest achievement so far, and *Stavisky* has added a new dimension to filmed biography as *Providence* has to comedy. Kreidl feels, however, that the lesser success of Resnais' more recent efforts may be the result of his having moved too fast, too far ahead of his audiences, and that only if we continue to take cinema seriously as an art form will other filmmakers and viewers begin to catch up with Resnais' achievements, as so far only some of the new generation of unorthodox West German filmmakers have.

Whether or not future developments confirm Kreidl's diagnosis, Resnais clearly stands apart from his contemporaries as an artist who has refused to repeat himself and has rather moved ahead—as he has been granted the opportunities—to explore new creative possibilities. Because of the increasing difficulties of obtaining financing of expensive projects in this world of the conglomerates, Resnais has probably paid for his integrity and restless inventiveness by a slowing down of the opportunities that he has been afforded to experiment with new subjects and techniques.

In view of the unique pioneering aspects of Resnais' works, a thorough study of his achievement is essential to any comprehensive survey of the development of cinematic art. John Kreidl in this book avoids simply summarizing once more Resnais' complementary relationship to the New Wave and puzzling out a chronological arrangement of the events presented in his early non-linear films (an effort entirely at odds with the director's major concerns); rather he opens up such new subjects as the influence of American comic book style on Resnais' techniques and the relationship between his unique art and subsequent experimentation by others. Kreidl attempts to do for criticism what Resnais has done for film—break away from accepted models and fashionable preoccupations and see what can be done to make the work of a significant artist more accessible to curious audiences rather than exploit this work as a vehicle for projecting the critic's hang-ups.

Kreidl repeatedly stresses that Resnais insists that the audience must not be just passively entertained, but must participate actively, energetically in creating for themselves the story behind what transpires on the screen. Similarly, Kreidl's book seeks not to impose a limiting interpretation of individual films upon readers, but rather to provide liberating evidence that may encourage viewers to transcend their inhibitions and enter with Resnais into the creation of films as the transaction that he envisions. Surely if more filmmakers with such a challenging, open-ended vision and audiences equal to the demands that it presents continue to emerge, a significant future for film as an art form may indeed lie before us and our debt to Alain Resnais may be incalculable.

WARREN FRENCH

Preface

Alain Resnais is a hard filmmaker to place in the context of a movement. Unlike the New Wavers or Neo-Realists, unlike even Jean-Luc Godard or Alfred Hitchcock—who can be viewed as one-man movements—Resnais is difficult to locate in the history of cinema because he is at once ultramodern in narrative technique and old-fashioned in image construction. It is a bit easier to locate him within a French intellectual tradition. One could in fact ask the question: Resnais, Baudelairian dandy or artist? Is Resnais more of a descendant of Baudelaire and Proust than of Louis Lumière (1864–1948) and Georges Méliès (1861–1938)? Is not Resnais' *Providence* a lusty film closer to Auguste Renoir's heart than any of the films of his director-son, Jean? The answer is that Resnais does fit into French film history, but as a descendant of Louis Feuillade (1873–1925) rather than Lumière or Méliès.

One school of thought sees Resnais as a pessimistic realist and puts him with Italian directors like Michelangelo Antonioni. This is where, for example, the Marxist critics who like him, put him. I, however, see *Hiroshima Mon Amour, Last Year at Marienbad, La Guerre Est Finie*, and *Providence* as sad rather than pessimistic films, films which show tiny flickers of light at the end of their tunnels, but only after an overpoweringly skeptical discourse has told you to watch out even about that. Be an optimist if you can, Resnais dares you, after stacking the evidence to the contrary. This attitude, of course, is not inconsistent with Marxist materialism. There is, furthermore—not surprisingly—little evidence of any propagandizing for religion in Resnais' films. Yet his films are laden with a secular mystification (but not mythification) that I have not seen in any other cinema save that of Werner Herzog. Resnais' films seem then to fall outside both the realistic and the mythic, two of the prime areas in which cinema has operated. This failure to fall into a major, definable, consumer category has undoubtedly hurt Resnais commercially.

The critical attention Resnais' cinema has received is far out of proportion to its commercial success. (No Resnais film has ever appeared on *Variety*'s "grossed more than five million dollar" list.) One has to try and reconcile this discrepancy. Why are those of his films which have attracted so much critical attention not better known? Is he a "director's director," the analog to a "musician's musician," which is a polite way of saying that only directors, cineastes and critics understand him? Are his films even more complex than Jean-Luc Godard's—and aren't Godard's films really only tolerated in America because of their intelligence? Does a Resnais film not sell because of lack of sex? of youth? How does one reconcile Resnais' greatness with his relative obscurity?

One reason, obviously, is that Resnais, the man, is not a familiar personality. (He has never been an American TV talk-show guest!) Sad to say, in the United States, ten times as many people are familiar with the name Godard or François Truffaut than with his. Godard became a radical household word on the American campus in the late 1960s, and Truffaut has had an unbroken string of his films distributed in the United States from 1960 on and has conveniently provided one for every New York Film Festival since 1973. Resnais was on the verge of a reputation right after *Marienbad* in 1962, but *Muriel* which followed in 1963 was not what critics call a commercial breakthrough film in either France or America. A remarkably alive film, *Muriel* sailed over the head of the Pauline Kaels and under the legs of the Susan Sontag and failed to land on receptive turf. Also, even the critical success of *Marienbad* never made Resnais popular very far away from urban centers or the review pages of the slick *Film Comment* magazine. As a consequence, his name remains to most an incantatory word, uttered in the name of art cinema. The purpose of this book is to shatter this cliché—to make Resnais better known.

Its purpose is also to show why, among all well-respected, world-famous filmmakers, Alain Resnais is the most unique. Within the pantheon of Orson Welles, Ingmar Bergman, Federico Fellini, etc., Resnais is a singular talent, as this book will demonstrate, using his seven feature films as illustrations of his intent, as well as "reading" them as film texts.

What I hope will emerge is an explanation of the two ways Resnais modernized film narrative: first, on the level of preparing the narrative for filming, by using the most modern scripts with multiple metonymic and shifting narrators; second, on the level of filming and editing the narrative, by shooting his films achronologically —i.e., by making each shot not a piece of a preplanned spatial-temporal decoupage (a chain of glued-together storyboard frames or units put on a string), but a point-space "concurrence" left open for the spectator to put into a time-respecting text he makes up. In this way, a Resnais film deals with time through the spectator's recreating it. Thus Resnais has successfully solved the problem in film of how to show two or three stories that do happen at the same time, actually occurring simultaneously. (By destroying filmic time, Resnais can thrust the fragmented stories of several characters at us and ask us to re-create the time sense of the film.) Thus Resnais made, by his own choice, a major concern the evolution of a technique which he could only have dealt with in the film medium.

The advantage of his kind of "open" film over others is obvious. One can make films that discuss philosophical problems or "show what cannot be said," as Ludwig Wittgenstein would have phrased it. Wittgenstein's philosophy—which primarily concerns itself with self-help in thinking—is closely analogous to the goal of Resnais' films. Resnais' philosophic interests could have turned him towards any of the narrative arts. He could very well have become a theater director or a photographer. Instead, he chose film, as one would choose medicine or law, as an intellectual form rather than as a craft occupation. In fact, he could be considered to be more interested in the intellectual and aesthetic problems that a film could solve than in the filmmaking profession as such, as his only published essay (see Chapter One) strongly suggests.

Resnais is a consummate stylist. Style, we must recall, is the suppression of the arbitrary. A Resnais film, though it seems unmanipulative of the audience, is highly manipulated, but towards a freedom of choice for the spectator. Here we see Resnais' intellect superseding aestheticism. Resnais' films tend to fall into two patterns: they are either "operatic" *(Hiroshima Mon Amour,* and *Muriel)* or associative *(Marienbad, La Guerre Est Finie, Je T'Aime, Stavisky,* and *Providence).* The soundtracks of the first two films are as important as the images and make them operatic. Resnais' narratives unfold almost exclusively associatively. The associative strain in Resnais comes from his love of comic books, photoessays, and other image-narratives that he grew up with.

Resnais' cinema has mistakenly been appreciated for its formal quality, and many a film course has followed the error of looking at *Marienbad* as an exercise in form rather than one in narrative. The uniqueness of Resnais' film lies elsewhere than in its formal devices. His films are elegant but they are neither exercises in form nor are they "arty."

Resnais' trick—how he makes his cinema work—is based exclusively on how he forces themes onto his plots. His filmmaking process goes like this. First he selects a skilled writer to give him a screenplay (Marguerite Duras, Alain Robbe-Grillet, Jean Cayrol, Jorge Semprun, Jacques Steinberg, and David Mercer have all written for Resnais). He then forces his own theme on the screenplay. The film that results confirms that it is Resnais' theme and not the screenplay that he wishes to convey, and this is borne out by the way he shoots and edits the film. None of Resnais' films retains even half the intent of the original screenplay. The screenplays exist to provide a basis for Resnais' work; they are tools, means to an end.

The three big Resnais themes are (1) the impossibility of documenting, (2) the presence of the absent, (3) the return of the repressed. The first two of these themes are philosophical, basically ontological. The last belongs to psychology and is a Freudian concept. To write a successful critical book on Alain Resnais, we need to scan each of Resnais' seven feature films using each of these three topologies. For example, using "the impossibility of documenting," we will find a solid statement about this subject in four of the seven feature films he has made, as the following explanations show.

Hiroshima Mon Amour. The documentary film that is supposedly in process (i.e., the film within a film Emmanuelle Riva is supposedly an actress in) is never made. All we see of it are unmanned set-ups. The sense of this is that Resnais seems to be making a statement: one cannot document the day of the atomic bombing of Hiroshima.

Muriel. Bernard, the documentarist, quits in disgust near the end of the film and concludes his film-within-a-film documentary effort by throwing his camera into the sea after which he commits a murder. Bernard's confidence in exposing evil through a documentary film has, apparently, eroded to zero.

La Guerre Est Finie. What is a true Spanish revolutionary? the film asks. One who remembers the Spanish Civil War. But who remembers the Spanish Civil War accurately? The hero, Diego, admits he doesn't. He says that no one can document what it was.

Stavisky. Who was Serge Alexandre Stavisky? The film treats him as an enigma and leaves him an enigma. In fact, *Stavisky* is almost a film about the impossibility of documenting Stavisky. At a certain point, it meanders off to document Leon Trotsky, about whom more is known.

The most singular aspect of Resnais' cinema is how he has reversed the classic Hollywood relation of foregrounding actors against illusionary backgrounds. In his films, the background is the foreground. The skeptical reader may ask: Is Resnais the only director to have made a cinema with time-space as foreground and the incarnation of a character role the background? Is he the first to have made a cinema that requires the spectator to construct his own narrative and, therefore, to come closest to solving the fundamental problem of how to modernize film narrative? It is a problem that will at last be solved, if twenty years from now we are still taking the cinema seriously. In modernizing film narrative, Resnais became involved in reconciling the opposition of the novel and the film, a controversy that raged between 1935 and 1958 and about which we hear no more (see Chapter Three). In this area, his work was part of that of the New Wave.

Why credit Resnais entirely for this? Why not praise Bergman? Why not cite Fellini? Credit Godard? Is not the history of cinema mostly characterized by collective advances rather than individual breakthroughs? The above is generally true, but not in the case of the cinema of time that Resnais improvised. There are long, complex arguments to be made, showing that Bergman, Fellini, Godard, and Welles, despite each of their singular ways of complexly handling complicated themes, never "solved" (perhaps "resolved" would be a better word) the problem of inventing a new level of film discourse that would address the spectator—in Resnais' words, "in a critical state of mind."[1] Fellini stuck to mirror structures and "doubling" (thereby calling attention to himself) but never dealt with—for all his interest in creativity—man versus time. Bergman for his part mostly wanted to show the psychological state of mind of his characters and manipulated narrative to give us filmed Strindberg but never went much beyond the narrative ideas of Freudian plays and the manifestations of the unconscious. Bergman remains a great *second* generation director, moving from the conscious to the unconscious.

Jean-Luc Godard was also a second generation filmmaker until *Two or Three Things I Know About Her,* which is a film highly influenced by Resnais. Godard also did not repeat the structure of this film, though he proved he could admirably handle the approach. Godard has returned to discursive films and seems no longer to be interested in approaching reality Resnais' way. Perhaps, of Welles, Cocteau, Bergman, Godard, and Fellini, Jean Cocteau (1889–1963) is the only one who has successfully dealt with time in film. Bergman and Fellini are obsessed with dream structures, which is not the same thing as dealing with time. Their dream structure comes from the Expressionistic toolbox of filmcraft and is not an effort to restructure the film in order to make it an ontological exploration. Resnais has no "dreams" in his films.

We return then to Resnais' desire to address the spectator in "a critical state of mind." Clearly, this means he does not want to be just another maker of films of illusion: larger than life, and yet not of life, but just of the filmmaker. He depersonalizes himself in order to make the film more personal for you, the viewer. That is why I love Resnais' cinema. As I hope to show in this book, the effect is achieved by a style of authorial disguise known as metonymy. This is what gives the Resnais film its mystery (who is the author? who is speaking?) and at the same time, its privacy and clarity for the spectator. Clearly, Resnais loves the spectator, and because of this feeling he is back in the company of all great and mediocre film directors alike. But, I believe that Resnais stands alone, as the only major film director who believes that the film spectator deserves being addressed in third generation film language. As Resnais has said, "I love to get lost in a film for about ten minutes, and then discover what is going on." The spectator cannot love a film if it is made too easy.

Thus Resnais puts all his filmmaking eggs into one basket. All his films seek the same goal: "To address the spectator in a critical state of mind." Thus, above all, his cinema—every film—is a gamble.

While reading this book the reader should become aware of how Resnais' self-defined limitations with concocting narratives affects the scripts he chooses and the kinds of films he makes. One will gradually perceive (1) why he makes very few films, (2) why he must stick to "Resnais" themes: time, Proustian memory, Mallarmé's negative surrealism, and (3) why he must pick his screenwriter/co-authors very carefully. These are the doors that open up the method of Resnais' cinema, and once having entered, the reader will be well on the way towards interpreting Resnais perhaps in a more personal way than this book can suggest. At any rate the above are the interplaying forces which determine the success or failure of a Resnais film. In each of the chapters on the individual films, the reader should always remain aware of Resnais' unusual strength in conveying ontological explorations with the camera as well as his unusual handicap for dealing with conventional narrative.

Now a final word on the question of authorship. Resnais often does not want to admit publicly to what he does; therefore he hides behind his co-authorial relationships. But he has altered every script he has ever filmed. As a result of this intriguing paradox, *every* Resnais film transcends its script well beyond the impossibility of creating an isomorphic construct in one medium that has been taken from another (so that any film is naturally different from its screenplay). What we find is that whenever Resnais' manipulatory intents have been discussed, they are remarkably consistent with what he has finally achieved in the film. This revelation apparently confirms his entry into the authorial process right from the start of the story conferences. What is his interest and motivation in this manipulation? It seems that he is not concerned with "how the story will come out," but with what he can do to the narrative to make it into an experiment in film form. For this reason, he wants to begin with only certain pliable types of narratives. In *Marienbad,* Resnais transcended Robbe-Grillet's script; in *Muriel,* he enhanced rather than transcended the ideas in the script; and in *Providence,* a film which was concerned with a writer's problems but approached this concern in film form, Resnais used the extra-mediumistic approach to advantage. On the other hand, the scripts for *Hiroshima, La Guerre Est Finie* and *Stavisky* are of only average quality. The films Resnais made using these scripts vary in quality. *Hiroshima* is a superb film which transcends the limitations of its script; *La Guerre Est Finie* has fine moments but is, on the whole, an average film in which Resnais seems to have simply contended with the script; *Stavisky* is an average film which shares the strengths and weaknesses of its script. The script Resnais used for *Je T'Aime, Je T' Aime* was flawed by overintellectualization, a weakness that was carried over to the film.

Is Resnais, then, as successful an innovator as he is a daring one? The answer lies in the texts of his films wherein we will see both the earnestness of Resnais' attempts to solve the problems he set himself and the remarkable blend of intellect, character, and intuition that he brings to the task, as well as the extent to which he is successful. It is interesting to note, and perhaps appropriate at the closing of this Preface, that Resnais himself finds it difficult to describe his own films. Win Sharples describes this difficulty tellingly:

> Resnais' analyses of his own films seem to be those of another, betraying a strange and surprising sense of his own work's separate existence and unfathomability. He resembles a prowling archeologist, searching relentlessly through the shards and fragments of his own sarcophagus, striving to understand the meaning of his own existence, to unearth some key to the purpose for his life and work. Resnais is unique as the artist-critic, as post-interpreter set at a strange abstracted distance from his own work, indeed almost viewing it as the work of others. But not of other people; more of other forces both without (Fate) and within (Intuition) but in any case ungoverned, uncomprehended, and warily to be watched.[2]

The closest definition we can provide for Resnais, the man, is that he appears to be a realist with mystical—though not mythic—tendencies. The closest we come to defining his films is that they seem to represent the positive pole of the twenties-originated, anti-subjective art movement called *die Neue Sachlichkeit* (the New Materialism), something defined by G. Hartlaub as "an enthusiasm for naked truth, that stems from the wish to see things completely objectively and in their material form without their being burdened *a priori* with ideas."

I hope, then, this book will represent Resnais correctly and will introduce the reader more easily to the remarkable world of his cinema than would be possible merely from reading Resnais' interviews.

Acknowledgments

I would like to thank Nick Browne for letting me participate in a seminar on *Muriel* at Harvard University, and John Lvov, Resnais' second assistant on *Providence,* for information on the shooting of that film. I would like to thank Julia Rowe for assisting me in the fine points of translating some of the interviews with Resnais into English, though I take full responsibility for their accuracy. I wish to thank French Canadian filmmaker, Michel Brault, for insights into honesty in the documentary process and German filmmaker, Hark Bohm, for reminding me of the real purpose of film. I would like to thank the late Dr. Ekkehard Kreidl for discussions on time-space.

I would like to thank Andre Gadaud of the French Embassy Cultural Section in New York and Mary Corliss for stills and Boyd A. Norcross, Jr., for frame enlargements.

Finally, thanks to A. H. v. C. for giving me the patience to deal with Resnais not just as a filmmaker but to try to define what makes him an artist.

Chronology

1922 Alain Resnais born June 3, in Vannes, Brittany.
1938 Completes High School.
1940 Moves to Paris, studies acting, lives on Proust's old street, the Rue de Courcelles.
1944 Attends Institute des Hautes Études Cinématographiques for one year.
1945 In the French Army.
1946 Makes first feature film and first documentary in 16mm.
1948 *Van Gogh*, first film in 35mm.
1955 Makes *Night and Fog*.
1959 *Hiroshima Mon Amour*.
1961 *Last Year At Marienbad*.
1963 *Muriel*.
1966 *La Guerre Est Finie*.
1967 Contributes to *Loin du Viet-nam*.
1968 *Je T'Aime, Je T'Aime*.
1969 October 7, marries Florence Malraux, daughter of André Malraux.
1970 Spends most of two years in New York City.
1974 *Stavisky*.
1977 *Providence*, first English language film.

1

Alain Resnais

Resnais: The Early Years

RESNAIS WAS BORN A BRETON. He speaks the Vannetais dialect of lower Brittany and claims he speaks French with a slight Breton accent. Unlike many other French directors of his generation (and we should consider him the eldest member of the Godard-Truffaut generation, rather than one of the older generation that includes Orson Welles, in the United States, and Jean-Pierre Melville, in France) he was not a Parisian nor even ever more than a visiting intellectual in the French capital. There is something markedly peripheral about Resnais' cultural geography. He belongs to the western European world of culture more than to any one place, something that should be quite obvious if one considers the geographic loci of his films. Like his same-age colleagues, Chris Marker or cinematographer Sasha Vierney, Resnais was old enough to have been a veteran of World War II and to have known the sweetness of life before the atomic revolution, yet young enough to share in the grand adventure of reshaping the course of cinema that swept France in the late 1950s. As it did for Eric Rohmer and Jacques Rivette, Paris represented for Resnais an upward mobility, a place where the action was, and thus something to conquer.

The Breton, like Resnais, in France, is thought to have a particular character—that of a traditionalist who works hard—a person who is more likely to be a DeGaullist than a Marxist, someone austere, concrete, yet with a mystical tradition (the Bretons like the Welsh are Celts). France's supermarket king is a Breton. Other famous Bretons were Jacques Cartier, who gave the name to Canada, Chateaubriand, and Bertrand du Guescelin, who drove the English out of southwestern France. For seven hundred years, until the

'annes, Brittany, Alain Resnais' birthplace.

ervices Culturels de l'Ambassade de France

sixteenth century, Brittany was an independent country; and Resnais grew up only a half mile from the ancestral castle of the former Dukes of Brittany.

Resnais was born in Vannes, a town of thirty thousand people, on 3 June 1922, the son of Pierre Resnais, a pharmacist, and Jeanne Gachet, one of those mothers important in the development of artists. It is of paramount importance in understanding his shaping as a filmmaker to note that Resnais grew up in calm isolation and that he gathered around him—amidst aloof, quiet calm—the toys he would use to adult effect: an 8mm camera, comics, and the novels his mother, possibly out of compassion for his asthmatic condition which seemed to develop when he was around eight, taught him to love: the novels of the asthmatic Proust and the short stories of the tubercular Katherine Mansfield. From Proust he would come into the world of Bergson's *Time and Free Will,* thereby learning Einsteinian space-time relativity without even knowing it; and from Mansfield he would learn the prosody that makes things look transparent, that lets their significance break through the surface and become highly visible and accessible.

His temperament was the paradoxical one of the Breton: concrete action-orientation touched with and tempered by Welsh-Celtic mysticism, Flying Dutchman legends, and a belief in startling coincidences as the norm of life. In Resnais' world, one works hard while allowing oneself to be haunted by visions. Many such generalizations about Bretons seem pertinent to Resnais, for one sees them displayed in his films as much as one sees tough provincial Catholicism and Germanic precision in the films of Eric Rohmer as a function of *his* unusual background as a Franco-German Lorrainer.

Resnais was a child during the French cinema's great avant-garde period of Louis Delluc, Germaine Dulac, René Clair, and Marcel L'Herbier, during which a powerful tradition was laid down and the second generation of French cinema strove to make film into the "seventh art." When Resnais was six, the era of the sound cinema began. Never a devotee of more than the visual style of 1920s films, especially L' Herbier's, Resnais once said that he considered the silent black and white film era "an accident. Film should have sound and color normally,"[1] he said, rejecting Kracauer's claim that cinema originally grew out of black and white still photography.

When Resnais was seven, the Great Depression began; but France was the one country in the Western world that was never seriously thrown back on emergency measures (France never had more than eight percent unemployed). Thus Resnais was personally little affected by the tumult of the decade. The pessimism of surrealism, which made itself noticeably felt in France, surely came to his notice; but by and large he and the French cinema continued as inexorable a middle-class existence as if the stability of France had changed not at all since the time of Auguste Renoir and the impressionistic era of peace and confidence.

During Resnais' childhood, Proust died in his cork-walled Parisian apartment on the Boulevard Housmann. Earlier, before his mother's death, Proust had lived on the Rue de Courcelles, where Resnais (out of some strange homage) would later live. Because his school attendance was affected by asthma, he received something of a home education; and, as we have mentioned, his mother's strong predilection for Proust was passed on to him.

Yet I find it curious—with so much written about Resnais and Proust, and an entire book, *Resnais and the Cinema of Time*, by John Ward, on the theme of Bergson in Resnais, that Resnais, in his numerous interviews has never mentioned either of them. Is the influence more indirect? Or coincidental? Was Resnais merely swept up by the same ideas of time and narrative, to which *we* have

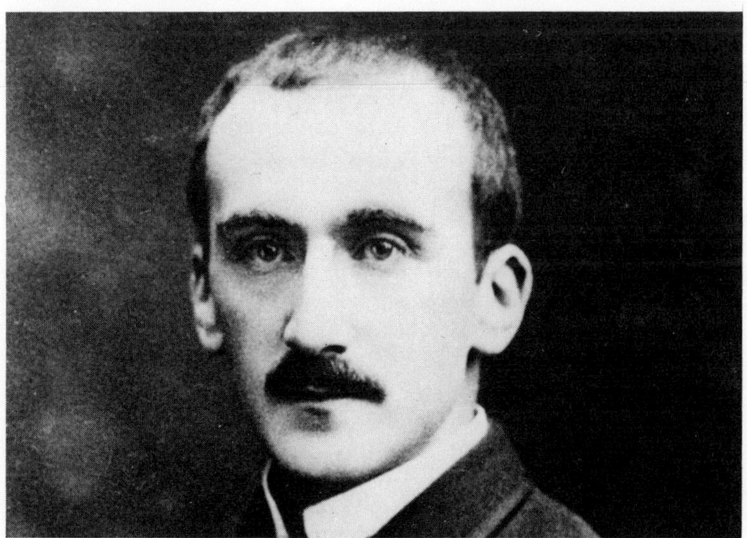

Henri Bergson, anti-rationalist philosopher whose theory that time is elastic anticipated relativity and gave the cinema the concept of psychological time.
Services Culturels de l'Ambassade de France

assigned the labels of "Proustian" and "Bergsonian"? After all, Baudelaire invented the literary equivalent of the dissolve in cinema (via secondary correspondences); yet no one speaks of Baudelairian influences in thematic analyses of films. It is hard to say accurately. Perhaps Proust and Mansfield, who came close to being contemporary authors for Resnais, were liked by him for their story telling value? At any rate, we have to try to trust him when he says he does not want to be thought of as the father of a cinema of memory and that he prefers the word "imagination" rather than "memory" to describe his films.[2]

There is also no evidence that Resnais ever liked the great "peasant intellectual" writers, like the novelist Henri Alain-Fournier and the poet Jean Arthur Rimbaud, both of whom wrote terse, breathtakingly concrete dialogue. Proustian and Mansfield-like images seemed to have remained in Resnais' consciousness because of their ideational power, for the logic of the secret garden, that logic sung about so well by Charles Trenet in his song, "Jardin."

> ...Garden of the month of May
> where are you, tonight...
> ...Garden of my memory
> of my first rendezvous...

Thus we can not treat Resnais' digestion of Proust like François Truffaut's ingestion of Balzac. As for Bergson, he is only useful for a reading of Resnais' films, not as an explanation of why they came into being. The cinema of Resnais is not just a series of Bergsonian problematics filmed with a movie camera.

By 1934, when he made his first 8mm short—a film of his classmates in a version of one of the adventures of the master criminal, Fantomas, a fictional French villain of the 1910s, whose adventures had sold over ten million copies, making the name literally a household word—he had already accumulated the resources of an independent researcher and the attitude of a private and privileged character. Resnais was not like the other children. Perhaps his mother's instinct to strengthen him and protect him from the world because of his asthma gave him more than Proust's cork wall, that special security of the child who knew no fear and could plunge deep into the world of day dreams. At any rate, Resnais began to draw from the outside world the stimuli *he* wanted. One of the stimuli he absorbed was the desirability of being an *author* of something. One can easily demonstrate how terribly author-consious Resnais became at an early age. In a way, he thinks of all his artistic friends as authors, as *Fahrenheit 451* characters, who walk around, reciting their texts, their life histories. In Gaston Bounoure's mini-biography of Resnais, there is a great and telling story, told to Bounoure by Resnais' Breton childhood buddy, George Hilleret, which reveals this:

> He remembers everything, retains everything. Back then, I was writing a novel. An adolescent's novel. Yvonne Suzur—one of the girls in our middle school, who today is a pharmacist—was the heroine in it. It was called *L'Obus*. Me, I forgot about it. But Resnais, one time, introduced me to Delphine Seyrig by saying: "This is the author of '*L'Obus*.' "[3]

Vannes, the ancient Breton capital was also not entirely cut off from the world. French and Italian comic books were available at the railroad station news kiosk, and Resnais became an avid reader of these strips as well as of "The Adventures of Harry Dickson," a dime novel series with numbered issues, whose author Resnais, years later, went to great pains to meet. The train to Paris also took

Marcel Proust who brought to narrative a style of fluctuation of tenses. Resnais incorporated Proustian and Bergsonian ideas in his cinema.
Services Culturels de l'Ambassade de France

only twelve hours; so Resnais, precocious child that he was, began while he was erratically attending St. Xavier high school in Vannes to make trips to the French capital, that, when we read about them today, seem like nothing less than artistic pilgrimages of the highest order.

In general, one could argue that Resnais had five major artistic interests: theater, painting, cinema, still photography, and the art of the comic strip (graphics and narrative), and that he admired the first two but felt he had no talent for them (witness his abrupt termination of his theatical acting career). Gaston Bounoure, Resnais' earliest biographer, records that in the late 1940s career stage, some critics went so far as to consider Resnais just an art groupie; but what was Resnais to do?[4] He has more the intellectual sensitivity for painting than the actual skill. On the other hand, he was extraordinarily talented in film shooting and editing, and especially in still photography. Resnais, with his Leica, often scouted geographic locales he later would film or planned to film. Over a thousand of these photos have been printed and thousands of others exist on contact sheets. Most of them are stylistically overexposed and underdeveloped, and highly original.

Jorge Semprun, later one of Resnais' screenwriters (on *La Guerre Est Finie* and *Stavisky*) was to write the introduction to a collection of some two hundred of these remarkable photos which were published without commentary in 1974 as *Repèrages*. Semprun said of these *repèrages* (references or landmarks):

> These are photos of places—of sets—where one would like an action to take place. It is this deceitful presence of a possible action which gives Alain Resnais' photos their dramatic intensity.[5]

Semprun went on to say,

> The insidious beauty of Resnais' photos, the disturbing beauty there, comes from an explosive mixture of every day platitudes and furtive interrogation that bring them their depth . . . . At the beginning [of photography] people, animals, cars were added in to the photographs because they [the public] couldn't stand empty urban landscapes. Alain Resnais, on the other hand, takes the opposite path. He doesn't add the appearance of life to his images, the illusion of the human reality of life. On the contrary, he does everthing necessary to wipe out this illusion, this appearance . . . . Alain Resnais' photos catapult us back into this original anguish, this uncomfortableness [with the empty frame], this illness, this restating of the question

[whether to "doctor" the image with human extras or not], this absence of man lived by man. For ourselves, in this case, [we are left as] spectators of our own absence.[6]

The theme of absence, so notable in all Resnais photos, would become the key to all of his films.

The "explosive mixture of everyday platitudes and furtive interrogation" in Resnais' photos can be attributed to his interest in the silent films of Louis Feuillade, an interest that stimulated him toward preferring elliptical to straight narratives.

His interest in theater stemmed from his desire to be a stage actor. Accordingly, though he has never acted in any one of his films (in strong contrast to that ham Godard, and the zany Truffaut), he learned the craft of theater as well as any minor stage director. I doubt that any other film director working today understands the application of Brecht's theories to film as well as Resnais.[7]

The portrait then that emerges of Resnais at eighteen in 1940 shows a complex, precocious individual with a Renaissance man's overview. The Modernist in Resnais seems only to have emerged later.

Resnais and the French Directors of His Generation

Resnais, we now should mention, belongs historically to a movement including Jean-Luc Godard and François Truffaut as its brightest lights. Godard, born in 1930, and Truffaut, born in 1932, do not differ from Resnais as much due to their later birth as we might expect. Truffaut, for example, has reached back into the 1930s to make Jean Renoir into one of his influences. None of these three is impervious to Cocteau, despite their age difference, and the fact that Cocteau was a darling of the 1930s and 1940s more than of the 1950s. Cocteau, of course, is an influence on all three, giving Resnais, in the same breath,the contiguous, direct cut flashback without dissolve (first used by Cocteau in *Orpheus* in 1951), and to Godard the jump cut. It is not surprising that Cocteau thought Godard's *Breathless* was a great film.[8]

As Truffaut told Peter Ladiges in an interview in 1974, in answer to Ladiges' question, "How was it then in 1958 with you, Resnais, Rivette and Godard? Later, all of you went in completely different directions,"

Each of us developed in his own direction. But I don't think for a moment that these developments produced any big surprises! If one took a look at which films each of us first made, which films each one of us admired, what kind of articles each of us wrote, then one could quite easily have predicted our development. It is completely normal that the gap between us has grown with time.[9]

Temperamentally, Godard and Resnais still have one striking thing in common: a sense of paradox. They also share, perhaps much more than Truffaut—who likes at times to rewrite history—a desire to confront history through confronting its language.

Renais is, on the surface, a Tolstoian when it comes to historic attitude, whether it is film or political history. He believes in (and the Breton background here helps in shaping this orientation) events moving individuals around—and one just finds oneself there. He preferred, he said on numerous occasions, to have his films commissioned by someone else—by Tolstoian historic inevitability so to speak. (Here Resnais differs from Godard, who has never found it painful to take history to task.) Resnais has never, it seems, begged anyone to let him make a film, never knocked down any doors screaming to anyone who would listen, that a "masterpiece" was about to be lost if he were not allowed to make *this* film.

Yet there is counter evidence that Resnais is really a "closet Carlylian," a believer that individuals determine historic results and that without the appearance of such individuals in the tableaux of history, there would be no specific history. In short, making a movie is an act of will. Thus the Renais paradox: He wills structure onto the films he makes, but he wishes that someone else would invent them.

The paradox results in such things as Resnais' refusal to call himself the author of his films,[10] his calling himself the *realisateur* (i.e. producer) as in the case of his film *Muriel*,[11] and his using other metonymic dodges to disguise the authorship for which he knows other people know he is responsible. It also leads to his elevating his screenwriters to the position of co-authors (a designation they all richly deserved) after which Resnais would comment on the film as if someone else had authored it: "I think she might stay with him a week or two longer,"[12] his comment about the ending to *Hiroshima Mon Amour*, or "I don't understand the film completely but eventually I might. . . ."[13] to *Les Nouvelles Litteraires* upon being asked about his latest film, *Providence*. Only Antonioni has been more metonymic (often saying, in effect, "why don't you ask Antonioni" to reporters who asked *him* specific questions about his films). This paradox results in some positive features in Resnais' cinema; Resnais' films are a concoction of the ethereal and the formal, a quality that led Julia Rowe to describe Resnais' style as "breathtakingly concrete."[14] Yet, one must ask "why the paradox?" Godard sets up the paradox of film in order to study it with us, as a kind of *Sprachkritik* shared by the audience. Resnais seems to use the paradox of authorship to hide behind, in order to retain a purity and unself-consciousness of purpose. Yet is not Resnais in the business and art of making cinema in order to seduce people into liking him? Perhaps his personality's native obsessiveness rather than a neurotic drive to succeed is responsible for our having Resnais' cinema to view.

He, of course, also grew up under the spell of a cultured country, which had produced one generation of dazzling avant-gardes after another—the one, in film, of the 1920s having just died, only to be replaced by another equally brilliant, the era of Jean Renoir's expressive Naturalism and the great late 1930s somber French cinema of *écriture*. Still staggering the imagination was the dazzle of Daguerre, Lumière, Méliès, and Resnais' great love Louis Feuillade.

Feuillade, to Resnais, represented the synthesis of thesis, Lumière (reality), and antithesis, Méliès (fantasy). It is interesting, on this note, to compare the way Resnais and Godard aligned themselves with the Grand Lumière-Méliès tradition that all French filmmakers had (at least until the elder Lumiére brother died in 1948) to contend with. Godard himself claimed that the dichotomy between Méliès and Lumière was a paradox and that they co-existed within each other.[15] Resnais resolved this paradox externally and less theoretically by claiming that the cinema of Louis Feuillade contained the essense of both, and that form could be copied as a legitimate, third, alternative. This kind of external resolution of paradox put as a problem to the spectator would become a key to the cinema of Resnais; the resolution of paradox by the filmmaker for the spectator to see how and why and to what effect, would become the key to the cinema of Godard before 1968.

What Resnais meant by this "third way" is difficult to assess. Feuillade's *Fantomas* films did have a style of moving characters via clever mise-en-scéne speedily into ever new situations and perhaps influenced Resnais with their confident pacing and aura of mystery, the two stylistic components of practically every Resnais film, long or short, and even an element of any given Resnais sequence. Yet Resnais was quick to add that he never followed one master filmmaker's approach. In response to the inevitable question, "Who were your influences?" Resnais has vaguely answered that no one has directly influenced him, but that Cocteau and Welles probably have indirectly and that Antonioni is someone he likes.[16]

There is no doubt that Resnais had the intellectual ability to teach himself cinema. He could have emerged, technically, without specific influences. He did not learn the vocabulary of the film shot from watching American films, as Godard probably did. We have every reason to believe Resnais when he said, "Everything I learned about the cinema already existed in comic strips.[17] He was one of the few French post-War directors to enroll in I.D.H.E.C., the French national technical college of film, but he learned nothing practical there and probably only some details about editing. How to use film narrative, how to document, how to cut in the camera, are all aspects of the cinema Resnais taught himself once he switched from his first love—the theater—to the art of filmmaking and the creation of "the film approximating thought."[18]

Resnais in Paris: Under the German Occupation (1940-1944)

In the winter of 1939-1940, having obtained his baccalaureate the spring before, Resnais moved to Paris, where he had already been lured to visit previously by the theater, the possibility of studying acting, and by the contact with more people similar to himself. Like Bach in search of Buxtehude, Resnais decided to move towards the proximity of those who could teach him.

Living on the Rue de Courcelles, near where Proust once lived, Resnais proceeded to live a classic kind of art school life, one oblivious to the German occupation and one attesting to the very mild experience Parisians had of World War II. In 1941, he enrolled in an acting school, the Cours René Simon, where he stayed for two years and met such colleagues as the future film actress, Danièle Delorme.

Delorme recalls Resnais at this period as a recluse: "I retain the memory of a person apart, who observed, watched and did not say anything. I never saw him on the stage or presenting anything at all.

But . . . outside the course, we talked, discussed a lot. He was, for some of us, a rallying point. . . . We used to meet in his room, and on his projector, he would show us old films, *Metropolis* for example, accompanied with music, like the 'Firebird Suite' [by Stravinsky]."[19]

If Resnais did not behave like an *apache* James Dean or a wall-leaping Belmondo, it was not because of his temperament, but because a defeated France under German occupation, while not financially ruined, was culturally moved towards sobriety. On the first of September, 1940, only four months after the invasion of France, German submarines plied into the ports of Resnais' native Brittany and Grand Admiral of U-Boats Karl Doenitz himself came to Paris and moved into headquarters at 18 Boulevard Suchet, Paris XVI (to begin the direction of the Battle of the Atlantic) only some two miles from Resnais' apartment. Resnais, as he later would explain, was totally oblivious to the war. He was far more concerned as to whether he could succeed in becoming an actor.

Resnais' enrollment in the Cours Simon put him into contact with the elite of the French theater and the milieu of the French acting student. Like many of his generation, he was bitten by the theater

Daniéle Delorme, who was one of Resnais' friends and fellow students in 1943, shown in her role of Gigi in the French production of Collette's story.
Services Culturels de l'Ambassade de France

bug (younger readers have to imagine as a comparable influence the fascination of rock and roll in the early 1960s or the film enthusiasm of the 1970s) because it was hard to achieve self-expression in a very bourgeois country like France without being either directly involved, or indirectly as a fan, with some kind of expressive art form. Like so many of his friends, Resnais—not yet interested in the directorial craft of the stage—which would come later, in 1947, when he discovered Brecht—wondered how he would do on the stage as an actor. It was his eventual self-critical decision that he did not have the skill to be an actor that decided Resnais against remaining on the stage. Instead, one could say that he compensated by becoming a particularly sensitive director of actors in the cinema. In his own words: "I have a great respect, a great love for the actor. He has a very difficult and delicate task and enormous demands are made on him."[20]

It is only speculation, but Resnais might never have turned to cinema had he shown at least an equal talent in one of the other arts. He drifted towards cinema in steps, rather than making one big gracious leap into directing like Truffaut, or after specious self-examination, like Godard. Somehow, one feels Resnais thinks of theater as glamor and cinema as an occupation.

An important factor in the development of Resnais as a film director has been his fascination with and respect for writing, for narrative. Now narrative and experiments in narrative are an area shared by cinema, writing, and theater, all three of which coequally tried, each in its own way, to push forward in the 1930s, 1940s, and 1950s, the last frontiers of the age of the avante-garde.[21]

Resnais' strangely exaggerated respect for writing and the written word (considering his occupation as a visual craftsman) needs some illumination. One often respects writing and speaking if one is not good at it. Resnais insists he is not good at narrative, which is why he employs screenwriters and has never written any narrative or even commentaries for his films himself. To such an Arthur Sullivan, Gilbert must be God! But, on the other hand, for a native of France, *the* country in the world with a grand tradition of belles lettres, to say he "can write a little," or that he "dabbles" at writing, is like saying one skis "just a little" in Austria. Resnais' caution is understandable. But we must raise the question: Does he protest too much on the issue of having no talent for narrative?

As we have pointed out, Resnais, one of the foremost filmmakers of France, of his generation, has distinguished himself even while never writing anything. Like a true Modernist, or even a post-Modernist, Resnais perhaps, better than most artists since Baudelaire, first deplored the new cocaine-like *momentum* of urban life, then realized how futile it is to write if one does not have an incredible gift, and how difficult writing, as such, is, when it attempts to express modern rhythms of life. Therefore, Resnais avoided doing anything more than writing down the meaning of the experiment of the film he was about to do. He wrote a short statement as to his intentions in *Van Gogh* (1948), one of his first documentaries; and he shared many a post-film observation. But Resnais has never written a complete script or a theoretical article on the cinema, and the absence of both from his work is a statement in itself. The goal of Resnais' cinema, we can deduce from this, has never been to produce a *Gesamtkunstwerk*, a total work of art.

We get as close as we ever can to seeing how Resnais would write, when we read his delightful interview with the critics of *Positif* in 1966, where, during a post-mortem of *La Guerre Est Finie*, Resnais almost accidentally got into narrating and holding forth on some of his ideas. Why then he chose never to write remains a mystery; for despite his claim that he expresses himself clumsily, he is never turgid, often illuminating, and sometimes quite gracious. As a gentle polemicist, he could have contributed invaluably to cinema criticism. It is a pity he has not for, like Truffaut—who is a finer film critic than filmmaker—and Godard who is not so astute a critic but who still brings a wonderful mathematical Apollonian perspicacity to film criticism, Resnais would have brought a unique point of view to film writing that would not have been sullied by an overanalytical approach.

In 1943 Resnais, having quit the Cours Simon, entered I.D.H.E.C., headed by a former director Resnais admired, Marcel L'Herbier. Was he on the rebound from his failure as an actor? Or did he fantasize becoming a director? We only have Resnais' terse comment that he never got to shoot any film there, and that, as a result, he quit in 1944.

Perhaps more important than any of his formal educational attempts was Resnais' education by Paris, a strange place during the occupation, where nothing seemed to have changed on the surface. Resnais himself, later, somewhat sadly and guiltily admitted he was so busy absorbing theater that he "didn't even know there was a

Resistance,"[22] something we can readily believe if we look at the many-sided points of view and recollections presented in *Memory of Justice* and other Marcel Ophuls documentaries, which, in particular, cite the veneer-like quality of Occupation Paris, where even the Germans were under some kind of spell. François Truffaut, though he was only between his eighth and twelfth years during that time, today recalls Paris under the German occupation as "a period of deportations" which depressed him, of repression for many, a kind of oblivion for others, concentration camps for still others.[23] At least three of Resnais' future collaborators were on their way to camps while Resnais was at the Cours Simon.

Yet, French cinema survived despite the occupation and the emigration of the cinematic Big Four: Jean Renoir, Jacques Feyder, Julien Duvivier, and Max Ophuls. François Truffaut, in his introduction to *Cinéma de la Resistance et sur l'occupation*, by the late André Bazin, listed at least twenty-five worthwhile films made during the occupation and in Vichy before it was occupied in 1943. Peter Cowie makes the fascinating suggestion that his cinematic experiences in Paris during this time may have taken Resnais away from one kind of cinema that he had admired and propelled him at least to have a good look at another kind of cinema, a more austere kind.

"During the 1930s the school of 'poetic realism' had exerted the predominating influence on the French film, and the austere, melancholy work of Carné, Prevert, Renoir and Feyder was only just past its peak when war was declared."[24] Resnais arrived in a Paris that had been deserted by Duvivier, Renoir, and Feyder among others. If Hitler had not occupied France, Resnais' work might have been completely different. As it happened, he was nourished on films like *L'Eternel Retour* and *Les Anges du pêche* that were born of a sterner attitude towards the mechanics and language of the cinema than was shown by the escapist melodramas of the later 1930s.

Eric Rhode describes Jean Delannoy's *L'Eternel Retour* (1943) as "condemned, somewhat unfairly, as Nazi propaganda."[25] He says that "with hindsight, it is possible to enjoy many Vichy films as autonomous and imaginative artifices that never quite avoid a sense of precarious studio carpentry. Jean Delannoy's *L'Eternel Retour*—with a screenplay by Jean Cocteau and very much a Cocteau film—is of this type. [And we have already mentioned Resnais' admiration of Cocteau.] Its Tristan and Iseult, idealized to the point of implausibility, are surrounded by envious grotesques. Yet Delannoy realizes the notion of transcendental passion effectively and puts over the mythic business of poisons and potions with enough conviction to make an improbable story acceptable as a sort of dream. Jean Epstein's influence is noticeable throughout and was to be even more marked in Cocteau's own *La Belle et la Bête* [Beauty and the Beast, 1946], which managed to sustain the atmosphere of a fairy tale on a minuscule budget."[26] Bresson's *Les Anges du Pêche* (1943), with its dialogue by Jean Giraudoux, was one of the remarkable films of the period, already displaying Bresson's noted austerity. Those two films also contain the combination of director and literary screenwriter that Resnais would follow throughout his entire feature filmmaking career.

While we do not want to overstress these perhaps minor influences on Resnais (they are less than Feuillade, Cocteau, and Marcel L'Herbier), they do give us a little better clue as to what Resnais absorbed during his incubative period when Danièle Delorme so aptly described him as a person (*A Bande?*) apart, who observed, watched, and did not say anything, "but when his turn came to make films, said everything."[27]

Resnais' watching films and his year at I.D.H.E.C.—this way of learning cinema—was interrupted by the liberation of Paris. The French army was rebuilt and needed for the occupation of Germany. Resnais, now twenty-two, was drafted and served in the French army for approximately eighteen months. While in the French occupation forces, he joined a theatrical troupe called "Les Arlenquins," which included several professional actors. There is a shot in Resnais' *Muriel* showing Bernard and fellow draftees from the Algerian War which recalls the cameraderie of this time of Resnais' life. Unlike Truffaut, who could not endure being a soldier, and Godard, who lived in Switzerland during World War II (and, besides, is hopelessly near-sighted), Resnais did not seem to experience any hatred for military service.

Resnais and the Short Film

In early 1946, after completing his military service, Resnais returned to Paris where his parents set him up in a sizeable apartment at 70 Rue des Plantes in the XIVth arrondisement, near the Gare de

Monparnasse, and, incidentally, not far away from a small Breton colony in Paris.

At twenty-five Resnais began his quest and picked up his dormant camera. His fascination with painters—we have already mentioned the writer who likens him at this time to an art groupie—led him to make a series of "visits" to painters: Lucien Coutaud, Felix Labisse, Hans Hartung, Oscar Dominguez, Cesar Domela, and Max Ernst. Of these painters only Max Ernst and Hans Hartung are known today, but they were all artists whom Resnais personally liked.

Interestingly enough, Resnais did not apply his "documentary" interests to African ethnographic projects and hippopotami, as did Jean Rouch (then thirty years old) nor did he go further in the formal study of some discipline, enrolling at the Sorbonne like the seventeen-year-old Jean-Luc Godard in 1947, to study ethnology for a certificate (B.A. degree). Resnais began to shoot film footage and soon amassed an enviable record of completed projects.

In 1947, he also began the second prong of his formative film career: the hiring of himself out as an editor on other people's films. Nicole Vedrès (1911–65) hired him as an assistant editor for her *Paris 1900* (1948). After 1952, Resnais would spend a considerable amount of time editing other people's films, and his reputation here became as formidable as his renown as a cameraman/director of the short or art film.

In 1948, with a bicycle and a 16mm camera strapped on his back, Resnais filmed the *Chateaux of the Loire* (1948), a travel film, during the shooting of which he passed through Nevers, which would so prominently figure in *Hiroshima Mon Amour*.

By 1948, his experimental side led him to try a further development of the short film. As he himself put it *Van Gogh* (1948) was an experiment. In one of the few written appreciations of his own work, the twenty-eight year old Resnais wrote,

> Since the release of *Van Gogh* (the 16mm version) I have incurred numerous criticisms. One, in particular, reproached me for being a traitor to the paintings of Vincent Van Gogh. I would thus like to take advantage of [the fact that the] Ciné-Club asked me to do an article, to clear up some misinformation.
>
> Above all, this short film represents an experiment, a test, for Gaston Diehl, Robert Hessens, Jacques Besse, Pierre Braunberger, Claude Hasser and myself.
>
> It concerns itself, in effect, with finding out if painted trees, painted

houses, can, in a narrative, thanks to the montage of the cinema, serve to take the place of real objects, and if, in this case, it is possible to substitute for the spectator, and almost without his knowledge, the internal or interior world of an artist, a world such as is revealed by photography.[28]

Resnais During the Pre-New Wave Period

Lack of money and plenty of ingenuity, small groups of friends helping each other, and a middle-class public for both art and pure entertainment helped struggling artists in France during the period from 1945–1960 in a way that has not existed at all in the United States since 1969. Each small circle of friends had its talents, its contacts, and its individual successes. Each artist was helped by the success of the group.

Pioneers in this approach, with its newer post-War requirements of utter self-confidence and innovative talent, quickly applied their talents and skills towards making the pre-New Wave films the most full-grown product possible. Jean-Pierre Melville made *Le Silence de la mer* in 1947 for twenty-four thousand dollars, but his merit was not so much raising the cash as using Henri Decae as cameraman and Howard Vernon and Nicole Stephane (a friend) as actors. Resnais would build up such a circle of friends too, and the first such valuable relationship for him was that with Chris Marker (the pseudonym of Christian Bouche-Villeneuve). Marker was a Marxist and an activist filmmaker who used a Vertovian approach, but on a level of culture. Marker's eclectic use of documentary style and abstract thought characterized a group which—overdogmatically, perhaps—became known as the Left Bank Group (as opposed to the *Cahiers*, or Right Bank Group, that grew up around the cineastes at the *Cahiers du Cinéma*, who were all at that time pure theorists). There was no opposition between the groups. The frequenters of the Cinematheque on the Avenue Messines, Eric Rohmer, who was Resnais' age, Truffaut, Godard, Chabrol and Rivette, who had come from Rouen, were just engaged in a different kind of activity, thinking about films, viewing them, saturating themselves with them, while other cineastes like Melville, Cocteau, and Resnais were working out ideas by making films.

Eric Rohmer has told the story that at the end of a theoretical argument with someone, the debater challenged Rohmer to do it better himself, on film; and Rohmer said, "I would, but I don't have a camera." "Well, you can borrow mine." "Fine, I'll do it."[29] This use of cinema to make a point is really an extension of the essay. The term *camera-stylo,* coined by Alexandre Astruc (1923–) in 1947, applies here: "camera-writing." This distinction between *camera-stylo* and scripting and shooting a film in factory-fashion has to do with a fundamental methodological difference: in the former case the film becomes a tight extension of the thinking of the author, his "writing." In the latter, a film is a film, and the specificity of the cinema medium is not only adhered to but is its own *raison d'etre,* and the film is made as a product. In Paris, both the *Cahiers* (Right Bank) group and the Left Bank group were, each in their own way, *camera-styloists.* Resnais, while having one hand in the documentary/art short film world, always had both feet in the world of *camera-stylo* narrative. The *camera-stylo* world existed on both banks of the Seine. Thus, one foot of Resnais was always planted on the Right Bank with the New Wave. The two worlds were not contradictory. It is needless and false to separate totally the *Cahiers* from the Left Bank group, as many writers have done.[30]

Resnais must have met Truffaut and Godard sometime between 1948 and 1951. Godard lived and worked in Paris from 1945 to 1952, and Resnais could have read his articles in *La Gazette du Cinéma* and *Cahiers:* "Joseph Mankiewicz," "Toward a Political Cinema," "*Que Viva Mexico,*" "Works of Calder and L'Histoire d'Agnes," "La Ronde," "No Sad Songs For Me," "Strangers On a Train," "Defence and Illustration of Classical Construction," "What Is Cinema?", or "Les Petites Fille Modeles." He was undoubtedly aware of Truffaut's article on the "Politique d'auteurs," written in 1954. All three were frequenters of Henri Langlois' Cinematheque. As Truffaut later told interviewer Peter Ladiges, "Back then [in 1958], the four of us [himself, Godard, Rivette, and Resnais] could have closeted ourselves in a room together and—say, for example—written a screenplay for Rivette, or one for Chabrol. But it's very obvious that after one has done a couple of films, one can see one's own progress line much more clearly."[31]

Resnais met Truffaut, for their worlds were on a collision course. Truffaut knew Marker and others. In 1955, Resnais was to serve as editor on Truffaut's first film, a "home movie" (all prints of it, unfortunately have been lost), *Une Visite.* As Truffaut recalled the film to an interviewer:

Une Visite was my first film. It was a silent film in 16mm. But I didn't shoot it like a silent film, i.e. when the film was finished, it just lacked the sound. One saw people talk to one another, but one didn't hear what they said. For that reason, one couldn't show the film anyway. Today, it's gone. We only had one copy and no one knows where it went. It was a little film in the manner of certain Cukor's comedies. That is, the opposite of the 16mm avant-garde film that they were making at the time. There were no corpses in it, no blood, no suicides. The images were knife-clear as in the American comedy film. Jacques Rivette was my camerman [and Resnais the editor] and I asked him to shoot it in the way that Cukor did in his Judy Holliday comedies, such as *It Should Happen to You,* and ones like that.[32]

The Resnais-Truffaut relationship remained a friendly one (which it still is today), leading Truffaut to champion Resnais in the French cinema press, In May, 1956, Truffaut highly praised Resnais in *Arts* magazine, listing him with Alfred Hitchcock and Vittorio de Sica as "celebrated names." In February, 1956, Truffaut had interviewed Resnais for *Arts,* and drew out of him that "we owe everything [pertaining to the art documentary] to Luciano Emmer and Chester Gould."[33] Likewise, it was Resnais' colleague, Godard, who reviewed Resnais' *The Song of Styrène* [*Le Chante du styrène*] in *Cahiers* in 1958 (which I shall quote from later, for it is an important review from the viewpoint of understanding both Resnais and Godard). By 1955 Resnais' reputation as an editor was second to none. As a filmmaker, his reputation progressed more gradually. After producer Pierre Braunberger (who later produced *Vivre sa vie*) commissioned Resnais to remake the 16mm version of *Van Gogh* (1948) into a 35mm version (1949), and the film immediately won a prize, Resnais could have said to himself that he had mastered an area of endeavor and could now dare to do something else. Yet only slowly did he shift from documentaries to explorations in narrative. Even then, his entire expertise up to *Hiroshima* was limited to films under one hour in length.

From 1951 to 1953, he and Chris Marker filmed *Les Statues meurent aussi (Statues Also Die),* which was banned by the French government censor because of the war in Indochina. Resnais recalls, "they misinterpreted that the film was anti-colonialist whereas the film was really anti-racialist."[34] The form of this film is similar to that of the later *Night and Fog,* Resnais' next and most celebrated documentary, in that it experiments with giving animation and life to what other people consider objects. In its subjective-objective form, this film anticipates Godard's early approach and bridges the gap between Resnais art films and his documentaries.

Henri Langlois, the founder of the Cinematheque Française, where French filmmakers and critics met to view Langlois' vast and various collection of films.
Services Culturels de l'Ambassade de France

Resnais in 1953 was still considering himself a maker of film shorts, and was on the executive committee of the society for the propagation of the French short which sponsored the yearly Tours Festival for such films. This activity shows that Resnais was not a hermit, that he took an active interest in the affairs of French cinema. In fact, Resnais never shirked a public role if it were absolutely necessary, especially when his professional competence made it a foregone conclusion he would have to make common cause with a group. In these cases, he would always sign up. With success—and one should keep in mind that practically every Resnais film has won some kind of an honor or prize (with the exception of his *Gauguin* [1950] which he rightfully considers a failure)—Resnais came more and more in contact with the "Who's Who" of French artists.

By 1954, his circle of friends included, besides successful authors and filmmakers, many of the associates he would later use in his feature films: Henri and Jasmin Colpi (editors) and Sasha Vierney (cinematographer). Within the next four years, he would meet the actresses and actors most useful to him, those who started out in the theater and moved to film: Jean-Paul Belmondo, Jeanne Moreau, Anny Duperey, Nita Klein, and the incomparable Delphine Seyrig.

Resnais was thus a working professional already in the early 1950s. Most of his friends were also. Particularly inspirational was Chris Marker, whose film, *Lettre de Siberie* (1957), a remarkable documentary, would become a landmark analogous to Resnais' *Night and Fog* (1955). Then there was Armand Gatti, who made films and wrote plays. Though the uncategorizable artist and free spirit, Agnes Varda, who was a type of beatnik jack-of-all-trades, would never advance to the high adventure level that characterizes Resnais' cinema, she has remained a good friend.

Then there were his cineaste friends from the Cinematheque, Truffaut, Rivette, and Godard, who were really different in the way they spent their social time; for they were younger and desperate for a cultivated social life. Godard, especially, by his use of Belmondo, instinctively tapped into a teenage sensibility Resnais never did. Belmondo contacted the sensibility of the teenagers of 1953–1957 when they became the young adults of 1957–1963, as well as those growing up just behind them.

Resnais did not seem ever to have gone through a period of being sexually deprived, bored, or just wanting a social life, as Belmondo describes the New Wave's being born during an era of freedom, prosperity, and boredom:

Those years at the Conservatory[1953–1957, when Belmondo studied acting there] were for me those of carefreeness and of the happiness of life without material care. We spent our days having nothing to do, and played with our youth. It was the great era of nights of love, the *caves* of St. Germain-des Près. We danced. We conned each other. We were happy without knowing it. In the intellectual magazines and papers the serious gentlemen already chatted back and forth about this "youth in danger" of which we were a part . . .[35]

But the New Wave caught, expressed, and held not only the hopes of Belmondo's subgeneration but of the most impressionable of the next generation (those who were the film-goers of 1959–1963 and the future buyers of rock albums) whom Belmondo lovingly characterized as "crazy." As Belmondo recalled, that emerging generation, the youngest ticket buyers to *Hiroshima* and the movies of the New Wave, were really an avant-garde generation.

I assure you I admire this generation of rhythm. They are more beautiful than we were. Never in France were the young boys and girls so crazy and so splendid. They love good humor and a good time, it is what I trust them on. The girls are no longer virgins at 16, and that may disturb you; but because of this they will not become anything less than good wives. It is necessary to embrace the sentimental potential of one's adolescence [which is what the New Wave films often depicted] in order to avoid to have to do it later. Young people aren't reading anymore and only think of amusing themselves: so much the better. They shall have an entire life for reflection, like those monks who spend years at debauchery before adapting to a civilized life that they have found so vile before.[36]

It is this subgeneration's folkways and mores that would be seen on New Wave screens, and Resnais' cinema—to be commercial—had partly to cater to them. Even though Resnais did not know it before the fact, this would be the subgeneration that would cheer his *Hiroshima Mon Amour*. From Belmondo's point of view, Alain Resnais was one of the "serious gentlemen" one heard about. Yet Resnais was distant and serious because he was busy, not because he gave in to his aloof temperament. At that time in his life, he was actually quite social, constantly making new friends, even though they largely came from the "up and coming" actor group, from media figures, and generally included "sophisticates" rather than parvenus.

How did Resnais, for example, meet Delphine Seyrig? By seeing her in a play. The same holds true for his discovery of the cinema acting talent of Anny Duperey, a Comédie Française actress, who had a small part in Godard's *Two or Three Things* and whom Resnais hired for his *Stavisky.* By 1960, Resnais had also met his future wife, Florence Malraux, the daughter of the writer, who became his second assistant on *Marienbad.* Since he was an active artist, French intellectuals naturally gravitated towards him; for he always had a project in the works.

In short, while the New Wave was incubating, Resnais was making short films, but within the New Wave group and strategy councils. Resnais was considered very much one of them at the time. In the sense that the New Wave so admired the "writing" of films, or writing, period, Resnais would always remain, at heart, a member of the school of authorial narrative, of *camera-stylo.* This led him, just like Truffaut, to seek out writers that he admired, and unlike Truffaut, who did his homages from afar, unabashedly to try to seduce

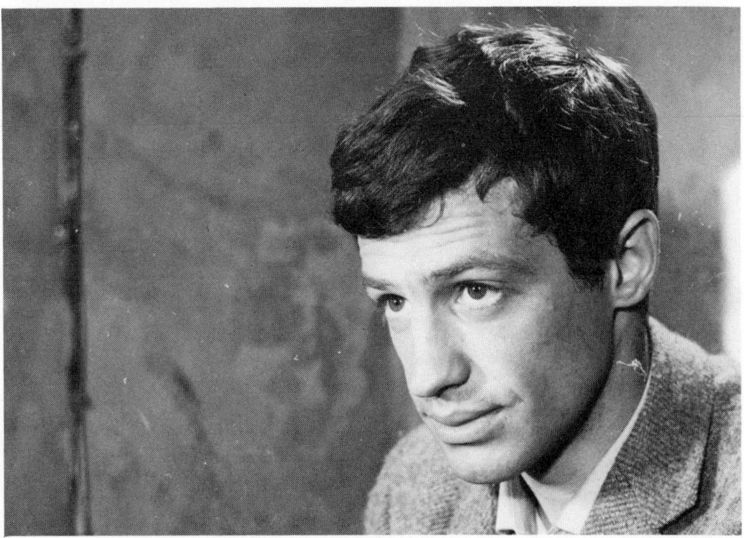

Jean Paul Belmondo, the key actor of the New Wave. Resnais did not get around to using him until 1974 in *Stavisky*. Belmondo was the "bankable" star that enabled Resnais to get the film financed.
Services Culturels de l'Ambassade de France

them into his projects. (And, as most French writers of the time secretly admired the cinema, it wasn't too hard to succeed.)

Starting in 1954, Resnais made a number of new, important acquaintances, such as the well-known authors, Jean Cayrol and Raymond Queneau, whom he admired from a distance. (Resnais was always a literary groupie.) Cayrol would soon be engaged to write the narrative of *Night and Fog* for Resnais and was a fascinating man in his own right, for his writing style was closer to being cinenovelistic than to that of Robbe-Grillet and "the New Novel" and almost begged contact with the cinema.

Cayrol, born in Bordeaux in 1917, was a literary review type, five years older than Resnais, whose activities in the French Resistance caused him to be arrested as a *Night and Fog* category prisoner and deported to Mauthausen concentration camp by the Germans. His brother, Pierre, died in a camp. He, himself, thereafter felt an urge to rewitness the camp experience which he had trouble remembering in its actuality; so he invented the Lazarian novel to deal with this—a style of fiction which examines memory lost and recalled, returns from the dead, and which is particularly and equally interested in establishing within the setting of life—which it equates to a cosmic nostalgic connections with powerful experiences and to investigate whether shattered lives can begin anew. The former consideration was the basis for Cayrol's *Night and Fog* script; the latter was the basis for his screenplay for Resnais' powerful film to come, *Muriel* (1963).

Cayrol's art was succinctly described in a press release sent out by Editions du Seuil (his own publisher), for Daniel Oster's biography of Cayrol. It reads as follows:

> Since getting the Prix Renaudot, which revealed him to the public, Jean Cayrol has been speaking to us. In a raised voice; in a low voice. The complexity and the simplicity of this voice, his frankness and his ambiguity, his sparseness and his trasparency, have carried along with them, the gist of our times.[37]

The role Cayrol was to play in Resnais' life was similar to that of mystic-in-residence played today by Bavarian novelist Herbert Achternbusch for contemporary Western German filmmaker Werner Herzog. At any rate, he was to become possibly Resnais' most interesting collaborator; and the two films which Cayrol participated in are, in my opinion, Resnais' finest documentary and his finest feature film.

Night and Fog (Nuit et brouillard) (1955)

This documentary is the definitive, perhaps the only Resnais documentary. Filmmaker and Beaux Arts graduate Dominic Benechetti said of this film that "in it, Resnais told us all we need to know about the genre."[38] Shot in black and white (past tense newsreel footage) and color (present tense location shooting in Osweicem [Auschwitz], Poland), the style of black and white/color has been much imitated—often unsuccessfully, but often quite successfully as by Marcel Ophuls in *America Revisited* (1972).

Since there is such a misconception as to what the title means, we should set the record straight that the title, "*Night and Fog,*" refers to a category of Nazi concentration camp prisoners, called *Nacht und Nebel* (or "night and fog") *prisoners.* The original French title for *Night and Fog, Nuit et brouillard,* means that category of prisoner specifically; thus the title of Resnais' documentary is *not* a poetic metaphor for the murkiness of concentration camps. Jean Cayrol, who wrote the script for *Night and Fog* and was its narrator for the spoken commentary, was himself a Night and Fog German prisoner from 1942 until 1945. In 1945 Cayrol had commemorated his own experience and survival by writing "Poems of Night and Fog." Ten years later, Resnais and Cayrol reused the "Night and Fog" title, but without the poetic intent. Resnais, one sees, was already convinced of the impossibility of remembering exactly such an event as Auschwitz.

There are, I feel, five views of "documentary" which we should keep in mind before going any further.

(1) First, there is objective camera, or straight recording. This is also known as the Frankfort School of documentary. The camera takes one shot in real time without cutting.

(2) Next, in order of objective to subjective, are the versions of documentary film dealing with the impossibility of documenting.

(2a) Resnais' position is that documentation is impossible. We forget. Therefore he drifts towards an artistic compilation film which subjectively says "objectivity can't be stated," or which uses a Wittgensteinian approach to "show the unsayable." This approach towards documentation is mystifying.

(2b) The Godard position, which originates with the ideas of Dziga Vertov, is that there are two realities; and a documentary reality can recreate and stand in for the other one. Vertov referred to two "Life-As-It-Is's." Godard says, quoting Brecht, "there is a difference between how real things are and how things really are." The filmmaker can achieve the latter, and thereby can document. Godard's approach is basically dialectic and Hegelian. In *Two or Three Things*, he said the way to document reality was to posit the subject of the film like an imaginary number in the form of $\frac{a}{b}$ plus $\frac{b}{a}$ plus i. The a/b b/a reversal would give you each character's reaction to the other and i would represent off-screen similar characters, whose lives would have to be taken into account to explain why and how the couple a plus b behaved. The documentation, according to Godard, must always have confrontations which lead to disjunctions.

(2c) The Brechtian documentary, which Resnais tried out in *Muriel*, is another form of dialectic documentation. Brecht originally borrowed the idea for the distancing effect (*Verfremdungseffekt*) from Piscator, who developed an approach which attempts to place the burden of arriving at the meaning, the burden of documenting, on the audience. This approach relies on giving the spectator only raw material, never the finished product. A finished product will always be an illusion, according to this theory.

(3) Then, uncomfortably in the middle, between objective and subjective, is the compilation film, an edited film of factographic newsreel shots.

(4) Dangerously subjective, because of its pretense at one hundred percent objectivity, is the recreated but fictitious film of facts, like *Algiers* (1967). This is pure subjectivity masquerading as objectivity.

(5) Then there is, at the other extreme, the unabashedly subjective cinema, such as the Maysles Brothers films. In this form of "documentation" the subjects are invited to enter the film and do what they want, even to the point of taking over the authorship of the film.

The title *Night and Fog* has a strange origin, which, if we trace it can tell much about the film. Because *Night and Fog* is an art documentary or a "documentary" film which falls into the category of the impossibility of documenting (exactly the opposite of what some critics have called it),[39] the title of the film must somehow convey the impossibility of knowing, which it does exactly; for a "night and fog" prisoner was made to "disappear" and was never confronted with his crime in a court of law.

Heinrich Himmler, Reichsführer SS of the German Reich, invented the term "night and fog" prisoner, with the intention of making the term itself mysterious and undocumentary. Taken from the prologue to Wagner's *Der Ring des Nibelungen, Das Rheingold* (1853–4), it refers to the dwarf Alberich (the character with whom Himmler identified) and his theft of the Rhine maiden's gold. Assisted by his cretinous brother Mime, Alberich now succeeds in forging the Tarnhelm, the magical helmet that allows its wearer to assume whatever shape he desires, and says,

> Dem Haupt fügt sich der Helm:
> Ob sich der Zauber auch zeigt?
>
> The helmet fits my head:
> Now will the spell work?

Alberich softly says the magic incantation:

> Nacht und Nebel—
> Niemand gleich!
>
> Night and Fog—
> No one remains as he was![40]

Alberich is then transformed into a cloud of mist and fog and becomes invisible.

With *Night and Fog,* French filmmaker Dominic Benechetti has rightly said that Resnais told us everything we need to know. Cinematically, the film lays bare all the future cinematic devices of Resnais' arsenal: montage, the travelling shot to show the director's disguised authorial presence walking around and taking a look, straight temporal jump cuts without dissolves, use of color to starken rather than aestheticize reality. The film is both in black and white (past) and in color (present). The film is told in the present tense and it evokes a parallelism in one's own mind, the sense that one is experiencing all that one sees in the present. Despite its illusionist structure, *Night and Fog* works as an anti-illusionist film (barely) and functions as a thinking film without losing itself in abstract propositions. Resnais, laying down no theory for how to make such a film, nevertheless established, with *Night and Fog,* a film typology he was to follow rigorously.

In his study of the French National Library, *Toute la mémoire du monde* (1957), he uses the same approach: the camera tracks down information. It finds it is there, imprisoned inside four walls.

Whether this being there is "good" or "bad" or what there is to do about it is left to us.

With his last short film before beginning *Hiroshima Mon Amour* (1959), the film that put Resnais on the world map, *Le Chante du styrène (The Song of Styrène)*, Resnais made one more innovative advance over his own technique (or, more accurately, invented a variant of it: all the Resnais films really should be seen as variants of one master technique, even though they are not to be read quite as narrowly as variations of one master film).

The innovations of *The Song of Styrène* have best been described by Jean-Luc Godard. Writing a review in *Cahiers du Cinema*, Godard said:

> *The Song of Styrène* is a film that is ingenuously edited. Or, what is saying the same thing, without a bit of the goldsmith's craft at work. On first viewing, I said to myself: "It is impossible for Resnais to go futher than *Toute la mémoire du monde*, it is time for him to make the jump across the water into feature films." I was wrong. I was incorrect in believing that *The Song of Styrène* could not be, could not work as anything other than negatively, as more than decoration (non-existent besides). Seen on the CinemaScopic screen at the Tours festival [in 1958] *The Song of Styrène* appeared to me to be an olympian film, a serious film without equal. "Make documentaries and film the mountains," said Lubitsch. "Afterwards, you will know how to film people." *Hiroshima Mon Amour* will be one of the most beautiful of films because *The Song of Styrène* has proven that Resnais has definitively mastered the secret of matter. Such a film discourages excess.[41]

With *Night and Fog* and *The Song of Styrène*, Resnais at thirty-six emerged like Lieutenant Napoleon Buonaparte, as far as he could go without the intervention of Tolstoian history. As Carlylian as his intentionality was, it took a Tolstoian sweep of history, "the loosening up" of the French film scene, to bring Resnais to the realm of making feature films. Later, when queried what he felt like making short films, Resnais replied, "I told Marguerite Duras it would be a miracle if we actually got the money to film *Hiroshima Mon Amour*."[42] From this comment, it is obvious Resnais wanted to make features earlier than he got the chance, and made as many shorts as he did just to keep his hand in; but I wholeheartedly concur with Resnais' biographer, Roy Armes, who said that the delay in Resnais' career was fortuitous and that the delay of his first feature film was to his and our advantage.

It is always sad to see a film director frustrated by commercial restrictions but it is difficult to see how Resnais could have developed as he has done, if he had been able to begin a feature career as early as 1951 with an adaptation of a novel by Vailland or Queneau. Had he begun then he would surely have followed the normal patterns of film construction with their emphasis on plot and character. [As it happened] when, in *Hiroshima,* he came to include people in his films for virtually the first time, he had already had, formed and fixed, structural patterns that owed nothing to the conventional film, novel or drama and were therefore to prove as revolutionary in 1959 as Orson Welles's experiments in *Citizen Kane* had appeared in 1940.[43]

As Resnais perceived, well ahead of his time, the director of the modern narrative film needs the skill of the very visually oriented (as opposed to the audio-tactily oriented, in McLuhanistic terms) who can construct an associative language. His perception came, quite obviously, because of some structuralist goal, the "film of thinking." The key to the message of a film, Resnais seems to have decided, is not in the flow of images but in how the narrative component works with the flow of images, i.e., the image/narrative correspondences in his narrative component. Resnais avoided them by using clear, concrete, powerful images in conjunction with his metonymy and indirection in the narrative. In short, a set of powerful images that are not part of some obviously precomposed symbol system to communicate visually a fixed intellectual concept to the viewer (as in the lifeless film version of *Lord of the Flies*). Even to get a narrative he could make metonymic, he needed a screenplay which would offer possibilities for narrative indirection and which could be informed by powerful iconic images set somewhat adrift from the narrative thrust. He thus sought and obtained in his films an image/narrative thrust that was fascinating to watch; for it seems to have produced those beautiful subtle chunks of meaning through Baudelairian secondary correspondences, subtle signifiers that reward the prescient, the spectator who doesn't want the narrative held under his nose. It was Resnais' genius to effect this just when the New Wave threatened to throw out the novelist-screenwriter and replace him with the director's ego. Instead, Resnais sought out the best cinenovelistic talent then available in France. (Resnais thus not only crafted his films better but advanced the careers of Alain Robbe-Grillet, Jean Cayrol, and Jorge Semprun.)

2

Hiroshima Mon Amour

The Genesis of the Film

Marguerite Duras' original scenario, *Hiroshima Mon Amour*, as well as the one she wrote in collaboration with Gerard Jarlot, *Une Aussi Longue Absence*, constitute, then, transpositions to the cinema screen of topics close to the novelist's and playwright's heart. While her first excursion in movie-writing has been viewed by many as one of the finest examples of her work, the second, more limited in tone, did not enjoy great popularity. For Madame Duras, who had already used motion-picture techniques effectively in a number of novels, the cinema was no stranger territory. Her flair for movement, for the clever lighting of cameras, for the interplay of shadows and lights, and for the construction of haunting dialogues, lent itself splendidly to *Hiroshima Mon Amour*, if somewhat less admirably to *Une Aussi Longue Absence* [not filmed by Resnais]. It is not easy to duplicate a work of art that comes very close to perfection.[1]

It is no exaggeration to say that *Hiroshima Mon Amour* has established the international reputation of Marguerite Duras. It is not merely the fact that the movie had received the International Critics Prize at the Cannes Film Festival in 1959 and the New York Film Critics Award in 1960; it is more the popularity of this work of art in countless countries throughout the world, popularity with the elite and with the average moviegoer, which has made of it an unqualified success. The usually unsafe barometer of box-office receipts, added to the official acclaim, is proof, in this case, that a finely nuanced and authentically wrought screen portrait can be pleasing to the intelligentsia and the mass audience of many a nation.[2]

HIROSHIMA MON AMOUR, a full-length black and white feature film, announced to the world that Alain Resnais had come of age and would remain a formidable filmmaker. That *Hiroshima* became a feature film is ironic. Resnais was originally approached by a company to make a documentary on the way Hiroshima appeared twelve

[M]arguerite Duras, author of the screenplay for Hiroshima Mon [A]mour, *as a young woman.*
[S]ervices Culturels de l'Ambassade de France

years after its destruction by an atom bomb. As Resnais made it, *Hiroshima* turned out to be a film about the impossibility of making a documentary about Hiroshima. After several months of trying the documentary approach, Resnais abandoned it because he had already seen from his own *Night and Fog,* that one cannot document a memory.

The film now became a fiction film with the same producers. The genesis of this film grew from Resnais' admiration for novelist Marguerite Duras' book, *Moderato Cantabile;* and when *Hiroshima*'s producers offered Francois Sagan the opportunity to write the script for the revised version of the film and she declined, Resnais selected Marguerite Duras. Resnais, at the time, told Richard Roud that *Hiroshima* was also intended to be something of that old Hollywood cliché, the woman's film. "I wanted to make a film for women, and I more or less forced Marguerite Duras into going her 'own' way. She was an essential factor in the 'grand opera style' I wanted to achieve."[3]

Duras finished the script in the summer of 1958. Resnais then went to Tokyo and Hiroshima with his script girl, Sylvette Baudrot, and supervised the Japanese cameraman for the Japanese sequences. Simultaneously, the cameraman for the French sequences at Nevers shot those sequences under instructions from Resnais without ever knowing what the Japanese cameraman was doing. The film really achieved its final form during the editing stage.

The Script

As Marguerite Duras scripted it, *Hiroshima* tells the story of "the emotions of a woman of thirty-four [Emmanuelle Riva] who, because the brutal war evidence at Hiroshima evokes her first love affair fourteen years previously, confesses the secret tragedy of her youth to a Japanese architect. Love grows between her and the architect, but she refuses to sacrifice herself to it. She claims that forgetfulness is a stronger force and that she will forget him just as she has forgotten her first love—a German soldier shot on Liberation Day—and as the people of Hiroshima have subdued their memory of the atomic explosion."[4]

As Resnais made it, *Hiroshima* keeps the plot in all its essentials but changes the narrative line so that the stories of the actress and the architect run as conflicting narratives. The non-synchronicity of the two narratives produces a double disjunction: we doubt them both. However, Resnais gives a seductive and affirmative quality to the woman's narrative not only by the way he handles framing (giving her choice placement in the frames) or mise-en-scène (having her lover walk in her shadow) but also by using her vocal incantations as a kind of superordinary narration above the ordinary dialogue that she carries on with her lover. Nowhere in the film is the presence of Resnais the author directly felt; but the superordinary narrator—the actress—takes on the function of a metonymic narrator standing in for the author of the film. This narration is nowhere and everywhere chronogeographically, and its temporal-spatial origin in the film is always mysterious; for we are never certain from when or from where this superordinary narrator is addressing us. This symbolic signification gives *Hiroshima Mon Amour* its timelessness, its universal quality.

Hiroshima was first shown, out of competition, to thunderous acclaim, at the 1959 Cannes Film Festival; and it premiered in the United States to equal acclaim in May 1960. Practically every reviewer praised it.

As A. H. Weiler said in *The New York Times:* "If Alain Resnais, producer-director of *Hiroshima* may be classified as a member of the French 'New Wave,' then he also must be listed as riding its crest. . . . As a director who set himself an extremely difficult task, he expertly sustains the fragile moods of his theme most of the way."[5]

Hiroshima as a Film "Whose Time Had Come"

I predict "*Hiroshima Mon Amour* is a film that will still be important fifty years from now." The rave reviews it received showed in what high esteem the film was held, but they tell only that Resnais' first film was a success. Most reviews of the film right after its release praised its confidence, its beauty, but did not really locate it in the stream of film history.

Let us look at the smash success of *Hiroshima* from two angles. First, was it better cinema, say, than the bulk of the films made and released in France and the United States between 1957 and 1959? Second, did it represent some startling innovation in film narrative? Did it give us an innovation that would correspond, say, to a generational advance in computers, cars, airplanes, or some technology—one that would have received almost automatic praise from the public just for its very existence? Was *Hiroshima,* in effect, a film "whose time had come"?

The answer to the first question is an unqualified yes! One has to recall what the output of films between 1957 and 1959 was to appreciate the impact *Hiroshima* made. On the one hand, there was *The Bridge on the River Kwai,* which featured the fine acting of Alec Guiness and the blowing up of a bridge: in short, a special effects film. This film was a success with the public. On the other hand, there were the intriguing 1957 box office failures: *The Sweet Smell of Success* and *A Face in The Crowd,* both made in stark black and white by Hollywood directors Mackendrick and Kazan. Both films were, by American one-dimensional standards of viewing, depressing. They were not bittersweet.

Something in between the colored fairytale-like *Kwai* and the dark *films noirs* of the fifties was lacking, missing, a new kind of film the public would gladly go to see. (The public often wants a work of art to corroborate its progress.) A part of the American filmgoing public by 1959 was restless, was ready for more bittersweet resolution and a more ambiguous kind of narrative, provided the overall effect of the film was not completely negative. *Hiroshima* owes its commercial success to its not being a negative film and to its providing the bittersweet purge of the emotions that makes one feel lighter. For that, the 1959 audiences, and not necessarily just the art house audiences, were ready. The American audience's love of *Gigi* (1958) showed this to be true.

As *Hiroshima* is that rare blend of a serious love story and a moral tale, the audiences found—often much to their surprise—that not only did they enjoy the film but also that they accepted being morally instructed as well. The moralizing tone of *The Sweet Smell of Success* and *A Face in The Crowd* annoyed the American public, and yet the object lesson in *Hiroshima* was accepted and appreciated. Resnais had managed this, largely through using new subtleties of narrative. Quite a feat!

This brings us to our second question of locating *Hiroshima* in film history: Did it represent an advance in the form of film narrative? The answer to this second question is a bit more complicated. Yes, I would argue that *Hiroshima* represents a sea-change in how a film is narratively constructed, but the advance is in the form of a quantum leap. The film's popularity and its instruction as to how to take its own narrative both stem from this.

If we could, for example, go into a screening room and project Welles' *Citizen Kane* (1941), Jean Cocteau's *Orpheus* (1950), and Resnais' *Hiroshima* (1959) back to back in strictly chronological order, we might find that *Hiroshima* does not seem to be such an over-whelmingly great advance. But, if we were to make that conclusion, we would be forgetting that we were comparing it with two of the most remarkable narrative films ever made before that. Besides, since Resnais was heavily influenced by Orsen Welles and Jean Cocteau, as well as by Alfred Hitchcock (see Chapter Six), there is perhaps an extraordinary (and narratively misleading) kinship among the three films.

In *Citizen Kane* Welles pioneered an unusual kind of flashback by using multiple stage dissolves with non-identical aural and visual temporalities. Cocteau, in *Orpheus*, pioneered the direct cut flashback, where a cut, without any cue, suddenly jumps us to another year. Resnais borrowed the technique of changing tense with sound without having to do it with image from Welles. He learned the glib, direct temporal jump cut from Cocteau and experimented even further with those methods. When we finally get *Hiroshima* on the screen, we see Resnais has actually pioneered a new style for the film's narrative in order to make it fit into a schema of tense changing that he wishes to play with. In *Hiroshima*, the past impregnates the present often through musical themes on the soundtrack that are associated only with the past. At other times, Resnais has the past impregnate the present in the form of flash cuts showing the past but with the voice-over narration associated with them belonging to a narrator in the present.

Both these methods used by Resnais are associative. Thus, while he took cues as to how to narrate from Welles, Cocteau, and Proust, his cinematic rendering of a story line owes entirely to his own personal development of a vocabulary of associationism specifically geared to the cinema. (See Chapter Eleven for the influence of this technique on younger filmmakers.)

This achievement is comparable to developments in the computer industry when, trying for greater memory, the computer people abandoned a second and a half generation computer, which used a mixture of vacuum tubes and integrated circuits, for a third generation computer which used integrated circuitry exclusively.

Why did Resnais want to make a narrative film using uncued tense jumps, showing a Proustian interplay of past and present in

Resnais directing Eiji Okada and Emmanuelle Riva in *Hiroshima Mon Amour*.
The Museum of Modern Art Film Stills Archive

dealing with the plot? Was it that he wanted to show the plot of everyday life? No, far from it. Was it not more because he wished to continue to explore the solution of a film-aesthetic problem? Did he not wish to continue to demonstrate, as in his *Night and Fog*, that one simply cannot document the past? Was not *Hiroshima*, then, made to show one could not really document the atom bombing of Hiroshima in August 1945? There is much evidence to support this theory.[6] Resnais was fascinated with solving the aesthetic, non-political problem in film of how to depict parallel narratives convincingly and beautifully.

As we have seen, he did this by developing a novel way to use the parallel narratives. By having his two characters' stories cast doubt on each other, and by keeping them separate to the end, Resnais was able to suggest that *Hiroshima* did not answer the larger, all-encompassing question of what really did happen to the world after the atomic bombing of Hiroshima. This non-documentary quality of *Hiroshima Mon Amour* is clearly shown by the way Resnais handles the peace documentary the French woman has come to Hiroshima to act in. We never see it being filmed. We see camera equipment set up. She says she is in such a film. But we never see this film—it would be a film within the film—being made. Resnais seems to be saying that he did not wish to make such a documentary and chose to make *Hiroshima Mon Amour* instead. This pretty much corresponds to what Resnais himself has admitted were his motives.

Hiroshima as the Radical Solution to a Film Problem

One of the outstanding features of *Hiroshima* is that though the two narratives of the actress and the architect never become one, Rivas' narratives of the past and present occasionally fuse into one story, one moment, one *moment priviligé*. *Hiroshima* can be considered to have three narrations going on intermittently and often simultaneously: the actress' Present, her Past, and the architect's Present. As we have mentioned, the actress' narratives and the architect's narrative clash. Her Present and her Past narratives often clash but occasionally fuse. But her narratives never fuse with his to form what Proust considered a momentary triumph over one's own lost memories. Aside from its aesthetic value and the excitement this structure brought to *Hiroshima*, it was also a wonderful addition to the arsenal of filmmaking devices that Resnais figured out how to replace narrative informed by character with narrative informed by time.

One has to digress momentarily to film history to recall that the problem of showing not one narrative linearly, but two separate narratives which come together somewhere had been solved in film as early as 1903 by D.W. Griffiths in *The Battle of Elderberry Gulch*. But not until *Hiroshima* was a really major narrative advance made beyond Griffith's accomplishment. The leap from a film like *Citizen Kane* to *Hiroshima* for example, is considerably more startling than the leap from *Elderberry Gulch* to *Citizen Kane*. The reason is that no film before 1959 was yet anchored in the slipstream of time.

The groundwork for the interpretation of time in *Hiroshima* was basically done not by filmmakers but by novelists and physicists, by Marcel Proust and Henri Bergson. Proust gave novelistic expression to Bergson's "anti-rational" interpretation of time as expressed in *Time and Free Will.*[7] By Proust's day, Bergson's concept had been demonstrated—by Einstein in 1905 and others—to be quite rational.

Proust's skill was to make narrative that was evocative of time, and he posited in the 1910s and 1920s that events are therefore what they are because of time. Time was thus the subject of Proust's *A la rechevche du temps perdu*. By 1929, in Alfred Döblin's novel, *Berlin*

Alexanderplatz, in the modern Czech novel of the 1930s, and James Joyce's *Ulysses* (1939), the shifting narrator became the chosen form; but no one had gone as far or further than Proust. In the United States, however, William Faulkner was rapidly approaching the same point; and he eventually came to the conclusion that it was vital to the modern novel to give all narrative experience a fourth dimension.

"In 1954, French New Wave director Agnes Varda placed together two separate plots in her film, *La Pointe court,* in an imitation of Faulkner's novel, *The Wild Palms;* Alain Resnais, who edited *La Pointe courte,* was to develop this technique of parallelism further in his first feature, *Hiroshima Mon Amour.* . . ."[8] Many have since considered Varda's Faulknerian *La Pointe courte* a break-through, the first New Wave film. (A breakthrough she has inexorably repeated: vide *One Sings, The Other Doesn't* (1977). At any rate, *La Pointe courte* certainly broke narrative convention; and Alain Resnais helped confirm, by his skillful editing of the film, that Varda need not have regretted her radical narrative experiment.

When, some four years and three successful short films later, Resnais approached the Indochina-born Marguerite Duras—a successful novelist who specialized in locating her often nameless characters in superprecisely designated geographic locales—to write him a film script for *Hiroshima,* Resnais showed it was not only playing with the parallelism of narrative, as in *La Pointe courte,* that fascinated him. Resnais, as Eric Rhode observed, "had already begun to experiment—in such documentaries as *Van Gogh* (1948) and *Guernica* (1950)—with the tensions that an editor can obtain when he places images of the past against images of the present. . . ."[9] Resnais was definitely in search of a narrative to use as a departure point for the visual-aural discourse on memory that he wanted to make, and he selected Duras as a tool to make the word part—the semantic part—of the narrative function properly in order to achieve the effect he desired. Duras accordingly gave him such a script, the salient feature of which was its repetitive, incantatory style and its banal use of emotion and detail. All went well and the script remained the cornerstone of the film.

The Present Tense as an Imposter in *Hiroshima*: The Presence of the Absent

> To see emptiness means to place into a precept something that belongs there but is absent and to notice its absence as a property of the present.[10]

Virtually everyone who saw it recognized that *Hiroshima* was about the past tense impinging upon and influencing present reality. But more so, in its very structure, *Hiroshima* treats the present as if it were an imposter, one assaulted by a vital past. This is experienced by the spectator as a kind of removal of an overcoat, as the present slowly sheds its lies. As Gaston Bounoure, Resnais' first biographer, put it, this happens rapidly and rhythmically in *Hiroshima:* "memory and desire are commingled and seem to withdraw at vertiginous speed."[11] Bounoure's apt comment refers to the way the film (thanks to its editing and "leopard-linking" style of montage) breaks down the certainty of its own present tense and denies its own future tense, a narrative technique Resnais brought to cinema, but one already existing, and called autodestruction in many of the other arts. A continuing series of disjunctions destroys the plot of *Hiroshima;* finally we realize we must give ourselves over to the narration and believe it. *Hiroshima,* like Resnais' next film, *Marienbad,* replaces its self-destruction by seduction. *Hiroshima* is seductive in its music and its metonymic narration by the actress on an aural level which constantly substitutes for the present tense of plot. This narration continuously destroys the plot in the way it blithely edits in non-chronological shots or shots of uncertain chronology. It "covers up" its own skeleton of shock with a velvety soundtrack that spirally holds the film together. *Hiroshima* is a trick, not done with mirrors but with *vertigo.*

The reference to Hitchcock here is quite literally true and should get the reader away from comparing *Hiroshima* to Fellini's cinema of self-reflection and move him towards seeing that Hitchcockian allusions are Resnais' film's real spiritual godfather.

The word "vertigo" should also structurally evoke Hitchcock's *Vertigo* (1958), a film so similar to *Hiroshima* in one sense, that if it were not for the fact that the Hitchcock film had not yet been released in France when Resnais shot *Hiroshima,* one should call it a copy. Not only does *Hiroshima* have the same premise as *Vertigo*: to give the spectator some priveleged information about the main character—the actress in *Hiroshima* and Madeleine/Judy in *Vertigo*—but also, later to confound him with multiple allusions of uncertainty that render suspect any certainty of motive for an action by any character.

In so doing, both films honor the surreal. This is less surprising when one notes that *Vertigo* was concocted as a screenplay for Hitchcock by two French novelists, influenced by surreality.

Why surreal? Because surrealism can and usually does connote a transparent, fabricated reality that one is invited to see through by the way its structure is arranged. The surreal is a form of charlatanism, of pictorial translucency revealing yet another picture which sets up an imposture obvious to the spectator (as anyone who has ever viewed a surrealist painting, like a Delvaux, can attest to). *Hiroshima* is surreal because its heroine's imposture is clearly perceived.

The major difference then between *Hiroshima* and *Vertigo* is not on the level of structure, but on that of seriousness of style. It is between Hitchcock's asking the spectator to see his narrative premise through the eyes of "the world of entertainment" (Méliès) and Resnais' asking his spectators to see it through the eyes of his "investigative" approach (Lumière-Feuillade). It is simply not true that *Hiroshima* is more "arty" than *Vertigo;* it is just more serious. Stylistically they are equally surreal. Both films can be understood by similar alert perceptions of a kind of structure common to both.

Vertigo's two stories—of Madeleine in the first half and Judy in the second, both played by Kim Novak—bear some retelling to demonstrate just how *Hiroshima*-like they are. In *Hiroshima,* the actress (Past) and the actress (Present) are likewise played by the same woman, Emanuelle Riva, but the dichotomy is split not between two characters but between two time zones. In *Vertigo,* Kim Novak is successively Madeleine and Judy, who turn out to be the same film character, Judy. Judy has impersonated Madeleine and later appears as herself, a fact soon apparent to the audience but not to the protagonist, played by James Stewart, who falls in love with her twice. Hitchcock reveals her identity by "leaking" information to us—if we are observant—when we see Judy finger a necklace that once belonged to Madeleine, thus demonstrating that she is indeed Madeleine. (In *Hiroshima,* hands switch ownership in the same way: the Japanese has the German's hands, and imposture is suggested.)

Once we know that Judy impersonated Madeleine, we see the film's narrative autodestruct; for all the time there really was only Judy, so now there is nothing more to tell. Hitchcock's surprise, if one had not suspected it all along, is that what we think is mainly a story about Madeleine is actually a story about Judy and her masquerade as Madeleine. If we think about it in this context and compare the confrontation between the two tenses of the life of the actress in *Hiroshima,* the Emanuelle Riva character, with Judy's impersonation of Madeleine versus Judy-as-herself, we find a striking similarity in how the actress (present tense) is an impersonation of a woman whose fiction is seen through by the spectator. The common surreal structure of both films should now be obvious.

Next one should be alert to how the structures of the two films are very similar, even though the ontologies of one's experience seeing both films will, of necessity, be different. While Hitchcock was telling a story psychologically, Resnais was philosophically showing the effect of time on love. The difference: Resnais has introduced a fourth dimension to the narrative. But this should pose no problem for the spectator; it should be much easier for him to understand the way in which Resnais builds his ontological film if the understanding begins with the fact that its basic structure shows that the woman we encounter, the actress, is going to be undermined by her own past and exposed as a fraud by herself. Resnais' moral is that one cannot remain frozen in memory, despite the strongest act of will. The actress' imposture immediately then implicates her Japanese lover as well.

In *Hiroshima,* the imposture in the film is precisely located. It is the actress' present tense love affair with the Japanese architect. He seems, at first, to be the other important character in the film; but as the film progresses, the true main character of the film appears, the German soldier who died in Nevers, and he becomes dominant. This causes the actress in the present tense in *Hiroshima* and the actress of the past in Nevers to clash. This "missing" main character is paralleled in *Vertigo* by the criminal Elster, who is rarely seen but who becomes the dominating character because he controls Judy and has put her up to impersonating Madeleine.

Resnais, in *Hiroshima,* thus gave a brilliant twist to the same structural device that was used by Hitchcock in *Vertigo.* He added the vital dimension of absence, not only an absence of character but of time. A mythic, self-created character, the actress-in-the present tense impersonates the authentic one; the fusion of the actress-past and present appears gradually. And when we extrapolate this to a political dimension, as Resnais does not require us to do but hopes we will do nonetheless, we end up with this formula: We gradually perceive that we were not witnesses to the atomic holocaust at Hiroshima, as we were not witnesses to the German soldier's death at the hands of French partisans; so the banal story of what the

Japanese architect does with the woman in the city of Hiroshima functions as an imposture that suggests, through its very fictiveness—its surrealism—that we have missed the main event: Hiroshima destroyed by the atomic bomb. This presence of the absent is vital to *Hiroshima*, and we will see that it is equally vital to Resnais' third film, *Muriel*, which has as one of its themes the way the French ignored the real war in Algeria.

Accordingly, when we begin to view *Hiroshima*, we feel we are involved in a story of modern-day Hiroshima; but then the story becomes one about Nevers—*Nevers Mon Amour*, if you prefer. Life is not just being; it is also becoming. *Hiroshima* shows how as one changes and grows older, one's memory, even of specifics, is qualified. It does not belittle Resnais to point out that this technique of the past falsely recalled is one often used in ghost stories. *Hiroshima* could be taken as a mystical narrative of the type often found in Welsh fiction and Breton legend. Considering this, Resnais can be seen as having bathed the Duras story in a Celtic surrealism, a revelation of Nevers under a Druidic spell, an impression enhanced by leaving out most of the woman's real psychological pathos and substituting a kind of psychic state and by not allowing a real psychological interaction between the actress and the German soldier.

The actress is not permitted to narrate her past in a normal, continuous flashback of the kind that ordinarily offers a grand opportunity for dramatic bathos. In fact, if Resnais had allowed either genuine interaction between the actress and the soldier or the more usual sort of flashback narration, the film would have become too melodramatic. By the end we would be crying with the heroine over our own lost loves, not because of her acted-out pathos, but because the film is so evocative of her repressed emotion. Because *Hiroshima* is narrated as a universal metonymy that never allows us a clear metaphoric "way out," it denies us an excuse to weep in sympathy. That is why so many who saw the film cried.

The way Resnais finally made it, *Hiroshima* turned out to be a film about the impossibility of making a documentary about *Hiroshima*. This was not stressed in contemporaneous reviews. Now it seems, this is historically the really significant reason for respecting this fine film.

3

Last Year at Marienbad

YOU CAN'T GO TO MARIENBAD, expostulated Alain Robbe-Grillet (after a journalist kept referring to the film's locale as though it were real.)[1]

It makes better sense in explaining the connection between all of Resnais' films to consider *Last Year At Marienbad* as an Alain Robbe-Grillet script which Resnais only shot and edited. Thus it need not be considered as a typical Resnais film. It was, in every sense, an experimental film, but one in which Resnais did not have his cinematic hand free in the very beginning. "Robbe-Grillet gave me a choice of four scripts, and I picked the one of them that was the most austere."[2] Though there were story conferences over shooting the film, the *Marienbad* type of narration is strictly Robbe-Grillet's. How can we say this so easily?

Because *Marienbad* is a perfect example of autodestructive art of the type that Robbe-Grillet was employing in all of his novels immediately prior to his undertaking the *Marienbad* project.[3] In autodestructive art the narrator appears at the beginning; disappears at the end; destroys himself. The narrator in *Marienbad* is the voice of the character called X. The voice disappears at the end of the film. The last words of the film are his, as well as the first. Significantly the voice only disappears after announcing it will leave, an act having the same significance, as when Peter Townshend of the British rock group, the Who, destroyed his guitar (a thing) at the end of the Who's 1964 concerts. He destroyed it at the moment the music ended or "disappeared." Townshend's guitar smashing and Robbe-Grillet's *Marienbad*, considered historically, exemplify the popularity in French and British avant-gardes in the late fifties and early sixties of autodestructive art, which became almost a fetish. In

ain Robbe-Grillet, author of the screenplay for Last Year at
arienbad.
vices Culturels de l'Ambassade de France

Britain, this movement came out of the art schools; in France it stemmed from a group of novelists such as Robbe-Grillet.

Resnais' Intentions

What were Resnais' intentions in making *Marienbad* with Robbe-Grillet? First, Resnais wished to avoid repeating himself and making another film like *Hiroshima*, and *Marienbad* seemed a very different project. Second, Robbe-Grillet's script was a challenge. Resnais is more interested in solving aesthetic and intellectual problems in cinema, with cinema, through cinema than in making films for the sake of making films, i.e. as cinematic self-expression. *Marienbad* posed some dandy problems for him to solve on the level of film narration.

Thus, first and foremost, Resnais' fascination was with tackling the problems posed by Robbe-Grillet's script. Hence, it was for him an experiment with specific goals; and Resnais has expressed several times that unless a film is an experiment, making it bores him[4]. The experiment was not making his own film, but experimentally filming a Robbe-Grillet narrative and co-opting it into his own experiment. History and fifty film reviewers have adjudged that Resnais' experiment worked.

After the film was completed and had become both a critical and commercial success, it seems that Resnais and Robbe-Grillet were satisfied and delighted with the result of their collaboration. In ecstatic press conferences and in a long joint interview in the September 1962 issue of *Cahiers du Cinéma*, they discussed the film, praised each other and expressed their solidarity in finding a unified approach, satisfactory to both, that enabled them to work together and collaborate so well.[5]

Years later Resnais expressed some second thoughts about *Marienbad*, but he never, even remotely, suggested that he and Robbe-Grillet had different conceptions of the film. Robbe-Grillet, as we shall see in the next chapter, was less charitable. In 1975 he told interviewer Brad Burke that originally he had a much different conception of *Marienbad* than had Alain Resnais.

A second, familiar motive for Resnais' making the film—that resulted in some differences with Robbe-Grillet—was his desire as conjurer and entertainer, to please the audience rather than just the artist. This motive, absent from *Hiroshima Mon Amour*, will run through all of Resnais' features after *Marienbad* and up to the present, including *Providence* (1977). It will color all his films, often causing dipolarities that are never quite resolved. In *Marienbad*, the dipole between experimenting and pleasing is, for the only time in Resnais's case, resolved; and the film stands—on the level of structure rather than content or ambition—Resnais's masterpiece. However, I believe that it is not his most important film; I reserve that distinction for *Muriel*.

In *Marienbad* Resnais achieved a one-to-one correspondence between what he set out to do with the film and what he ultimately obtained. His intention was to show, experimentally and in a way pleasing to the audience, in the form of film, Robbe-Grillet's notion of showing a multiplicity of narrative possibilities packed into one story, none wholly true, none wholly false, some more probable than others—a story told by a narrator who disappears at the end of the tale, after announcing that he will vanish.

Marienbad as Film Made Up by a Spectator

So much has been written about *Marienbad* that reviews of it would fill a book. Therefore we must ask what new light can be shed on this film fifteen years after it was made. Let us compare what Resnais himself said about the film in 1961 and in 1976. In 1961: " . . . I am concerned with trying to reach the spectator in a critical state of mind . . . "[6] and "With the film, I should like to recover, without theory or manifesto, the conditions of reading, that is to say, the spectator should feel himself alone, like the reader."[7] In 1976, he added, in response to the question, "How would you analyze today the shock that was felt when *Marienbad* was released in 1962?": "I recall the violence of the reaction, with a bit of surprise, because the film was mostly rejected by those who were brought up on 'cultural baggage' and liked by those who were not. Though *Marienbad* uses some different devices from normal film, it wasn't such a break with traditional cinema or narrative."[8]

There are three characters in *Marienbad:* a man, X; a woman, A; and M, who may be her husband, guardian, or protector—we are never told the exact nature of their relationship. X appears to be trying to persuade A to leave with him, and as a device (excuse or fact?) tells her she has already met him at Marienbad a year ago and had agreed to go away with him a year later. She denies this but at the end agrees to leave with him. A less probable but wholly possible reading would be as follows: A wants to go with X and imagines he is forcing her in order to overcome her own feminine reluctance and inertia. Within the film there are also bits of information that could fit into different versions of what was happening. These include an episode in which M kills X with a pistol, which suggests that the whole thing is only A's fantasy. Unlike the film *Rashomon* (1953) in which three conflicting stories are told in a syntagmatic, one-two-three order (thus disjuncting the film's apparent paradigmatic structure almost totally because we are manipulated into believing the third version more than the first or second), *Marienbad's* multi-stories are all paradigms of a root story which we are never told. Thus we are invited to invent the story of *Marienbad* as it goes along; indeed, we should not shirk from doing so if we want to make any sense of it all. Resnais' achievements in constructing the film are the plausible ways in which he linked the subtexts or possible stories and in sustaining our interest in a ninety-minute film that could as easily have been sixty or thirty minutes long.[9] He does this by montage tricks; by a general austerity of movement; by using organ music that rhythmically matches the tracking shots; and by reserving his most dynamic travelling shot for the key narrative sequence, the imagined rape of A. The montage is less the "leopard-linking montage"[10] of *Hiroshima* than a classic Eisensteinian analytic montage, and it is particularly effective in sequences like one in which a glass breaks and we do not know whether it really broke or A imagined that it did. The net result of the way Resnais uses analytical montage in *Marienbad* is that we get analysis without synthesis; we do not know what actually happened, and our point of view is thus manipulated so that we feel her alienation. The process by which Resnais edited *Marienbad* thus gives us the opposite of the Hollywood approach to character point of view. A Hollywood film could not have left unresolved what happened in the sequence with the broken glass. It would have to have given the audience privileged information so they could resolve it. Either A imagined dropping the glass; X imagined A was upset and dropped the glass; A dropped the glass; or, A went insane at that moment. In *Marienbad* we are not given such privileged information; the montage will fit any of these four conclusions without eliminating any of them.

Overmuch has been made of the possibility that *Marienbad* is a story of sexual persuasion, and that all its content deals with X trying to seduce A. It could also be that X is mixing up in his mind his attempts to seduce several different women and is, as in fiction, assigning all the properties of various desirable women to one fantasy woman who is A. In *Providence* (1977), Resnais' most recent film, Resnais makes more obvious use than he did in *Marienbad* of how we mentally assign variable roles to other people and how these roles change from time to time. It could thus also be that in *Marienbad* X is casting A in several roles and is more interested, in fact, in persuading himself that she exists in the way he imagines.

What it comes down to is that the filmmakers, Resnais and Robbe-Grillet, are giving us beautiful but conflicting images of a luxurious resort coupled with information intended to makes us doubt that this locale, "Marienbad," (which is actually an architectural composite of two Bavarian castles, Nymphenburg and Schliessenheim)[11] exists. This is intended to subvert our falling for a narrative too easily, too quickly, too intellectually. In a sense all of *Marienbad,* every shot of it, is, what only one or a few shots are in some films, privileged information for the audience. In a tremendous turnabout from usual procedures, it is the characters who are stripped of the normal information they have about themselves, whereas we, the audience, have all of it. We can, then, make up *Marienbad* as we go along.

As Roy Armes suggests, "seemingly insignificant incidents like the game played by M may be irrelevant, nothing but elaborate traps, while casual interrupted conversation, like that of the guests at the beginning, may contain the germ of the whole film."[12]

Not everyone called *Marienbad* a masterpiece. It has also been criticized as formal, narrow, and oppressive. Eric Rhode says, "it celebrates little more than Resnais' gift for mise-en-scène, being a semi-abstract excercise in which camera movements and editing conspire to create a splendid mystification. Resnais was to find more substance for intricate techniques in Jean Cayrol's screenplay for *Muriel* (1963). . . ."[13] While I agree that *Muriel* has more substance, I think the fault in *Marienbad* is not in its being "semi-abstract." I don't find the film abstract at all. I think that it is, if anything, too concrete, too concerned with objects. The "factory of facts" shows through *Marienbad's* veneer, and they do not form a coherent whole. As an excercise in "the camera lies," it is fine; as an excercise manual to show how film can manipulate narrative, it is superb. *Marienbad's* beauty is its dialectic; it tries to seduce you even while it disjuncts its own seduction. (In Robbe-Grillet's *The Man Who Lies,* by contrast, the same approach is tried again; but one has to concentrate too hard on the narrative to allow the image flow to create its own patterns of recognition.) The problem with *Marienbad* is, then, not lack of content, but what one does with its content in one's mind. Everyone—even the unadventurous *New York Times* critic, Bosley Crowthers, seems to have been able to deal with *Marienbad.* Critics like Crowthers, who did not basically see the film as a para-logical narrative, took it as showing us a dream state. In the dream state rules of logic are customarily suspended. So Crowthers could explain the film to himself as a dream. Many other critics also seized upon the oneiric quality of *Marienbad,* possibly being encouraged to do so by their previously having seen and heard analyzed Bergman's *Wild Strawberries* (1957).

Marienbad as Cinema of Pessimism

There is another aspect to *Last Year at Marienbad* that I believe has never been much discussed, and that is the film's projection of its pessimism by virtue of its making objects and not people its center. One could, of course, blame this aspect of *Marienbad* on Robbe-Grillet But I think Resnais shares complicity here for one good reason, and that is the generally reductionist and metonymic aspect of his next five films. I propose, therefore, to spend the remainder of this chapter in discussing *Marienbad* as an example of a pessimistic school of art called *Die Neue Sachlichkeit* (The New Materialism). In this way we can also demonstrate more precisely why Resnais' and Michelangelo Antonioni's cinemas are cousins and followed similar paths at this time. Eric Rhode, in *A History of the Cinema,* describes "The New Thing-Ness" as follows:

> In 1925 G. F. Hartlaub, director of the Mannheim Kunsthalle, organized a large exhibition called *Neue Sachlichkeit,* the new objectivity or matter-of-factness, which John Willet characterizes in [his book] *Expressionism,* as "a nonutopian even rather prosaic concern with clarity, accuracy and economy of means, biased towards the collective rather than the personal and informed by a realistic social analysis." It is possible that the model for this objectivity was the kind of newspaper in which reports on events, often of a violent nature, are incongruously placed side by side without comment. G. W. Pabst [in the 1920s] practiced such a treatment, clipping off shots or sequences at the moment when the feeling in them appears on the point of welling up.[14]

This cutting style is also evident in *Last Year at Marienbad.* In

Marienbad we find not only Robbe-Grillet's "new novel," anti-style style but also Resnais' paralleling Robbe-Grillet's script with a reified, formalist building block style of his own. Drawing on Eisenstein's analytical montage for his decoupage Resnais not only filmed Robbe-Grillet's instructions for a filmed Robbe-Grillet novel. He also invented cinematic equivalents to it that are anti-personal, visual-aural "New Materialism" equivalents, thus giving *Marienbad* a heavy, weighted, pessimistic feel.

Another aspect of *The Eclipse* and *Marienbad* that permits a useful comparison is the fact that both films can be seen as part of a brief, pessimistic era of the "art film." This era, from *La Dolce Vita* (1958) to *Marienbad* and *8½* (1963) revelled in using the "New Materialism" as a banal response to a banal decade, the 1950s—a pessimistic, but not unrealistic, equation of man with his possessions as basic to the films' structures. In most of the "art" films of this mini-epoch, 1958-1963, the protagonists literally drown in their possessions.

As *The Eclipse* opens, the harsh heavy piano chords of Giovanni Fusco's score lurk sonorously behind the credits and the austerity of the credit sequence is replaced by a series of shots of Riccardo (Francisco Rabal), Vittoria (Monica Vitti), and inanimate objects in an apartment. *Marienbad* similarly opens with the harsh, heavy organ chords of Francis Seyrig's score; and the austerity of the halls of the interior of the castle are replaced by a series of shots of the guests (who are like inanimate objects) until finally we see X (Georgio Albertazzi), A (Delphine Seyrig), and a series of objects.

In *The Eclipse* we next see that the atmosphere is heavy with frustration. A director's point-of-view close-up of an ashtray overstuffed with butts suggests a night wasted in arguments and self-analysis, as does a still fan. The camera pans across a cluster of intellectual books; included among them is Georg Lukacs' *Destruction of Reason.* (In *Marienbad,* the equivalent to this is the play poster for Ibsen's *Rosmersholm.*) Riccardo is slumped in a chair, his sleeves rolled up. Vittoria paces the room nervously, spasmodically, like a caged tiger, while Antonioni's camera cuts and travels to show her architecturally and to show where she can't go, so as to emphasize her discomfort. We witness what Ian Cameron has called "her determination compared to Riccardo's abstraction . . . and unwillingness to come to grips with what is happening to them."[15] Next, as Peter Cowie described it, "after what seems an eternity [a year, perhaps?] she draws the curtains open. Through the massive window a grey dawn landscape is revealed and is dominated by a water-tower shaped like some preternatural mushroom. The unsettling music, the fan, and now this are the initial clues to the sinister feeling that haunts *The Eclipse* and rules its concluding section entirely."[16]

Compare the above descriptions with what transpires in *Marienbad*, and striking similarities emerge. We have X's determination, A's abstraction—"an unwillingness to come to grips with what is happening to them." A paces the room nervously—initial clues—sinister feelings (*Destruction of Reason*). The scene suggests a year "wasted in argument and self-analysis." Very quickly *Marienbad* has consumed its shock devices, as does *The Eclipse*. Both films, after their first ten minutes, must merely extend these devices. *Marienbad* must now beg to draw you in by having you join X's attempt to "persuade" A. If this works for you, as it does for many spectators, you have a good chance of staying absorbed through the film. But if it does not, and the content fails to absorb you, the form will not give you any fresh information. All you will find throughout the remainder of both films is an accumulation of objects associated with the two main characters to no new purpose.

Antonioni's contrived spontaneity in *The Eclipse* works better than Resnais' formal style in *Marienbad* only because the spectator is more accustomed to unclear characters than to clear information not clearly connected with characters. *Marienbad* is, in a way, a documentary about the making of a film. *The Eclipse* is a completed work. In *The Eclipse*, furthermore, Antonioni is very sure of the length of the film. He knows just how long to linger, and though he uses contractions and extensions of psychological time, *The Eclipse* never loses the spectator in timelessness as does *Marienbad*. Finally, both films begin as *films noirs*, but *The Eclipse* suddenly has an Act Two in which the sun shines, while *Marienbad* is doomed to stay in Act One forever. Obviously, the limitations of *Marienbad* are due to the limits of the experiment set by Resnais and Robbe-Grillet, not due to any lapses in carrying out the filmmaking.

Ultimately, the main point of contact between *Marienbad* and *The Eclipse* is socio-cultural. As part of a brief trend in European film labeled "European Pessimism," both are versions of a similar socioideological urge: to show a landscape where the characters are the backdrop and things, time-space itself, are the foreground. Culturally both films show a lapse of faith in man and humanism even amidst the prosperity of the Kennedy years. Vittoria's new romance will fail just as Vittoria and Riccardo's did. We will learn just a tiny bit why it will fail; it will not make it any better that Piero is an active person whereas Riccardo was too analytical.

Both films have reduced their characters to objects. Resnais has overwhelmed (and thus destroyed) romance with things, while Antonioni has used things to foredoom love. (The triumph of romance in a film essentially about landscapes would be counterproductive; therefore, neither director lets it happen.)

The Eclipse especially, therefore, speaks the language of "The New Materialism." The newly-built section of Rome where Piero and Vittoria live is "reality without form"—one of the slogans of the "New Materialism" movement of the 1920s. The argument between Riccardo and Vittoria is "conflict without legitimacy." Piero and Vittoria's romance is in trouble because Piero is "a hero without pathos"; and despite one good day together, the communication between Vittoria and Piero is "speech without expression and answer," yet another slogan of the "New Materialism." The film ends with an eclipse of people—with a shot of a light (without people): *Marienbad* ends with a shot of the lit up castle, without people. Coincidence? Hardly! Antonioni and Robbe-Grillet (slightly softened by Resnais) were expressing a straight–from–the–shoulder contempt for man's ability to breeze merrily on. I don't feel that *Marienbad* is completely anti–humanistic, but there was a kind of faltering of faith about the future of man in the cinema at this time that the film subconsciously exudes. Resnais himself has suggested that "the claustrophobic atmosphere surrounding the shooting of *Marienbad*"[17] came from the internal political tension produced by the end of the Algerian War and, in particular, by a sudden violent burst of right-wing OAS activity in and around Paris, where the film's interiors were shot. In short, while the film shows extreme aesthetic self-confidence, it bears also some Marcusian touches in that it shows that modern tragedy is the result of placing on people controls they cannot escape, whether these controls be imposed by real life or fictionally by some narrator. (What one only senses in *Marienbad*, Resnais much more explicity brings to light in *Providence* fifteen years later.)

The ending to *Marienbad*, moreover, is black, ironic, even tragic, not pathetic, sentimental or hopeful. "She," as X's voice says, "is already getting lost, forever, in the calm night, alone with me." Lost in the recesses of the narrator's mind? "Perhaps he made it all up," one thinks; then, "Of course he did." But we are still saddened by the Marienbad experience, nonetheless. *Marienbad* examine a day in the life of the early sixties intellectual, the kind of intellectual whose life was superficially examined by Bergman and Fellini, the kind characterized also by the heroine and hero of *Hiroshima*. "The remembering X undergoes is something that the girl from Nevers would have experienced many times."[18]

So we see the tragic-ironic vein in the younger Resnais' cinema and its connection with the "New Materialism" as the fundamental premise that lies behind the structure of *Hiroshima* and *Marienbad*. (Resnais' next film will get angry and attack the New Materialism; and, as is the fate of many a film that turns its back on and goes against a trend, *Muriel* will receive less attention than the artistically safe *Marienbad.) Marienbad* was a catalogue of the reification of modern man according to the gospel of Robbe-Grillet, a "non-utopian concern . . . with clarity, accuracy and economy of means." *Marienbad* was a film without, Resnais admitted, "anecdote, witty dialogue, explanation, or chronology."[19]

If we can believe Roy Armes, Resnais' next film, *Muriel*, was to be for him an escape, a complete change, as Resnais "had felt that much of *Marienbad's* enclosed suffocating atmosphere came from the impossibility of talking about Algeria, inherent in the subject, as much as in the censorship situation of the French cinema."[20] To Resnais, *Marienbad* brought fame, but also the problem of being lionized for only one side of himself and his art. It is to Resnais' credit that he could shake *Marienbad* from his back, probably being helped in so doing by his falling short of the intelligent but sour Robbe-Grillet's complete pessimism, as he was "lacking Robbe-Grillet's absolute conviction of the futility of a commitment in art."[21]

There is, however, a sense of tragedy in *Marienbad* caused by the "New Materialism," a specter that was floating around Europe, perhaps rekindled by recollections of World War II and the childhood and adolescent experiences of the younger European directors, such as Resnais and Truffaut, who had lived in Paris during the German Occupation. Whenever it is screened, it remains a noisy witness to a period in which the post-World War II European cinema's love affair with the "New Materialism" hit its strong, startling, and final apogee.

4

From *Marienbad* to *Muriel*

Afterthoughts About *Marienbad*

AFTER *Last Year at Marienbad* was released—it premiered in Paris on September 21, 1961, and in New York City on March 7, 1962—*Le Monde* reporter Yvonne Baby asked Resnais "Had you thought of the public [that is, how they would react to the film]?" Resnais replied:

Without ever stopping to. I believe, to go back to the old formula of Marcel L'Herbier, that the director is the number one spectator of his film.

We would love to have the spectator let himself go and participate in continually creating his interpretation. The film is so made that fifty percent of it is what is shown there on the screen and the rest [comes from] the reactions and the participation of the spectator. Thus if one follows any possible self-determined interpretation, one arrives at this juncture, which [then] gives forth a realistic vision of life. *Marienbad* is an open [structured] film which proposes to everyone an experience, a choice. If one speaks to me of a gratuitous subjectivity, I will say, on the contrary, that we have wished to reach a large public, a huge audience.

Resnais continued:

Since what we're talking about is a film which tries to explore the unconscious [i.e., the subconscious], we preferred to adopt a style of game and narrative that is extremely free, reminiscent of, in a certain way, the opera. Thus as the oneiric limit of *Marienbad* is given [by Robbe-Grillet's screenplay], this necessitated the setting up of a mise-en-scène that indicated nothing but the essentials—a little like the murals of Giotto, where a stone of a certain size becomes a mountain and a large leaf becomes a forest.[1]

*'rench reservists in Paris in 1961 guard against a potential at-
ıck by Right-wing paratroopers from Algeria.*
ıgence Dalmas

Alain Robbe-Grillet and Resnais gave a joint statement of intention on the purpose of *Marienbad* to several *Cahiers du Cinéma* interviewers that made it seem as if director and screenwriter were in total agreement about their collaboration.[2] However, fourteen years later, Robbe-Grillet confessed to interviewer Brad Burke of *The New York Journal of the Arts* that he and Resnais fundamentally differed on how *Marienbad* was to go out to the spectator. The difference, said Robbe-Grillet, between himself and Resnais was the difference of sense between the two French words *plaisir* (pleasure) and *plaire* (to please). Resnais wanted to please the audience; Robbe-Grillet wanted to make the film for his pleasure. Robbe-Grillet further elaborated by suggesting that despite his thick as thieves attitude of common purposiveness with Resnais at the time of the filming, that he differed from him in unequivocally wanting to please the audience. "My goal was not to please," Robbe-Grillet-told Brad Burke. "What did you then mean by saying you are on the side of *plaisir*? Burke replied." To which Robbe-Grillet answered:

> For me, *plaire* would perhaps evoke even less than serious reactions. I saw this problem up close when I was working with someone else. I have done only one film as co-author with someone else up till now. I'm not speaking of Rauschenbeg. Rather I am speaking of *L'Année Derniere à Marienbad*, and the degree to which I found myself on the side of *plaisir* and Resnais on the side of *plaire*. He always felt like asking people around him: "Do you like this?" "Do you understand?" For me, it was really something else; pleasure was something completely different from this notion of pleasing.

"Just what do you mean by pleasure, then?" asked Burke, and Robbe-Grillet replied,

> I frequently adopt very current definitions, those which have been given by Umberto Eco, for example. On a coded horizon appears a displacement from the norm. This displacement is at first felt as a painful thing, a dissatisfaction, something which bothers you. You are thrown off. You are within an order, and you are thrown out. You are taken out of your repose, and from the time of the upset, there develops in the system of traditional literature, a return to the code by what in music is called a resolution; in modern literature, by repetition of certain displacements, a *new* code is formed in which one will again sense a certain fullness or fulfillment until there appears a new displacement with respect to this new code, which will again bother you, etc. Well, this definition of *plaisir* (pleasure) is something that has been dragged around a lot; I accept it provisionally.

> *Plaire* (to please), *on the contrary* [my italics] consists in respecting the code: that is, respecting the expectations of the person who is in his chair and who reads or watches the film and is calm and at rest.[3]

The End of the New Wave

The success of *Marienbad* in both France and America coincided with the end of the New Wave. "If the New Wave had a part in affording Alain Resnais and Marcel Hanoun the opportunity to make their first feature films," wrote Noel Burch at the time, "then we may easily forgive it for fostering some fake prodigies also."[4]

Two needs seem to have created the New Wave, which is usually looked at, not from the point of view of a public demand for it, but as an invention by a bold group of young French directors, "Truffaut & Co." who ranged between twenty-six and forty years of age and who made inexpensive films to suit their auteurish whims. These needs were a new generation's desire to see existential heros in films (Michel Poiccard in *Breathless*, Antoine Doinel in *The 400 Blows*), and second, a desire to see (on the part of a smaller part of the "new" audience) some of the serious concerns of the atomic age, including its effects on the institutions of love and marriage, deeply dissected (i.e., *Hiroshima Mon Amour*). The title of the films—in contrast to the same era of Hollywood films—are generically different: *A bout de souffle*, normally translated as *Breathless*, more accurately translates as *An Attack of Suffocation*, and *Les Quatres Cent Coups*, is better translated as *A Burst of Hell Raising*.

Does Resnais Really Belong to the New Wave?

All the New Wave films that succeeded in France (and England) between 1958 and 1962 either fell into one of the above categories or were a hybrid of both. Besides this, there was the American transmutation factor (as happened at this time in rock 'n' roll): The American art film circuit, founded on the strength of the Neo-Realist film's popularity, created the "foreign film" or "art film," and was thus prepared to receive the New Wave film as such. *Hiroshima Mon Amour* and *Marienbad*, Resnais' first two feature films, both succeeded in New York City and America as "art films," something that Pauline Kael deplored and wrote about at the time. Nonetheless, labels like "art film," "foreign film," and "New Wave film" brought young couples—a staple of the film business—to the box office to pay for Resnais.

The history of the term "The New Wave," is a strange one; for while the translation into English is quite satisfactory, the context in which the term was originally used was quite different. As Noel Burch put it, "Originally, the term *nouvelle vague*, as popularized by the snappy left-wing weekly *L'Express*, did not refer to cinema at all but to the generation of forward looking youth (mostly professional people, businessmen, and students) who were supposed to gather around Mendes-France and bring new ideas into French political life."[5] In 1958, *L'Express's* youth specialist, Françoise Giroud, wrote an article entitled "La Nouvelle Vague," where the connotation suddenly changed to meaning "The New Fashion"—clothes, behavior, the beat caves, new mores—and it, of course, included a statement about new expectations. Giroud's article also mentioned Chabrol's film, *Le Beau Serge* (1958), which was a low budget, "beat generation" type of film. The beat movement in the United States was well-known in France and was blatantly copied in French films, notably Carne's *Les Tricheurs*, which was roundly hated by the *Cahiers* critics among the New Wavers. There was also Roger Vadim's film successes with Brigitte Bardot. And one could now see that perhaps Jean-Pierre Melville had started it all with his personal films. By this time, *Cahiers du Cinéma* criticism was well-known among intellectuals and Giroud had undoubtedly checked out its pages. Thus the term Nouvelle vague/New Wave was ready for further application when *Hiroshima Mon Amour* and *The 400 Blows* appeared to the world via the splash of the 1959 Cannes Film Festival, and it gradually became applied specifically to the films made by the new young French directors. (Unlike England where its analog, the Modernist Movement, produced ideas, activities and products in all the arts except the cinema.) A cultural historian, while respecting the specific use of the term, the New Wave, as limited to film, would still resist calling it a style, and persist in looking at it as a Franco-American phenomenon, the French reaction with some borrowed Americanisms to the stagnations of their own urban culture.

What was then the New Wave film exactly? In 1964, when the fashion was no longer to make them, one writer described the New Wave like this:

> Style: Technically, a nouvelle vague film is generally recognizable by its fluidity (many directors—Godard and Demy, for example—resort to the

hand-held camera). The wide screen is preferred more than not—*Les Amants*, all Truffaut's films, *La Dénonciation*, *Le Petit Soldat*, *Adieu Phillipine*. Others concentrate on the theme of young people leading confused, nihilistic lives in Paris *(A bout de souffle, Les Bonnes Femmes, Les Quatres Cent Coups, L'Ascenseur pour l'echafaud)*. Others have tried to present a personal vision tempered by comedy or tragedy *(Cléo à 5 à 7, Tirez sur le pianiste, Lola, Les Dimanches de ville d'Avray)*.[6]

Sixty-seven new directors made first films in France in 1959 and 1960. (By the time of the Cannes Film Festival of 1962, we can consider the New Wave over.)

Is Alain Resnais, then, to be considered as part of the New Wave? I don't see why *Hiroshima* cannot be included in the New Wave. It meets the "fluidity" criterion of style; it meets the criterion of theme: "a personal vision tempered by comedy or tragedy."[7]

Last Year at Marienbad, Resnais' second feature, appeared in 1961, while the New Wave was still effervescent and some believed it was still to do its best work. Yet, it seems to owe everything to the nouveau roman and almost nothing to the New Wave.

Muriel Resnais' third film, can be seen either as having gone beyond the New Wave completely, or as a culmination of all of the techniques and styles of the New Wave film. In its daring to show the vision of the director, *Muriel* perhaps is a New Wave film; but its serious political content largely disqualifies it from such a category. Film historians would be better off not to consider *Muriel* a New Wave film but to consider it rather as a culmination of the New Wave tendency, such as is Jacques Rozier's *Adieu Phillipine*, a carefully crafted yet quite spontaneous seeming work of art. One can quickly find a similar use of Algeria as an off-screen event in both *Adieu Phillipine* and *Muriel*—two films made at the same time—that the former uses Algeria as a place where the young man, whose love life is made explicit, will go after the film is over, whereas *Muriel* shows a man who came back from there, who has no love life, and who must get on with the work of the world. *Resnais*, at any rate, has never called *Muriel* a New Wave film, though he has never disputed the inclusion of *Hiroshima* and *Marienbad* in such a category.

Significantly, Resnais had never commented much on *his* likes and dislikes in the New Wave cinema. It has been hinted that he did not even like the New Wave, that he did not like its "looseness," its hand-held camera self-indulgences. There is no hard evidence that

Resnais paid much attention to criticizing the New Wave. He was more of an influence on it than it was on him.

François Truffaut, for example—in his double role as a critic—suggested why Resnais refused to run with the pack in making a real New Wave film. Truffaut's theory, stated in the winter of 1961–1962 (thus *after Marienbad*), requires that we consider *Hiroshima* (and *Breathless*) as atypical, non-representative films of their directors. In other words, Resnais and Godard made these, their one and only New Wave films, and then turned their back on the fashion they themselves helped create and moved on. (Truffaut, by contrast, never stopped making New Wave films, as is illustrated by his latest childishnesses, *Small Change* [1976] and *The Man Who Loved Women* [1977].)

What interests us specifically here is how contemporaneous criticism treated Resnais' co-mingling with the New Wave. Was he considered in 1960 as: (1) part and parcel of the New Wave? (2) an elite component of the New Wave (i.e., one of the New Wavers who would go on to bigger and better things)? or (3) definitely *not* part of the New Wave? (Critics mostly thought the second or did other New Wave directors think of Resnais as part of the New Wave?

Truffaut's aesthetic conclusion as to where the New Wave could go and where it could not merits our serious consideration, especially as he so self-confidently locates Resnais' place in relation to it. And it is based on Truffaut's own classification schema, one he based interestingly enough not on the polar opposition between Lumière (reality) and Méliès (fantasy), as is customary in French film criticism, but surprisingly between Lumière (realism) and Delluc (avant-gardism). This is an extremely interesting and aesthetically sensitive way to locate Resnais' place in the complex topology of French film movements.

Truffaut put it in these words:

> Aesthetic considerations are what concern me most. I believe, for instance, that there are two kinds of cinema, one stemming from Lumière and the other from Delluc. Lumière invented the cinema to film nature or action (*L'Arroseur Arrosé*, etc.). Delluc, who was a novelist and critic, thought one could use the invention to film ideas or actions which have a meaning other than the obvious one, and so, eventually move closer to the other arts. And the result is that you have Griffiths, Chaplin, Stroheim, Flaherty, Gance, Vigo, Renoir, Rossellini (and nearer home, Godard) in the Lumière camp, Epstein, L'Herbier, Feyder, Gremillon, Huston, Bardem, Astruc, Anton-

ioni (and nearer home, Resnais) in the Delluc camp. For the first group, the cinema is essentially a show, for the second it's a language. The critics, incidentially, have always had more sympathy with the Delluc division [which includes Resnais].

Besides the two groupings based on the purpose of cinema, Truffaut also distinguished between two narrative camps:

The Sagan trend: attempts to be more outspoken about questions of love and sex; self-portraits of artists or intellectuals; cultivated, well-off, apparently chilly characters. One title: *Les Cousins* [Chabrol].

The Queneau trend: attempts to explore an everyday vocubulary; unexpected and economic encounters between people who are generally working class or a bit far out; a taste for mixing genres and shifts of mood; a kind of *rose et noir* [light and somber] tenderness: Some titles: *Zazie dans le metro, Un couple, Les bonne femmes, Tirez sur le pianist, Lola, Une Femme est une femme, Adieu Phillipine.*

Interviewer Louis Marcorelles then asked Truffaut; "Where would you put Alain Resnais?"

"His quality," replied Truffaut, "is that he escapes any classification. But all the same, let's imagine a third category which we would call the Editions de Minuit cinema [the publishing house of Editions du Minuit publishes the works of Beckett, Robbe-Grillet and many of the more experimental French authors, and also has many left-wing writers in its publishing list]. There we could group together those films which correspond to the 'new novel' and also those which have sociological aspirations."[8]

We have by now, I hope, established that the New Wave was not a cohesive unified movement of cinema, with its directors all shooting in the same style. In fact, as Agnes Varda claimed, the only thing the New Wave directors had in common was a lack of money. The New Wave was, like the title of an earlier Truffaut article, "Une certain tendence du cinéma français" ("A certain tendency in the French cinema"). Truffaut had written this article in 1954, criticizing "la tradition du qualité" in the French cinema. Here again in the New Wave was a tendency—a tendency to group around certain basic strategies and attitudes. One could say then that the New Wave was probably no more than a tendency associated with a new movie mystique—rather than a style of cinema—tailored just for the new young generation of Frenchmen. This activity, with its jump cuts as jazz messages was not what ever interested Resnais primarily. Resnais was thus one of the first to outgrow it. And one of the reasons he abandoned the New Wave completely was that during 1960–1961, while completing *Marienbad,* he began to pay serious intellectual attention to the Algerian War which, though one would never have guessed it from looking at the films—coincided with the New Wave. As a consequence, instead of ignoring Algeria, as most New Wave films did, or having it as an off-screen event—as did Jacques Rozier's *Adieu Phillipine,* Resnais faced up to his having hitherto ignored it in his next film, *Muriel.* Not a little of Resnais' own guilt in having ignored Algeria went into that film.

From *Marienbad* to *Muriel*: Towards a New Approach

Though critics have thoroughly analyzed the operation of *Muriel,* no one has shown why Resnais made it and how—if we look at Resnais' works in their entirety—it fits in. Various intellectual and or political motives have been assigned to *Muriel;* yet one of the reasons the film is a success is its human quality. No one has mentioned it as the unusual love story that—on one level—it is.

Resnais admitted this in only one interview, but his admission is important. "It [*Muriel*] is a love story. An exchange of sentiments. My desire is to cross-cut this exchange between characters and the audience, to pinpoint inside certain members of the audience their position by relating it to their normal life. The characters must be determined by the spectators in the audience: each one will take his shape as a function of the reactions of the members of the audience."[9] In *Muriel,* Resnais has (as we will describe in the next chapter) drawn on his theatrical background, particularly on the *Lehrstück* aspect of Brecht's method of involving his audience. Thus the big change between *Marienbad* and *Muriel* is how the latter addresses its audience in a different manner.

In *Muriel,* Resnais shifted to a different style of acting, which definitely alienated much of Resnais' public. The style was a mixture of Brecht and Comédie Française and was intended to work by getting the audience to "determine the characters." The film thus featured the raw material of the character, and not the fully chiseled character himself. This is what Resnais meant by "I am relying a lot on the phenomenon of sympathy" to reach the audience's favor. One of the key ways to get this device to function in cinema is the careful selection of the face of the actor.

In *Muriel,* Resnais did a superb job of this; his choice of facial types in *Muriel* was very discriminating: the evocative face of Jean-Baptiste Thierry, a face which was sharp in features and could show brooding; the dishonest face and the hang-dog look of Alphonse; the lyric face of Delphine Seyrig (without Riva and Seyrig, the cinema of Resnais seems empty, at times) and the marvelously impish but malevolent face of Robert, are all so well chosen as to be Eisensteinian *typages*.

Furthermore, a comparison between Brecht's *Mother Courage* and *The Three Penny Opera*, and *Muriel* (which is beyond the scope of this book) would be instructive on the level of creation of character. My guess is that a huge gap would emerge between Resnais' and Pabst's use of realism in cinema. In *Muriel* the distancing devices are constructed through use of a photographic reality, showing the disjunction and reassociation of real images with new real images, thus using the camera to stage the characters in real environments which are used like props. What results from such an approach is that only the dialogue of the characters remains felt as very stage-like and grand-opera theatrical. This is precisely what we feel the dialogue is like in *Muriel*. It stands apart from the film, and it is often used to address us, the spectators, directly. (In fact, the weakest Resnais film, *Je T'Aime, Je T'Aime* is the film in which we are never addressed.) It is the merit of *Muriel* that images function superlatively as obeying the desire to create a fine film at the level of cinematography while, at the same time, the dialogue succeeds as Kammerspiel-like intimate theater. The clever construction of a disparity between image and narrative in *Muriel* works, and this is what makes the film work as a conception.

Resnais, however, did not just conceive of *Muriel* as a Brechtian film for the sake of making such a film; *Muriel* was also conceived (on both screenplay level and final film version) as a political film. As Susan Sontag observed, Muriel perhaps tries to do too much.

> The reason *Muriel* is difficult is that it attempts to do both what *Marienbad* and what *Hiroshima* did. It attempts to deal with substantive issues—the Algerian War, the OAS, the racism of the *colons* [colonists]—even as *Hiroshima* dealt with the bomb, pacifism, and collaboration. But it also, like *Marienbad*, attempts to project a purely abstract drama. The burden of this double intention—to be both concrete and abstract—doubles the technical virtuosity of the film. . . . [Resnais] can not be said to have solved the problem, and in an ultimate sense *Muriel* must be judged a noble failure, but he has shown a good deal more about the problem. . . .[10]

This is, of course, what makes *Muriel* a heroic film, one which reaches for the level of the stars in what it wishes to accomplish. It is the film which, to me, represents the furthest advance of the narrative film beyond Griffith, and a film against which all other narrative advances or attempts at an advance, have to be measured. *Muriel*, in short, is the narrative frontier of the cinema it now stands.

For this reason, it is important to establish whether Sontag is right or wrong (and because of her incredible didacticism, one has either to agree with her or ditch her comments entirely). I would argue that Sontag is wrong here, simply, because without the political aspect of the film—is that what gives the film its sincerity? its investigative power? was the war in Algeria a better riddle than anything in fiction, i.e., the proof that "truth is stranger than fiction," as the cliché goes?—without its reality quest, *Muriel* would be a much weaker film, and in fact, might not have worked at all. If Muriel had been a character in a *serie noir* B-novel who disappeared, and the plot of the film had been an attempt to find out who did what to her, would we care? *Muriel*, it seems, is at once an elegant and honest (rarely in life can the two be combined in a work of art, but somehow Resnais has succeeded) combination of the search for an advance in film narrative with the problematic of the Algerian War. In addition, it is a good story of two parallel narratives' of two generations, as has often been seen already in good narrative cinema. *Muriel* is not, like *Blow-Up*, an epistemological quest disguised as a mystery story. It is the presentation of a political mystery for us to attempt to resolve or face. For a brief period in his life, a political conscience must have surfaced in Resnais, for him to have so constructed and conceived this film.

During the filming of *Marienbad*, which Resnais claimed took place in a claustrophobic atmosphere due to the Algerian War, Resnais signed the Free Algeria Manifesto drafted by Jean-Paul Sartre along with one hundred twenty-one artists and intellectuals, including Florence Malraux, his future wife. Appearing on October 25, 1961, it advocated deserting rather than continuing to fight as the true course for any French soldier in Algeria. Admittedly, the war was almost over, but this action—as those who have experienced the similar situation America went through with Vietnam—was still courageous enough. For example, as a consequence of this, Resnais' *Marienbad* was banned from the 1962 Cannes Film Festival by the French government. Resnais' producer on *Marienbad*, Pierre Braunberger, thinks that "Alain decided to make a political film because he felt guilty among his left wing friends, and did it to go along with his group of friends rather than because of any burning conviction to do so."[11]

Resnais himself supported Braunberger's view, when, on March 18, 1962 (after *Marienbad* and before *Muriel*) he confessed as much to Eugene Archer:

> I don't like to talk about World War II, because I wasn't in the underground, he revealed, explaining with considerable embarrassment his asthama-induced absence from the Army. 'During the[German] occupation, I was studying in the theater, and I was so immersed in it that I didn't even know there was an organized resistance. But I don't think that's a good excuse.'[12]

Muriel, as it emerges, is perhaps only a quasi-political film. As the critics of *Positif* observed in 1966, *Muriel* was a step closer to reality than *Marienbad*, and then *La Guerre Est Finie* was step over the line into becoming a real political film, and that *Muriel* is just a "social" film, as is *La Guerre Est Finie*. What we cannot deny is that both films are about politics.

Whether this is due to Resnais or due to his loyal transmission of the political intent of the two screenwriters who created the scripts for *Muriel* (Jean Cayrol, who was in the French Resistance) and *La Guerre Est Finie* (Jorge Semprun, Spanish socialist in exile because of Franco—who, incidentally, returned to Spain in 1976 after Franco's death) is an important question also, but one which we never will be able to resolve.

My guess is that Resnais, like Godard (and this is a much more severe criticism of Godard than of Resnais), swung into the political realm because the *Zeitgeist* seemed to flow that way. Thus, I tend to see *Muriel* as a more sincere effort than Godard's banned *Le Petit Soldat* (1960) for the latter is a message film, an essay, about how Godard feels about war in general, whereas Resnais at least, concretely addressed himself to Algeria. I would also read *Muriel* as well as *La Guerre Est Finie* as containing little or no mystification about the political problem they deal with; thus, while they are not in any sense Marxist films, they approach the Marxist ideal through their attempt to be material and concrete. No spiritual archetypes exist in either film, and no false exhortations are made. A comparison of Bertolucci's *Before the Revolution* (1964) and *Muriel* shows that Resnais—as opposed to young Bertolucci—is already wise in the ways of the world. *Muriel* is already a study of patience in an existential world, a film statement that does not stand on the side of the hasty observation, but one that indirectly suggests the value of a concrete-materialist analysis. The even firmer analysis (combined with a flat surface suggesting documentary reality) is what probably "snowed" the Marxists critics of *Positif* into seeing *La Guerre Est Finie* as a decidedly committed or political film. *Muriel*, of course can be overtly seen as an anti-OAS film, for in it, Bernard murders Robert, purportedly a member of the OAS. Bernard represents the non-Marxist fifty percent of the eighty-five percent of Frenchmen who were against the OAS at the time.

The *Zeitgeist* aspect of *Muriel* may be a bit obscure for viewers today. This is not only attributable to the fact that younger viewers have no memory of the Algerian War, but also to the grand reluctance of Resnais in *Muriel* to create a spokeman character, an authorial character to speak for himself. However, Resnais has, perhaps for the only time in his film career, come close to representing (but *not* incarnating) himself as a character. Robert Benayoun suggests "in Bernard, Resnais has invested all of his sympathies. Resnais might have once gone around and filmed like that himself."[13]

Yet, Resnais could have encoded Bernard with even more of himself. So covert is his likeness there that we never find any overt representation of Resnais. Yet, there is an equivalence of Resnais' personal political experience in *Muriel*. Shortly before work began on *Muriel*, the OAS was terrorizing France with periodic bombings, like those today of the Baader-Meinhof gang in Germany. In February, 1962, the OAS tried to blow away Resnais' future father-in-law, André Malraux, with a plastic bomb. Florence Malraux (André's daughter, Resnais' second assistant on *Marienbad*, his assistant on *Muriel*, and his future wife) had been a signatory of the Free Algeria Manifesto, and therefore to the OAS the Malrauxs were "leftists." André Malraux also had an apartment in Boulogne at the time, which may have had something to do with the selection of Boulogne as the site for *Muriel*.

These personal factors may have made Robert, Bernard's OAS-joining comrade, a larger character in *Muriel* than he otherwise would have been—even beyond the sketch of him in Jean Cayrol's script. No original "first version" of the *Muriel* script has been published; so we do not know whether its 1959 version was considerably different from its 1962 version. But, since the OAS did not exist when Cayrol fiirst showed Resnais the script, we may assume that Resnais, rather than Cayrol, was responsible for the emphasis on the veiled threat of the OAS. At any rate, the OAS types in *Muriel* are depicted considerably more realistically (through photography—not through words—for the term "OAS" is never spoken in *Muriel*) than are the fantasy soldiers of his *Providence* and are meant to be perceived as such by us directly. They are not meant to be seen as though through the paranoid vision of Bernard, as a character's fantasy. In short, all of *Muriel* is given to us as its author's narration; there is no narrator assigned to be the master of ceremonies for *Muriel*. It is this lack of a surrogate narrator that lets us feel the *Zeitgeist* emerge in *Muriel*.

The attempt to answer world problems which so enriches *Muriel* introduces such minor touches as Bernard's insisting to his mother, at the film's end, that he can now live without money. (This dates the film to a 1962-1969 *Zeitegeist*; youth claims it can now survive without money.) Touches such as this represent Resnais' desire, I believe, to please his audience. Upon viewing the film in 1978, one is conversely struck by the fact that the classic structure that is so strong is also there, is what still makes the film so pleasing. One need not know much about the Algerian War to understand the film.

With *Muriel* Resnais made a film with a formal, classical structure, one intended to remain valid for years; but, we must admit, it also used the Algerian War as a subject and did it justice.

Muriel is about the deep freeze the Algerian War cast on freedom in France in 1962, and the mood associated with that period. In viewing *Zeitgeist* films, or the *Zeitgeist* aspect of a film, historically, we should try to feel how they evoke the time period they were made to represent. *Muriel*, then, is one of those rare films that is both a time capsule and a classic. This shows Resnais can be a successful eclectic at times. It is a film to be respected particularly for this reason, especially because America never made its film about Vietnam; the *Zeitgeist* classic mix shows just how successful a similar film about Vietnam could have been.

Resnais and the War in Algeria

To conclude the discussion of the political character of Resnais' art it is useful to review the events of the Algerian War and corresponding political activity in France from May 1959 through March 1964. During this period, Resnais had completed *Hiroshima* and worked on *Marienbad* and *Muriel.* The following chronology provides a useful background for an examination of the political content of the films in work at this time and to Resnais' political commitments in general.

1959	
May 8	*Hiroshima* shown at Cannes Film Festival, out of competition
June 10	*Hiroshima* premieres in Paris.
	Resnais contemplated an adaptation of Daniel Anselme's "La Permission," which was soon abandoned because he felt that it would have been too difficult to capture the work's sociologically realistic tone. Resnais began work on script with Anne-Marie de Villaine for a film to be called *A Suivre a n'en finir* (To follow is not to make an end to it) about the "repercussions of the Algerian War on a young married couple when the husband is recalled to military service." This project was abandoned, probably because it was too explicitly political for Resnais. The ban on the subject of the Algerian War, if the work in question was considered detrimental to the government, was not lifted until January 1963. Resnais began working on the rudiments of the idea of *Muriel* with Jean Cayrol.
November 11	Anti-deGaulle demonstrations in Algiers.
1960	
Early 1960	Producers bring Alain Robbe-Grillet and Resnais together. They quickly exchange ideas, Robbe-Grillet suggests several alternative scripts for a film; Resnais finds all of them acceptable, but selects the most "austere formal" one. This will become *Last Year At Marienbad.*
January 7	*Hiroshima* premiers in Great Britain
January 24	Week of the barricades in Algeria. Right wing demonstration leads to a week of Captain Lagaillarde and Joseph Ortiz controlling a part of Algeria. Lagaillarde surrenders. Ortiz flees to Spain. Colonel Jean Gardes acquitted but banished to the interior of Algeria.
May	*Hiroshima* opens in New York City.
September–October	Resnais shoots exteriors of *Marienbad* in Germany.
October 25	Resnais signs Sartre's *Free Algeria* manifesto. (Also known as the *Manifesto of the 121.)*

November	Shoots *Marienbad* interiors in Paris. John F. Kennedy elected president of the United States.
November 11	Demonstrations by *colons* and police in Algeria. *Marienbad* in editing stage.
December 9	Violent *colon* demonstrations in Algeria.
December 11–14	Violent Moslem counterdemonstrations.
1961	
Early 1961	French government does not permit *Marienbad* to be entered in the Cannes Film Festival, because Resnais signed the *Free Algeria Manifesto.* Considerable OAS activity in France.
April 22–24	Four generals and four colonels stage putsch in Algeria They are arrested and De Gaulle wins. Algeria will be given independence. The war is virtually over because the army refuses to fight for a lost cause. The OAS goes underground.
May 1961	Cannes Film Festival. No Resnais entry; no Truffaut entry. Godard's *Le Petit Soldat* has been banned, so there is no Godard entry.
June 1	Salan, Jouhaud, Gardy, Argoud, Broizat, Gardes, and Yves Godard sentenced to death for their part in the attempted coup d'etat in April.
August 29	*Marienbad* entered in Venice Film Festival. wins the Golden Lion.
September 29	*Marienbad* premiers in England. DeGaulle commutes the death sentence of seven of the condemned officers.
1962	
February 22	*Marienbad* premiers in England. Heavy OAS activity in France.
March 7	*Marienbad* premiers in the United States in New York City.
May	Algeria becomes independent. Three hundred thousand *colons* are evacuated to France. *Colons* continue to leave and to settle in France.
Summer	Script of *Muriel* is finalized.
	Archer Winsten interviews Resnais for *The New York Times.*
November 1962–January *1963*	*Muriel* shot in Boulogne on loacation and in Paris.
January 25	French Censor Board and Ministry of Information releases Godard's *Le Petit soldat* with minor cuts; it is shown in Paris.

July 24	*Muriel* premiers in Paris.
September 18	*Muriel* is shown at the New York Film Festival.
October 23	*Muriel* shown at London Film Festival.
November	*Muriel* premiers in the United States.
1964	
March 19	*Muriel* premiers in England.

5

Muriel I

MURIEL emerges as a Hitchcockian film, a point which will be demonstrated subsequently. But before proceeding to analyze the film, I should like to set the tone of this chapter by relating an anecdote which reveals similarities in the directorial points of view of Alfred Hitchcock and Alain Resnais. The source of the anecdote is François Truffaut who reports Hitchcock's reaction to the news that Resnais was working on a film entitled *Muriel.* As you read the anecdote, keep in mind that there is no reason to assume any prior collaboration on the film by Hitchcock and Resnais. Hitchcock, on hearing the title of the film, spins a tale with remarkably similar feeling to that which Resnais developed in *Muriel,* demonstrating an intriguing instance of parallel concerns.

> When Hitchcock heard that Resnais' new film was to be *Muriel,* he told me to tell Resnais the true story of Muriel. "Two guys walk down a street and there, in the gutter, they see an arm. 'Why, it's Muriel!,' the one says after which the other, shrugging his shoulders, says: 'What do you know about it?' A little while later, they stumble upon a leg and the first guy once again recognizes Muriel, but the second one still remains skeptical. A second leg shows up a few yards away, but doesn't settle anything. They turn the corner and near the gutter, there is a head. 'There, what did I tell you,' said the first guy. 'You see very well that it is Muriel.' The second guy, viewing the evidence, bends over, picks up the head and takes it in his arms and says: 'But what is all this here, Muriel? There is something which isn't right!' An exchange of good ideas: the Hitchcockian presence is very important in *Muriel,* not only via his effigy (a gag in the same spirit) and by multiple allusions of references but also by, one might add, an influence of profundity, of several levels . . . which all honor the master of suspense.[1]

·neral Edmond Jouhaud (left) and General Raoul Salan in giers in 1961, leaders of the OAS, the secret army organiza- n that Resnais describes in Muriel.
·nce Dalmas

Resnais himself says, "It's a love story. An exchanging of feelings. My desire is, against this interchange between characters and spectator, to let some viewers check out their own life against that of the characters. The characters ought to be worked out in their relation to the spectator; each one will take his proper place as a function of the spectator's reaction. I'm really counting a lot on the phenomenon of the sympathy-antipathy as a dramatic [*sic* epic] device."[2]

Narrative Technique

Muriel is "a love story of blank pages,"[3] a story of missing emotions, a story of the frozen emotions of a provincial French city right after the Algerian War. The narrative is fragmented. All couples in the film collapse and dissolve. Only individuals survive. At the end of this pessimistic film, there is only a chance that any of its characters can make their way. We, the spectators, however, can emerge with the feeling of being satisfied witnesses to a month of crisis in the lives of six characters, and we can feel the wiser for it. *Muriel* is not a film that can make us happy, but it can make us wise.

Alphonse and Françoise arrive in Boulogne as a couple (Alphonse pretends that Françoise is his niece, whereas she is really his mistress). They have come to visit Hélène, who lives with her stepson, Bernard. Alphonse, curious to know why Hélène wants to see him after twenty years, forms a temporary liaison with her that is interrupted by her boyfriend, Roland de Smoke, the head of a wrecking company. Bernard and Françoise pair off at Françoise's initiative, until Bernard leaves her, announcing he is going to see his girl friend, Marie-Do. He has previously told Hélène he is engaged to a girl named "Muriel." At the same time, Robert, Bernard's old army buddy, attempts to get him to join a right-wing anti-DeGaulle organization. Bernard refuses. Alphonse and Hélène get along but their tête-a-tête is interrupted by Ernest, who declares that the film's narrative has made a mistake, it is *he* who had originally been in love with Hélène. This causes Bernard to expose film, which in turn exposes his tape recorded complicity in the torture of Muriel. He murders Robert and announces his self-sufficiency to Hélène, who ends up, instead of running to de Smoke for help, visiting an old, secure, couple she has not seen in years. In the meantime, Ernest tries to take Alphonse back to his wife, Simone, after Françoise announces she is abandoning him. At the first chance, Alphonse escapes Ernest and flees on the next bus to Belgium.

The Hitchcockian presence in *Last Year At Marienbad*, amusingly underscored in that film by what appears to be a full-size cardboard cut-out of Hitchcock, is followed by the presence of that master's influence in *Muriel*.
The Museum of Modern Art Film Stills Archive

Simone, meanwhile, coming to fetch Alphonse, enters Hélène's empty apartment.

The only common element of the story is the character, Muriel, whom we never see. *Muriel, or a Time of Return,* the film's full title, refers in part to Alphonse's return to Hélène, but even more to Bernard's return to France, full of remorse about the death by torture of an Algerian girl named Muriel. We only learn about this girl from Bernard's voice-over narration, and the girl only appears in the film in the form of Bernard's guilt feelings (the return of the repressed). Otherwise, the story is very much the chronologically told tale of Hélène Aughain, a woman living in Boulogne, during three weeks in October, 1962, with her adopted son, Bernard. Bernard's return from Algeria coincides with the return of Alphonse, Hélène's old lover from twenty years before. The two "doubled" stories of Bernard and Alphonse have two functions in the narrative. They contrast two French generations at war (World War II and Algeria), they contrast two psychological types of characters that perhaps are most often produced as an effect of war on a society: Alphonse the mythomaniac and Bernard the repressed. Alphonse represents the bigot who dislikes Arabs because he has come to believe in the myth of the "glory" of the Algerian War (the French are heroic: Arabs are evil). His mythomania shows all the symptoms of a religious faith that has collapsed into a secular belief no more answerable to history than to the tenets of religion.

But a film is more than its plot. In a peculiarly characteristic way, *Muriel* is, of all of Resnais' films, his one fling at expressionistic effects (though this does not mean the film has a closed structure; it does not). By expressionistic effects I mean those that stand for more deeply felt emotions. In the sense that *Muriel* attempts to show essence by effects, the film is very much reminiscent of Alfred Döblin's *Berlin Alexanderplatz,* the first major novel to use the expressionistic style in delineating the activities of a city. (*Muriel* is similarly a "cityscape.") Half of *Muriel* shows isolated incidents, which take place in Boulogne; similarly, half of *Berlin Alexanderplatz* puts Berlin into the foreground and makes it "the narrator." As with Döblin's masterpiece, Jean Cayrol's script (and Resnais' film) of *Muriel* is not just the story of Bernard Aughain, but simultaneously that of Boulogne. *Muriel* is the depiction of a totality, the mood of a town representing France, in which Bernard moves about while simulcasting his story coincidentally with those of the other inhabitants. The "tricky" thing about *Muriel* is how the film tries to give the illusion that many of the events it shows occur simultaneously, whereas on the screen they are shown sequentially. One sequence, for example, alternates shots of two groups of two men with the trivial conversations of each group so designed that they could also be attributed to the other so that the dialogue seems to belong to both. Sound dissolves segue the shots. The overall effect is one of totality. The narrative of *Muriel* can thus be described in the same fashion as a critic recently described that of *Berlin Alexanderplatz*.

> This totality [or narrative]—a favorite expression of literary expressionism—achieved by means of the montage or collage, as it is found, for example, in the pictures of the Cubists and especially in Kurt Schwitters' MERZ pictures: self-sufficient elements of reality are mounted into the novel and are given a new function and a changed reality in the context of the novel without giving up their true identity. Thus all sorts of "literary" productions which a person of our century encounters daily find their way into the novel: hit songs, advertising blurbs, news reports, weather reports, political slogans, theater programs, statistics, etc. Döblin cut such texts out and pasted them into his manuscript. In a manner previously unknown, the novel thus presents the world directly by going beyond merely describing it. Often these texts stand in apparent isolation as foreign bodies, and occasionally they appear in the stream of consciousness of the figures or of the narrator. Because the world in its immediate fullness forces its way into the figures from outside, because its governing consciousness is inundated by the automatism of the stream of consciousness fed internally or externally, the personality of the figures dissolves, and the dividing line between subject and object is obliterated. Here again Döblin's philosophical insight becomes visible. There is no isolated thing, no isolated individual. Everything is linked in a "real nexus" (*Realzusammenhang*) with the surrounding world. Thus even in the style the theme of the novel becomes evident: the guilt of isolation and the over-estimation of his own power on the part of the isolated individual.[4]

Resnais achieved the same totality as Döblin in *Berlin Alexanderplatz*. This "writing" of an idea, on film, is in itself a marvellous, historical, monumental achievement. Yet the way Resnais did it is crucially important. It was not so much a matter of using the shifting narrator technique but using the greater advantage of the film over the novel, which—as Döblin once said in a film script he wrote in 1921—would be first "to abandon the field of tension (*Span-*

nungsfeld) in favor of groups of scenes mediated by 'transformations,' so that an amalgamation of elements according to their meaning [might be] achieved, and [second] to create imaginary space beside naturalistic space."[5] In *Muriel* Resnais uses the sound track to create and connect falsely a loose non-linear series of images. For example, early night in *Muriel* becomes day, and day becomes night during a two minute conversation. If one argues: "Well, the conversation could have taken place over two days," one can counter with a semantic analysis of the conversation, which would show that either the conversation took place at one time or it was nonsense. Hence, as Hitchcock suggested, one cheats to get this effect.

Thus we as spectators sense that the reality of *Muriel* is more chaotic than we are "told" it is by the soundtrack's smooth segueing from event to event. We also see—as in *Berlin Alexanderplatz*[6]—the totality of the world—but we see a more chaotic totality. The narrative difference between *Muriel* and *Berlin Alexanderplatz* is considerable even though both were created to show similar things. Resnais—unlike Döblin—is not a "secular mystic" who believes in naturalism. *Muriel* is not naturalism seeking verisimilitude or documentation of reality—it is a suprareal (or Surreal)[7] film constructed not to show reality, but to force the spectator to confront reality.

Pierre Kast, a French filmmaker and critic and *Cahiers du Cinémapanelist*, has successfully fathomed, in my opinion, the reasons Resnais made *Muriel:*

What does Resnais propose [in *Muriel*]? To show, it seems to me, as never yet before seen, a certain reality: to oblige the viewer to confront himself with himself, [an act] which appears to him at once faithful and monstrously unfaithful to that which he has never thought about in looking at himself in this way. It is concerned above all with a profound reputting under analysis of all of the logical systems dealing with external reality concerning those people who live in the world today. Evidently, if one sets out to describe the subject matter of *Muriel* with a certain type of vocabulary, one arrives at a presentation analogous to that of *Elle* or *Marie-Claire* [magazines for young women on the order of *Madamoiselle* or *Glamour*]; but it is precisely that which is put to the question; in other words, the film obliges people to find themselves in the presence of—in regarding their own self-adventure—the same horror that springs forth in looking at the external world, this monstrous reality in which they live and to which they are normally accustomed. And the essential proposition of Resnais is to open their eyes and tell them: look at yourself, here you are in fact.[8]

If we take this "why" into consideration—to get the spectator to think—and relate it back to Resnais' "how"—to use a sympathy-antipathy program on the spectator—we see the beautifully consistent way Resnais' "why" and "how" fuse.

It should be obvious to the reader by now that *Muriel* represents a break with what Resnais was doing when he made *Hiroshima* and *Marienbad.* Neither of those two films is intentionally banal, as is *Muriel.*

Muriel is about ordinary middle-class people "in fact," as Kast suggests, and their ordinary stories. The plot is soap-opera. According to Resnais' biographer, Roy Armes, even the film's dialogue reflects this banality [screenwriter Cayrol seems to try for Sartre's goal of authenticity for each person by having each character sound as banal as he or she is; only Bernard sounds as though he might have some superior intelligence] and has none of the incantatory repetitions of the two previous works. But it is presented in theatrical tones and accompanied by stage gestures. The purpose of this method is threefold in *Muriel:* to increase the air of strangeness, to prevent us from identifying with the characters, and to unify the film, since all the actors in it adopt a common non-naturalistic style (in the same way that all of Bresson's actors share a non-theatrical approach). The unification is achieved by allowing the dialogue of one scene to overlap the next [recall Resnais' similar approach in *Hiroshima* and *Marienbad*] and more especially by the way he uses music.[9]

Why does Resnais not want us to identify with the characters? Is it for Brechtian reasons, to make us distance ourselves so we see beyond the characters, see through their self-deceptions? John Ward has said of *Muriel* that "it would be mistaken to call *Muriel* a stream of consciousness film, since there is no interior monologue in it and no evidence that the narrative is a reflection of the characters' sensations except on the few occasions when there are direct flashbacks. . . ."[10]

Yet Ward, for all his open perceptions about it, sounds as if he would have trouble dealing with, describing, and identifying himself with a film that avoids presenting the characters' point of view. "One of the ways," he says, "in which we understand what is going on in a book or a film is by the way the characters develop and by what is going on inside them. In *Muriel* almost all this is absent, and we have to look to situation, settings, objects"[11] (i.e., at objects and artifacts: cameras, guns, furniture, etc., like those that make up the core of the *nouveaux romans* of Robbe-Grillet, the object-oriented violently anti-subjective objectivity of *Die Neue Sachlichkeit* "art" exhibitions, the architectonic landscapes and buildings that present themselves as reality in Antonioni's films).[12] Very important—for here is where the Resnais film ontologically differs even from Robbe-Grillet's works, as well as those of the Bauhaus or Antonioni—we have to be sensitive to how *Muriel* compresses and expands film time through its quasi-musical-tempo-like structure of fluctuating ritardandos and accelerandos, and makes us see a landscape dated with the rhythms of 1962.

Yet Cayrol's script for *Muriel,* John Ward admits, does share a common narrative technique with the work of Robbe-Grillet. *Muriel* owes its technique, Ward insists, to Husserl's phenomenology and, in particular, to the theory of intentionality. Ward quotes Husserl,

> Consciousness is characterstically consciousness of something, it points beyond itself. Consciousness is therefore revealed through its directedness to objects; its intentionality. And the physical world discloses its significance to us through the intentions we have towards it. Things have no intrinsic meaning. A hill, for instance, is only steep because we want to climb it.

He concludes that "the physical details of appearance reveal character far more than dialogue."[13] This implies that some kind of semiotics more than semantics informs the spectator of what is going on in *Muriel.* This, however, is not true. *Muriel* is a complex mix of significations through signs and words, and Resnais uses an entire arsenal of both. It seems, then, that the viewer of *Muriel* is bombarded with more stimuli than usually delivered in the ordinary film. How does the spectator proceed from here and "figure out" the sense of the film?

The spectator in *Muriel* can make sense of the film because he/she is given a masterfully contrived program of information. One useful advantage of the third generation film, we can interject here, is that it usually gives the spectator such a wealth. Yet, the extent to which *Muriel* succeeds or fails depends not just on the quantity of information transmitted, but on the information system of the film. There are plenty of signs and much dialogue which tell fact. But making sense of *Muriel* depends additionally on whether the one-time spectator can learn the information transmitting system of the film fast enough to follow it. Resnais here has doubted that he began the film well. He later felt that he "lost" some of the spectators in the first reel, by not being clear enough.[14] I would be inclined to agree with him. A second viewing of *Muriel* is essential;[15] it shows how unfruitful parts of the first viewing—especially of the beginning—are.

The big risk or liability, then, of the third generation film like *Muriel* is that it usually starts out without giving character point of view in the very beginning of the film, just when the spectator most needs it.

Yet critics like Ward are wrong if they think *Muriel* lacks character point of view throughout. There are, for example, during the film repetitive occurrences of ever more vehement bickerings between Alphonse the mythomaniac and Bernard the inquisitor which give us characters' points of view, both semantically and semiotically. (See the sequence analysis in this chapter.) Some of these conflicts integrate information into the more epic and less dramatic sequences of the film, where the overall sequence gives the spectator a Brechtian "activating effect," a thought to think, a suggested action to take.[16]

Muriel is a highly manipulated film, and Resnais uses character point of view as well as the director's disguised metonymic third person point of view[17] in a mixed bag of narrative effects to attempt to draw in the spectator.

Analysis of a sequence from *Muriel:* Shots 516–540

The purpose of this analysis is to test first the empirical assumption, obtained after watching several screenings of this sequence, that the character, Bernard, is directly addressing the spectator and not the other characters. Another empirical observation to be tested is whether Bernard and Alphonse, when they have a verbal confrontation, are addressing each other: why are they not felt to be addressing each other? The assumptions to test are thus whether Bernard is addressing the spectator while Alphonse is addressing another dinner guest or perhaps no one in particular. Are all the other guests addressing whom we think they are, thus giving us a background against which we sense that Alphonse and Bernard are not addressing each other, nor any other dinner guest? By our test, we will attempt to discover how Resnais manipulated the sightlines of his characters when they are addressing each other in each of shots 516–540. By this, we will ascertain the way he situates the sight-line gazes of the characters, in respect to whom they seem to be addressing, by actually drawing sight-lines from the characters faces in each shot to whom they would be addressing in the master shot of the sequence. After we do this, we can see how Resnais manipulated the text. After we ascertain the how, we can speculate on the why.

We begin the analysis by drawing the master shot of guests at the dinner table. We then draw the sight-line vectors and record who is at the end of them. We then compare this diagram with the dialogue and see if, when the dialogue is matched to the sight-line addressee, the "one addressed," the dialogue makes "sense." If it does we record it. If it does not, or the sight-line vector contacts no one, or the spectator, we record it as an anomaly.

At the conclusion of the following analysis, we find that Bernard is addressing the spectator, Alphonse is addressing no one, all the other guests are addressing the other guests we think they are. Our reading of the sequence is then this: Bernard is demanding the spectator's direct attention; Alphonse seems to be semiotically confirmed as a mythomaniac; the conflict between Bernard and Alphonse is referred to the spectator by an epic device rather than a dramatic device. We sense the conflict, not in a *Spannungsfeld,* (a field of on-screen, in-the-room conflict) but in the form of a direct appeal to the spectator. This is then furthered by Bernard's leaving the room rather than driving Alphonse from the room, something that could be done in a normal dramatization of a sequence with the same information content. Resnais' manipulations then seem to be, first, to "abnormalize" two characters, Bernard and Alphonse, By foregrounding them against normal characters—who do what one would empirically expect of them at a dinner party; second, to formalize Alphonse as one who addresses no one; third, to formalize Bernard as one who addresses the spectator.

At the dinner table, Bernard is the only one who faces the spectator. Since Bernard and Alphonse do not fight or conflict with each other through on-screen exchanges of points of view, their semantic interchange and their visual exchange are "distanced" from each other. This "distancing" invites our intervention. How we react is our business. But note that Resnais seems to want us to decide how we feel about Bernard and how we feel about Alphonse and not just

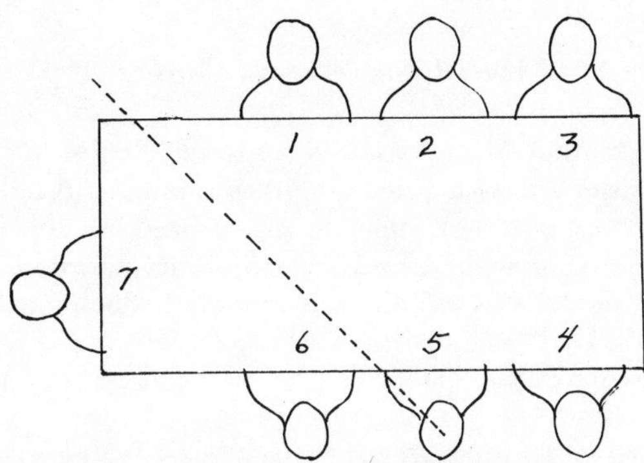

This vector diagram reconstructs a master shot for the sequence in which Alphonse and Bernard engage in a heated argument about politics and demonstrates how Resnais' editing informs us that Alphonse is lying. It shows, via the arrow, that when we think Alphonse is replying to Bernard and addressing him in countershot, with the words, "I respect all races even though I hate Arabs," he is actually not looking at Bernard or at anyone. The averted gaze implies that he is lying. In the diagram (1) is deSmoke, (2) is Helene, (3) is Claudie's husband, (4) is Claudie, (5) is Alphonse, (6) is Françoise, and (7) is Bernard.

to take for granted that they are in conflict. The latter technique would be dramatic; the former is definitely an epic device described in the body of theory attributed to Bertolt Brecht as the *V-Effekt*. Thus the structuring of the sequence suggests an epic intention.[18]

To Resnais' credit, he resists using cheap effects and makes his manipulations "elegant." The "right" conclusion, the grasp of what has happened (to the Algerian girl, Muriel, to Bernard, to Hélène, to Alphonse, to Françoise) does depend in the end entirely upon the spectator's reading of Resnais' manipulation, which depends of course mostly on the success of Resnais' narrative manipulation of the film. But it is wrong to assume Resnais does not help us enough, give us enough information to sort it all out. *Muriel*, unlike *Marienbad*, which was a paradox, is just a puzzle. It can be solved if we wish, but we are wrong if we think we can solve it with only the information provided within the film.

As with the solution of Antonioni's *Red Desert*, *Muriel* requires that we take in and use information exterior to the film. To understand *The Red Desert*, it would help considerably to know that Antonioni is pro-technology. To understand *Muriel*, it would help considerably to know that France had just ended its Algerian War and that there was rampant in France an OAS rightist movement outraged by the war's end.

Muriel: Success or Failure

Before evaluating *Muriel* as a success or a failure, one has, I argue, to consider it as a third generation film, with all that that implies. Whether one then analyzes it as a Brecthian epic film, as I have tried to do, or whether one considers its narrative as a text, independent of author, as one remarkable French book entirely devoted to *Muriel* has,[19] matters little as long as one considers the position and role of the spectator, the role he/she must play if the film is at all able to be a success.

With a third generation film, it is particularly valid, then, to look at one factor that is only of modest importance in the second generation film. It is necessary to defend the requirements the film makes on the audience. One could ask the question this way: Has Jean-Luc Godard been more successful than Alain Resnais in making the audiences of his films react predictably and positively to them? And considering that Godard's *Two or Three Things I Know About Her* in Godard's eyes is a remake of *Muriel*,[20] this is a particularly pertinent question!

Also, if a carefully thought out film such as *Muriel* fails to make audiences think and conversely, a flawed, pseudo-third generation film such as Robert Altman's *Nashville* (1974), reaches audiences, then what does this say about the validity of the third generation film? Do audiences react to *Zeitgeist* more than structure? Is the necessary conclusion that the film audience has been overestimated?

Let us turn for a moment to the Godard approach of requiring audiences to think and react. That Godard wished this to happen can be documented in his own word, in a conversation with novelist Michel Vierney in 1965 while shooting *Masculine-Feminine*, Godard said: "The extreme essays [e.g., essays geared to extremes], I don't believe in them. That's good for flattening political candidates, but it doesn't accomplish anything. I ask *them* [my emphasis] what *they* think. *Think of what you think! That's all*. I do not ask for anything else."[21]

We might then conclude there is more than just a secret little bit of Truffaut-isme (the audience is God) in Godard. Godard seems to be implying that he doesn't give a damn what people do with his films as long as they think about them at all. But, perhaps, I would argue, Resnais is more hopeful than Godard that the public will get exactly what he means. Only he is (secretly) more fearful than Godard that the subjects and formats for his films are a bit too obscure for the mass film audience. Yet, unlike Godard, Resnais refuses to despair, nor does he load his films with *Zeitgeist* clichés to get the audiences to come over: the newspaper cut out, etc., so often used in the American cinema to give the film the feeling of "current events." (The Sam Fuller, Nick Ray, Fritz Lang approach.)

When he made *Muriel*, Resnais was fully conscious that it did show a *Zeitgeist*, largely created by the Algerian War, but that this influence might work negatively on the spectator. The American mass audience, we can easily ascertain, did not want a film about the Vietnamese War, either, unless it was of the harmless love story kind, like *Coming Home* (1978). We can therefore understand the lack of popularity of the more painful Viet-nam film, like *Hearts and Minds*, in this context and compare how it was ignored to how *Muriel* was shunned in France.

We can, however, praise Resnais for ignoring the "let's forget Algeria" *Zeitgeist* in France only up to a point. A much more serious charge leveled against *Muriel* we must also answer is the traditional one levelled against all Resnais films, namely that Resnais did not care whether it had an audience at all. One could say, as Jacques Rivette succinctly observed in a *Cahiers du Cinéma* seminar in November 1963, that one of the "problems" of *Muriel* was that as a film it was "too French, too singular."[22] Yet this, as some of the other *Cahiers* participants observed, is precisely what made the film so valuable:[23] *Muriel* was like a well-written minority report. Nowhere in the *Cahiers* seminar did it come up that the film was too obscure in its information system. Thus I would cite this seminar as an argument against such American criticisms as Susan Sontag's contention that *Muriel* does not deliver what it promises.[24] *Muriel* is a thinking man's film, but paradoxically, not an intellectually predicated film. How one must think about the film—and there can, of course, be a failure to see its message if the spectator and the film do not come together—depends not upon whether we line ourselves up to work with it intellectually correctly, but whether we give ourselves over to how the film presents itself. As far as I am concerned, that throws *Muriel* into the category of entertainment, not purposeful polemic.

Unfortunately, the negative stance *Muriel* took against a French *Zeitgeist*, and the critics' confusion on how to address themselves to

(Top) Bernard, returned from Algeria.
(Bottom) Bernard begins a documentary film about Algeria.
Frame enlargements

the film, put "two strikes" against *Muriel*'s commercial success when it was released in 1963. A third strike against *Muriel* came from those who felt it could only be appreciated by the "arty" spectator.

In 1978, we should be free of the "art house syndrome" and be able to enjoy *Muriel* more as the Hitchcockian suspense film it is. Isn't the following dialogue from the film very typically Hitch suspensful?

ROBERT: But you, with your camera . . . what can you film at night? You don't have enough light.

BERNARD: Don't concern yourself with my camera. I'll get it all straightened out.

ROBERT : Are you going to tell it to Muriel? You can't tell Muriel anything.

BERNARD: (as voice-over) Leave me in peace on the subject of Muriel![25]

Robert is accusing Bernard of not having enough light! Not enough *illumination*, not enough *information* on the subject to set the record truly straight? Bernard insists that he will get it all straightened out. Get what straightened out? Not only the low light situation but also the Algerian cover-up? Robert finally has to play his one and only trump card. Muriel is (probably) dead. Robert's line here is the only indication in the film that Muriel actually could have died after being tortured—it is still an assumption, even though at least five critics writing on *Muriel* have declared she died from the torture and assume it as a fact of the film. So he now tells Bernard that he cannot summon Muriel as a witness to appear in the witnessing documentary film he might be making with his camera. Bernard, brought to a cold factual realization that this is so, can only reply that he wants to be left in peace on the subject, which immediately raises the wider questions: Do most Frenchmen want to be left in peace about Algeria and forget it ever happened? In a still wider sense, the word peace implies "peace on earth." The iconic, indexical, and symbolic connotations of the word contradict. But they show the how and why of those who want the Algerian cover-up.

What we see above is only a conjectural interpretation of the interchange of words between Bernard and his ex-army buddy Robert. Yet, knowing *Marienbad* to be a film where several solutions fit the facts, can we safely stop at one interpretation of *Muriel*? Can we say as Joseph Losey does, "I understood Muriel perfectly"?

6

Muriel II

Film Within a Film

THE MOST POTENT DEVICE a filmmaker has at his disposal for moving a film either toward or away from a spectator's sensation of an ontological exploration, is the use of a film within a film. It is so frequently employed—the technique goes at least as far back as *Tillie's Punctured Romance* (1914)—and so obvious, that it has been neglected by film critics seeking to study the significance of a film. This chapter will concentrate on the three films within the film *Muriel*, for this device sets *Muriel* apart from all other Resnais films and makes it something of a maverick among his works.

Marie-Claire Ropars, speaking of the self-referential quality of the three films within *Muriel* (as well as such scenes as the one of Bernard carrying a movie camera), a quality that she calls "self-representation," observes,

> The analysis of self-representation in *Muriel* can be approached through the phenomenon of "mise-en-abyme" ("text within a text"), which has been widely studied in literature; by this expression, I mean the "enshrining" within a surrounding film (for example, *Muriel*) of a miniature film (for example, the film Bernard projects) which would reflect it in a reduced form. One notices that in Resnais' film, this device undergoes a dismantling process, so that the film image cannot be stabilized in a single fixed reflection; the "mise-en-abyme" in *Muriel*, which is multiple, shifted, always displaced and passed around from place to place, belongs more to a generalized and conflictual "mise-en-écart" [setting apart]; the "enshrined" film apart from itself (the Algerian images), apart from its project (the im-

eneral Maurice Challe (left) and Andre Zeller were the ar-
hitects of the Algerian generals' revolt. To defend against such
ien, as them, Resnais signed Sartre's Manifesto of the 121
hich encouraged French soldiers to desert.
gence Dalmas

ages shot in Boulogne), apart from *Muriel* itself; *Muriel* is set apart from its own internal production. The film is always already done, and always to be redone. *Muriel's* narrative [development] is impossible, for want of an initial [thing] signified.[1]

Muriel is an excellent case study for the concept of "mise-en-ecart" for it contains three discrete films within the framing or "parent" film. Before describing these, we need to consider one bit of film theory. It is a well-known phenomenon that when people watch a film where the people within it are also watching film or TV, they begin, by association, to identify with the viewers watching the film within the film or TV within the film; they feel less detached than if they were simply watching a straight film. Hollywood has taken advantage of this phenomenon to shape some of its more preposterous plots.

Resnais, on the other hand, decided that this approach is primitive and useless. Instead, he decided to oppose three films in order to make it less easy for us to fall for the plot. First, there is a "documentary" or documentary-like film. It was shot by Resnais in 8mm and then blown up to a grainy 35mm for all to see that it is, in effect, a home movie. This "documentary" is shown by the film's narration to be a false documentary, an imitation of a documentary. Here Resnais again introduces his concept of the impossibility of making a documentary.

Furthermore, even if the "documentary" film footage were made up of real footage of the event purported, it could not have been a document made by the character, "Bernard," to whom it is ascribed simply because he does not exist. Thus Resnais tells us graphically that this is but a clever directorial device. In *Muriel* this type of film within a film appears once, and we shall call it film-within-a-film I.

To show how complexly this film within a film I functions despite its humble appearance camouflaged as a grainy home movie, we must first recall that this type of device is often used in fiction to suspend disbelief. By drawing the spectator, or in this case the reader, away from reality, it helps to protect the fiction from being unmasked. Thus the film-within-a-film I functions as an authenticator, one of the two prime ways the device can work in a narrative film.

The second film-within-a-film in *Muriel*, Alphonse's "exposure" of Bernard's diary (film-within-a-film II)—is also of this authenticating type. Film II is yet another form of the director's disguised authorship, another director's device, and completely equivalent in function to the metonymic 8mm documentary over which Bernard narrates. The purpose of both I and II is to make us believe that there was actually a soldier named Bernard in Algeria, and then to make us see Bernard as an icon or index of a French soldier who served in Algeria during the Algerian War of 1954–1962. As we shall see, the length to which Resnais goes to establish this fiction is amazing, especially when we consider how much this works against film-within-a-film III which is the opposite type from I and II, a distancing film-within-a-film. Yet, the opposition of these films-within-a-film is what makes it impossible for *Muriel* to proceed as narrative fiction or in Mme. Ropar's words, makes its narrative "impossible" and makes *Muriel* the truest film ever made about Algeria. In fact, film-within-a-film III seeks its referent not within the film but outside, the very audience of the film. It is a film-within-a-film which never "doubles-back" on itself to establish the authenticity of the fiction of the framing film, namely *Muriel,* for which reason it may be defined as a distancing device. Film III is not, formally speaking a film-within-a-film at all. We never see it projected on a screen; we only see it being shot. Yet it provides a series of images within *Muriel* that deters us from taking that film as a finished, finalized product. It functions within the context of *Muriel* as a narrative subtext like I and II. Film III, or Bernard's film (for it is attributed to him), is the one that *he* begins to make early in *Muriel;* in fact it commences with the very first shot where we see him with a movie camera. There are several specific non-contiguous shots (see frames) in *Muriel* belonging to Bernard's film-within-a-film III in which Bernard is "the man with the movie camera" who shoots footage of Boulogne, as if he and not Resnais were making a documentary of that city in 1962. Finally, after sporadically recurring in disparate shots, film-within-a-film III clearly ends with the shot, near the end of *Muriel,* in which we see Bernard forcefully throw his camera into the English Channel below in an image which, at least graphically, also joins it to the subtext of the main narrative, that of Bernard versus Robert and the OAS (Secret Army/Organization), Hélène and Alphonse, Alphonse's fraudulent claim of having been in Algeria, and all the other flotsam and jetsam caused by the Algerian War; for Bernard looks as if he were throwing a hand grenade. (See frame enlargement.) This shot, then, returns us to the main narra-

Having concluded that it is impossible to document what he experienced in Algeria, Bernard throws his camera away and decides to take more dramatic action.

tive, and signifies that Resnais is reaffirming the impossibility of documenting. This event also moves the plot towards the killing of Robert. (Recall: the first time we saw Bernard, he was opening a drawer containing both a pistol and a camera. He now opts for the pistol.) Thus this shot serves the dual function, as do many others in Resnais' films, of being the junction for the main narrative and one of the films-within-a-film, with the shot having meaning for both.

Film III is also analogous, contextually, to "the movie being made" in all those films which are ostensibly about the making of a movie. Some examples are *King Kong* (1933) where the film-within-a-film is the animal film a director wants to make, and which, for lack of an animal, "forces" him to sail to Skull Island to look for King Kong; Fellini's *8½* (1963) whose film-within-a-film is Guido's film; and Truffaut's *Day For Night* (1973) whose film-within-a-film is Ferrand's "Pamela." It is necessary to say here that none of the films of this nature is automatically an authenticator or a distancer. Films-within-a-films can function either way, though the classical function in Hollywood cinema was to authenticate a blatant fiction, or, even more primitively, to serve as a narrative excuse as part of the plot, as is true in the 1933 *King Kong*.

From an historical point of view it now seems that Frederico Fellini, in 1963, wished to deal with a film-within-a-film that did not neatly occupy the middle portion of the parent film. In *8½*, a film-within-a-film developed, Guido's film, because we watch him making it, and reached the spectator in fragmented form, in sporadic shots, and not as one block of contiguous narrative and continuous shot order. Fellini's technique of "doubling back," of having Guido's film mirror the parent film, even when it most threatened to take on a life of its own, became a fashion for a while, as a way to use the film-within-a-film. Yet, in *8½* Fellini was not doing anything remarkable or particularly schizophrenic. He was simply developing the potential of film narrative towards a function it could quite easily assume.

In *Muriel* Resnais uses Bernard's film quite differently from the way Fellini used Guido's film. Guido's film is still an authenticator, a justification for *8½*'s being made. Bernard's film is a distancer; it distances us from *Muriel*, and owes much of its style in doing so to Brechtian *Verfremdungseffekt*. How so? The proof is on two levels. Bernard is, first of all, on the level of narrative, quite unsympathetic to all the other characters, as if he were not even in their film.

Second, acting as a film device and not as a character, Bernard turns the results of his camera's findings directly to the audience, and not to another character in *Muriel,* not even to his confidante, Marie-Do. When Marie-Do asks Bernard if he is making a documentary, he answers: "worse." Here, again, Resnais implies that he doesn't think a real documentary can be made.

It seems also that Bernard's film is meant by Resnais to direct itself to the audience and not to "double back" onto the parent film. Is there any hard evidence for this view? There is evidence, in fact; but it tends to emerge as the cumulative effect of a variety of subtle details.

First, take the character, Bernard. Resnais' statement that he finds a character most interesting if he says three sentences and then contradicts himself in the next three sentences should be looked for in *Muriel* as a Brechtian *Verfremdungseffekt* that shatters our illusion of the character. We find this effect associated with Bernard and only with Bernard in *Muriel:*

HÉLÈNE: You never told me where you met your girl friend. Her name doesn't sound like she's from around here.
BERNARD: At the moment she's sick . . .
HÉLÈNE: Oh.
BERNARD: No, she's not sick.[2]

This contradiction makes us wonder, not who Bernard is, but what is going on behind Bernard, particularly if this distancing is reinforced by what we see on the screen. In the case of Bernard, it is reinforced. (In the case of the Rogers-Astaire films, where Ginger makes the same kind of smart remarks, what we see on the screen reduces them to romantic comedy.)

The mythomaniac Alphonse's words are, by contrast, never contradicted by him. We have to wait for them to be disjuncted by Ernest's in order for us to learn that Alphonse is a liar. Near the end of *Muriel,* Ernest belatedly supplies the truth that exposes Alphonses's falsehoods. Furthermore, Hélène does not function like Bernard either. She is the subject of an investigation, not an investigator. Bernard is the sole investigative character in *Muriel.*

Next we should note that early in *Muriel,* Bernard begins to reveal his function as a witness, and Resnais establishes this by association: From the first instant we see him Bernard is associated with a camera, a tape recorder, and a projector; Bernard's secret room in old Boulogne where he meets with Marie-Do, can be considered his film studio-in-miniature. Bernard is thus isolated from the other characters and formally distanced from them, suggesting that he has a unique function in *Muriel.*

Now, Resnais having "disrupted" Bernard from becoming totally a character or creature of the narrative for us, reassociates him, ordinary discourse) has to make Bernard attractive and seeking, yet the unknown quantity of place called Algeria. Thus, Bernard is implanted in our minds as the locus of the mystery. He is a place as well as a person; therefore Resnais, to set us on our quest to find out for ourselves what happened in Algeria (and why, in metropolitan France in 1962, the topic of Algeria was absent or surpressed in ordinary discourse) has to make Bernard attractive and seeking, yet curiously fulfilling and knowledgeable. This last purpose, perhaps, suggested to Resnais that he must incorporate within the parent film, more information that Bernard has (disclosed by Bernard's narration in film-within-a-film I) and more information that he might have (suggested by the fragments of rich information that Bernard's diary holds in film-within-a-film II) in order to make his curiously fulfilling side attract us to him.

Note that film III only becomes a full force in the narrative after we have become quite attracted to the contradictory Bernard, and only after we have seen the two authenticators, films I and II.

The other side of Bernard's personality, his function as a seeker, is neatly tied to the film's narrative level by the device of Bernard's search for a girl to be a new Muriel. (This "return of the repressed" theme here is one of the three main themes running through all of Resnais' films.)

It seems likely that Bernard may make up several fantasy Muriels. How many Muriels are there in *Muriel?* There are at least three: the tourtured Algerian girl, the one Bernard pretends to Hélène is his fiancée, and one who is called to by a woman passerby on the streets of Boulogne. The gist of *Muriel's* multiplicity is that everywhere Bernard goes, there is Muriel again. The repressed returns with a vengeance.

This all keeps alive the ontological quest that the spectator should pursue while watching the film, one in which the spectator is asked to find out what happened in Algeria. Was Bernard as well as Robert guilty of torture? Were Bernard and Robert French paratroopers in a protective custody unit (the French official euphemism for interrogators who used torture was *Groupment Protectifs* or GPs for short, a term reminiscent of the Nazi SD, or "protective service").

As we now should see, the *manqué* of the film's narrative, what is missing, is designed to lead us to search for an epistemological answer: what did France perpetrate in Algeria? The art of *Muriel* is how Resnais makes the narrative admit its epistemology. The narrative yields its place to the humanitarian question of Algeria only once *we* start the process. Resnais thus avoids delivering an Eric Rohmer-like or purely philosophical *conte morale* (i.e., an intellectual discourse) on the subject of the Algerian War. How he accomplished this is best described first in a broad sense.

Why does Resnais invent a fiction to discuss Algeria? Why did he not shoot a documentary? Or film a re-creation of the events, such as Gille Pontecorvo with *The Battle of Algiers* (1967)? I argue that the flaws of *The Battle of Algiers* are what Resnais voided in eschewing the semi-documentary approach of Pontecorvo's film. For even one factographic error, recognized by the viewer of a semi-documentary, puts the whole film into jeopardy and under suspicion, risking a disjuncting effect wherein the spectator throws the true facts out with the false—the baby with the bathwater so to speak—and rejects the whole film.

Muriel, not being a factographic film in intention, can never be factographically incorrect in an obvious way; thus it avoids all the pitfalls of the semi-documentary approach. Since it does not claim to be a factual presentation, *Muriel,* from the start, can use a combination of allusive fact (Bernard, saying that he was in Algeria for twenty-two months, could have been either a draftee or a volunteer; but when his diffidence is made clear, we guess he was probably a draftee) and some authentication of the narrative fiction (Bernard's fictive "Colonel Quonia" under whom he served). We do not doubt the product of the allusive fact and the fiction, for we know no fact to refute it. We also know there was an Algerian war at that time, so we accept the fiction that Bernard was a soldier like those who fought in Algeria.

The neutral world of Boulogne, in which all the allusions about Algeria are made, works well. Resnais made, in my opinion, an impeccable choice by filming the story of the Algerian War in a neutral *Welt,* and not in Algeria, simply because it does not precharge our expectations. There is a strange connection here between the affectlessness of this universal town of Boulogne and the mansion in Providence in *Providence*, Resnais' most recent film. As Chaim Calev puts it, "Resnais has decided to use an abstract location which could be anywhere in Western civilization. He deliberately detaches the visuals from the specifics of an identifiable landscape, destroys the illusion of a documentary presence in space-time, fights authenticity. This tendency has been growing throughout Resnais' films . . . He has never sympathized with New Wave or Neo-Realist aesthetics."[3] Resnais further reinforces our tendency not to doubt what little factography he incorporates in *Muriel* by keeping the background of Bernard, who was supposedly in Algeria, somewhere between the general, symbolic, and uselessly vague and the hyperspecific documentation of one French soldier. Resnais' Bernard is indexical enough to be seen as representing an entire class of men who served in Algeria. (He does not function like one of Hollywood's solo war heroes.) Bernard, then, is the index of a group of men—as French journalist Jean-Jacques Servan-Schreiber so eloquently described them—who collectively found themselves in a tragic situation:

> Communist propaganda has compared some of the behavior of the French Army in Algeria to that of the SS in Hitler's army. That is wildly untrue. What is true is this: when you have seen in Algeria how easily men can become helpless playthings of the set-up into which they are thrown, you don't feel you have the right to condemn the men of the Wehrmacht anymore. Individual behavior can be called reprehensible only when the behavior occurs within a collective undertaking that is not itself blameworthy.[4]

Thus, Bernard is an index of *all* French soldiers in Algeria, and Resnais' film here displays the Brechtian collective character rather than the Hollywood individualistic character. If Robert, Bernard's buddy, represents the worst of the lot, Bernard represents the average. In so constructing Bernard, Resnais approaches a new, higher level of aesthetic honesty, than is customarily found in the Hollywood film.

On the other hand, Resnais does not, like Neo-Realism, balance this generalizing tendency by having Bernard shot in an actual location. Rather, he resorts to a New Wave convention, a kind of updated Expressionism, and asks us to accept Bernard's killing of Robert on the fictive, allegorical level of a *Welt*. This moment in

Frame enlargements from the sequence in which Bernard kills Robert, who has become a member of the O.A.S.

Muriel is highly theatrical, hardly authentic, and an unlikely way of showing Bernard shoot Robert—we never even see a gun. In fact, it would ordinarily be seen as a New Wave, "bang, you're dead!" cliché, were it not for the fact that Resnais integrates this sequence on a visual level with his over-all plan of keeping things symbolic, indexical, and non-iconic: he makes (manipulates) Bernard's raincoat and packstraps to look as though he were in his army uniform again. Therefore, on the level of a *Welt*, again, we see Bernard, the soldier, kill Robert; and we of course expect soldiers to carry guns. (See frame-enlargement below.) It is the mixing of shots like this with frank, factographic dialogue such as Bernard's voice-over narration of Muriel's torture that correctly led filmmaker Pierre Kast to comment,

> What is Resnais' purpose? . . . to oblige the viewer to confront and compare for himself, that which appears at the same time to him faithful and monstrously unfaithful to that area which he has not yet thought of to look at in this manner.[5]

Resnais gives us the truth through a Brechtian theatrical shock effect rather than through a compendium of facts and fact-oriented narrative, such as is attempted in *The Battle of Algiers*.

The objective, then, of film III is to address the spectator, directly inviting him to take the pieces of film liberally sprinkled throughout the narrative and to add his own shots to it, thus completing it with Bernard. As Resnais has said, his objective in *Muriel* was to make a "non-linear film" in the present tense, that gives us the rhythm of modern life. "A classical film cannot translate the real rhythm of modern life. In the same day, you do twenty-six different things, you go to lectures, to the cinema, to your party meeting, etc. Modern life is fragmented. Everybody feels that, painting and literature bear witness to it, so why should the cinema not do likewise, instead of keeping to its traditional linear construction?"[6]

But unlike such truth-searching films as, say, *Blow-Up* or Welles' *The Lady from Shanghai* and *Touch of Evil*, Resnais' work does not disguise his epistemological quest as a banal mystery story but presents it as a completely self-justified representation, as the banal story of an actual city, Boulogne. He tries to catalyze us (by impregnating our minds through haunting images: he hopes that, months later, we'll get "the message"); and to achieve this, his strategy seems to be first to lay down a factual substrate, aiming to reach our consciousness later, to an unhurried fashion, at a moment chosen by us.

Bernard's film seems to be the major means in *Muriel* by which Resnais tries to achieve this "impregnation of our consciousness." For this reason he has Bernard recite his memories of the torture of Muriel while we watch hauntingly beautiful 8mm images of French soldiers at play in Algeria or of a minaret of a mosque, the symbol of an alien culture. The sense that "something is wrong" should come to us, though not by Resnais' overt persuasion.

Film III is a film to which we can associate our own images. It is there to catalyze them. It is there to invite us to supply shots from our own experience and memory external to the film. By showing us Bernard the cameraman, we are invited to get behind the camera, too. The presence of Bernard's film is the prime reason that *Muriel* is both a realistic film and, in non–agitprop fashion, a political film.

None of Resnais' other films shows a cameraman. *Muriel* thus stands outside Resnais' other films because they are never as self-referential. Yet, Bernard's film stands, in the larger body of Resnais' work, for one of his three major themes: the impossibility of documenting.

It is my belief that it is precisely Resnais' large experience in the documentary film area, with what the documentary could and could not achieve, that led him to the approach of *Muriel:* a documentary is attempted with great passion, only to be finally discarded with an angry gesture.

The reader will recall that *Night and Fog* taught Resnais the impossibility of remembering, a theme equally thoroughly examined in Ottakar Runze's *Messer im Rücken* (1975), a West German film that brilliantly justifies the approach Resnais used for *Muriel.*[7] If Bernard can not remember, how can we? We cannot know perfectly what happened in Algeria, but we can always collect information and come to a working hypothesis. I imagine that Resnais would wish a viewer of *Muriel* to assimilate information and add his own to the already existing body of facts, much as Resnais' personal revolutionary character, Diego, in *La Guerre Est Finie* goes about it: in solitude, but in depth, with patience, and a long-range goal in mind.

Now, understanding some of the mechanism of information transfer Resnais proposes in and for *Muriel,* we can next direct our attention to the contrast between Resnais' *Muriel* and Pontecorvo's *The*

(Left) The fictitious "Colonel Phillipe Mathieu" in Gille Pontecorvo's *The Battle of Algiers.* (Right) The real paratroop colonel who won the battle of Algiers, Colonel Yves Godard.

Battle of Algiers and in so doing draw some final conclusions about Resnais' approach to reality.

Pontecorvo's film is a reenactment of the Battle of Algiers fought in 1957, filmed nine years later with one of the Arab participants, Yaacef Saadi, playing a role in it (though not of himself). Resnais' film is the story of the effect of the same event—the Battle of Algiers and Algeria itself—on the political atmosphere of metropolitan France in 1962, specifically on the city of Boulogne. *The Battle of Algiers* uses professional actors (with the notable exception of Saadi) to play real people. French Colonel Yves Godard is called "Colonel Phillipe Mathieu" and is played by actor Jean Martin, in a role originally conceived for Paul Newman. "Mathieu" is also evocative of the last name of French paratroop commander General Jacques Massu, Godard's sector commander. "Mathieu" in the film—to make him more "real"—even has a fictive biography: he is made to come from Rennes, Brittany, which is made into a "right wing region of France" for the sake of the film. "Mathieu" is also commander of the Third Colonial Paratroop Regiment, a real regiment which was in Algiers (though the film never refers to it by name) actually, at that time, commanded by Colonel Maurice Michel Bigeard. "Mathieu," then, is a fictitious composite. By voice-over narration, Pontecorvo has a speaker tell us, over the image of Jean Martin:

Family Name: Mathieu.
Name: Phillipe. Born in Rennes, May 3, 1906.
Rank: Lieutenant Colonel.
Schooling: Politechnic; degree in Engineering.
Campaigns: Second World War, Anti-Nazi Resistance.[8]

This fictional biography does *not* match the real background of Colonel Yves Godard at all, even though it would match a composite biography of the French Algerian politically oriented colonels: Colonel Argoud went to the Polytechnic, Colonel Godard was a World War II officer, etc.

By contrast, when Resnais tells us Bernard's Algerian history, he makes it hard for us to take it as false, for he doesn't give us obviously false information, and thereby avoids disrupting our concentration on the film. He does not give Bernard a shaky, composite biography. The moral seems to be: don't claim to the audience that you are giving them fact, and then slip up and let them see a factual error.

Ironically, the fictive Bernard, by a method Jean-Luc Godard (no relation to Yves Godard) calls "fact-to-fiction, fiction-into-fact," is believed by us precisely because we do not doubt his credibility either as a character or as against known facts external to the film. Credibility of character in a realistic film is built by "fact-into-fiction" (Bernard is assigned factual attributes: he was a French soldier in Algeria—there really were French soldiers in Algeria) and "fiction-into-fact" (the fictitious Bernard represents French public opinion against the OAS, there were Frenchmen against the OAS, including Resnais, the director, even though there was no one named "Bernard" against them). By rejecting overt labels, Resnais built up a subversive film that waged psychological war against the Right in France. A film like *Muriel* is a fair film. Its "propaganda" does not require an *a priori* agreement before seeing the film. *The Battle of Algiers*, on the other hand, requires us to be sympathetic to the cause of Algerian independence as a pre-condition for enjoying the film. Pontecorvo was deluding himself if he thought he was making an objective film. And if he thought he was, why did he not call his Colonel "Godard." For Colonel Godard was such a well-known public figure that *some* of the audience would know "Mathieu" never commanded in Algiers.

I would like to reemphasize that Resnais was wise in not making his Algerian soldier a debatable person. While Bernard is fictively located in a specific Algerian context, no extra information in the film disjuncts it. Though we never learn for certain whether Bernard was a draftee or a paratrooper—important information, for the former case would decrease the probability that he helped torture Muriel—nothing Bernard says or that is said about him makes us think that he could not possibly have been in Algeria. Our facts are kept straight. Thus, as the film progresses, we become increasingly suspicious that Bernard did help to torture Muriel, we sense that it was his own choice which makes him responsible, not his being under orders as a paratrooper or some such stereotype. The "fiction-into-fact, fact-into-fiction" approach of Resnais and Godard avoids stereotyping, and breaks with the Hollywood system of treating such matters. In *Muriel,* then, our suspension of disbelief regarding Bernard is never halted by an "ah ha" reaction: false fact!

There are, furthermore, no blatantly false facts in the film-within-a-film I, Bernard's diary as seen by the eavesdropping Alphonse, where we are shown, in brief shots averaging three seconds, pages of Bernard's diary thumbed through by Alphonse, a device Resnais uses so we can see the diary. Through slow motion analysis on the Steenbeck, we can read this diary as Resnais fabricated it. We can discern that even in these shots which the audience is not expected to read word for word, Resnais does not put in misleading information. In the diary, where Bernard describes his life as a soldier in Algeria, all the entries are plausible. Resnais counts on the fact that a single word or a phrase subliminally perceived could work in favor of or against reality. As we view these frames at normal projection speed, any random tidbit of information we pick up, such as "it all began with Muriel" or "I rolled back the tarpaulin" or "her eyes were not shut," makes sense within the context of Bernard's typical experience in Algeria.

We can learn either subliminally or deliberately by slow motion analysis that Bernard typed some of his witnessing notes on French Army stationery. Resnais either found some Army issue stationery or made exact reproductions and then had the information typed on a standard French Army typewriter with pica type. From these notes we learn that Bernard might have been in Bone, Department of Constantine, in Algeria, as a member of a "Colonel Quonia's Tactical Group N." No date is given for Bernard's service under this Colonel, who, however is a correct index of the class of Colonels deployed in Algeria and commanding similar French tactical groups around the years 1958–1961, the time when Bernard supposedly was in Algeria. (See frame enlargement.) At any rate, even if we succeed in reading this (impossible at normal speed, but important to analysis of the film; for Resnais did supply the film with this information), the reference to "Colonel Quonia" is so obscure as to cause no doubt to be raised whether there was such a Colonel. (In fact there was not. Resnais made him up.) There is, thus, no comparison between the vastly different ways Pontecorvo used the fictional colonel. In Resnais' case, the invention is harmless and analogous to Dziga Vertov's concept of the reorganization of a "life fact" into the structure of a film; in Pontecorvo's case, it was done with the obvious hope that the public would accept the myth of the semi-fiction. (See frame enlargement of the army stationery used in *Muriel* versus a photo of actual French army stationery.)

In the case of *The Battle of Algiers,* some people (myself included), instantly perceived the fiction of "Colonel Mathieu" and proceeded to demote this otherwise well-filmed narrative work to the limbo of semi-fiction. The solution here to this kind of film, the one proposed by Michel Brault, French Canadian documentarist, would have saved the day. Brault would have had the actor playing "Colonel Mathieu" briefly turn to the audience when he first appeared and say, "I am (or my name is) Jean Martin, I am playing Colonel Yves Godard."[9]

Brecht, the Distancing Effect, and *Muriel*

One could argue that, because of its opposition of two types of films-within-a-film in order to create distancing, *Muriel* is a Brechtian film. Resnais was always fond of Brecht's theater; and there is some external evidence that around the time of the making of *Muriel,* he was interested in seeing whether Brechtian effects (always a tricky business to carry over into film form) could be used to advantage in making *Muriel* didactic and non–illusionary, a kind of *Lehrstuck.* In 1962 Resnais said, "I don't know whether I sufficiently understand Brecht's theater. . . . But it's certain that I would willingly find and see incorporated in film something that would be an equivalent to each freedom [to decide how to take it] that I sense in

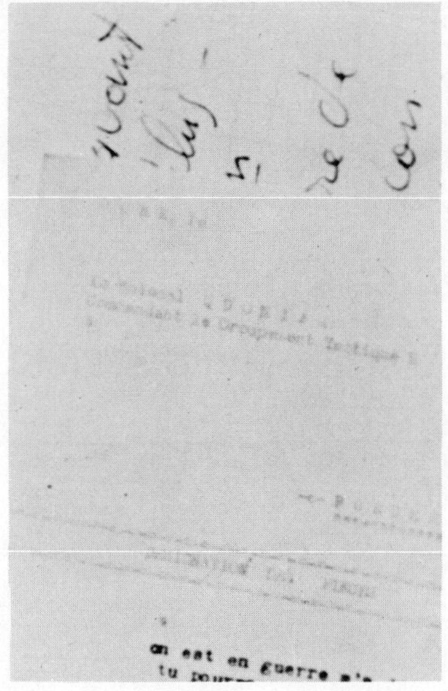

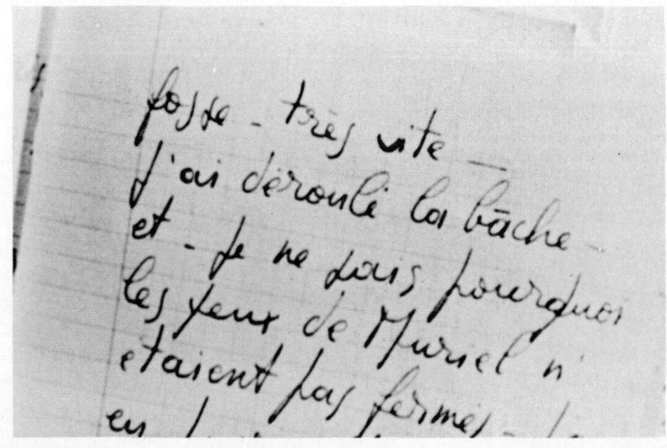

Frame enlargements showing excerpts from Bernard's diary. Note that one part is typed on army stationery.

all of Brecht's pieces of theater. . . . Naturally, I don't mean an adaptation [of Brecht to film, literally]."[10]

There have never been any famous Brechtian films, and perhaps *Muriel* is one of the few that works at all. It seems that to make a Brechtian film, the director must commit himself to combatting any illusions before he even starts. The failure to induce in the spectator a critical state of mind ruined the G. W. Pabst version of Brecht's *The Threepenny Opera.* Pabst, apparently, had a confrontation with Brecht over how *The Threepenny Opera* should be filmed, saying to him, "one has to consider the backwardness and stupidity of the public."[11] This was Pabst's excuse to film his way, and he failed ever to understand why Brecht did not like his film. *Muriel,* in this light, has to be considered exceptional. Resnais does place the spectator in a critical state of mind before addressing him. In addition, Resnais has avoided using dramatic effects for the conveyance of the major lessons of the film. Instead, these lessons are all conveyed through another procedure which Brecht calls "epic" but which has a very special sense in cinema.

As Resnais uses the term, an epic film is one in which the spectator is addressed by a series of "sympathetic-antipathetic" characters and participates in structuring the information they provide.[12] Thus, the Brechtian *Verfremdungseffekt* is very close to the special sense in which Resnais uses the term epic.

Despite its containing a film-with-a-film, *The Battle of Algiers,* has neither epic nor any Brechtian character whatever. Marsha Kinder has further pointed out that Pontecorvo himself may have felt a straight documentary film approach suspect, when she commented that

> in a scene where Mathieu is briefing his troops, they look at moving pictures of Algerians crossing the checkpoints into the European section of the city. This "documentary" footage reveals the image of one of the women who was carrying a bomb in her purse, a fact that is known to us in the audience but not to Mathieu and his men. Perhaps Pontecorvo is suggesting the limitations of the straight documentary and showing the need for interpretation which his own film supplies.[13]

This last point is precisely what makes *The Battle of Algiers* a semidocumentary and not a documentary. The film-within-a-film in Pontecorvo's work merely authenticates its fiction; it does not, as Kinder falsely suggests, help us in interpreting a straight documentary if

Pontecorvo tries to cover up for its lack of truth by adding on to it authentication in the form of a device. Resnais' *Muriel* avoided all this by including a distancing type of film-within-a-film, one that keeps us at a healthy distance from the illusion we see presented on the screen throughout the showing.

Resnais, in *Muriel*, successfully, I argue, avoided the trap that I believe Pontecorvo fell into when he invoked an event through character incarnation rather than through addressing the spectator "in a critical state of mind." As a result of its epic approach, *Muriel* is the more honest reproduction of the reality of the French side of the Algerian War of 1954–1962.

Perhaps one lesson in documenting a war can be drawn. One should perhaps document only one side per film, and try to do this honestly and well. If one senses one has an extraordinary insight to share, one might try to document both sides of the conflict. In that case, it should be done dialectically. *The Battle of Algiers* fails to show, for example, that Colonel Godard, the leader of the French, and Yaacef Saadi, an Arab leader, secretly admired each other. The film only shows Godard's respect for the Arabs, never the Arab's respect for the French. In the final analysis, the fault of the film is its attempt to capture objectivity by too primitive methods. Particularly revealing is Pontecorvo's admission that *The Battle of Algiers* originally started out as a fiction film project about French paratroopers and was to star Paul Newman.

How *Muriel* Achieves Its Sense of Reality

We can now summarize how Resnais thinks reality should be presented in film. The method is clearly epic. The devices are the films-within-a-film. Resnais elegantly incorporates three of them so as to make the epic quality less crude. Like Brecht with his bloodless and grim ideas for films, Resnais wishes the epic device to lure us to *Muriel* and to give us a sympathetic, feeling but, at the same time, one that is not achieved by falsehoods. Thus, the maker of the distancing film, Bernard, is made an attractive character, even while he is given a bloodless and grim dimension. Marxist critic Robert Benayoun has quite rightly found Bernard to be Resnais' most attractive character, when he said

> Resnais has clearly invested in Bernard all his intellectual sympathy. Bernard, like Resnais himself, tries to make Muriel talk. "Impossible task," says Robert, "she can't talk." Resnais does *Muriel* without getting caught up in

an orthodox form of narrative, in accepting just losing one's way into the subject as the way. In order to demonstrate his being denied affection, Bernard wears large, grotesque eyeglasses, MAD-style, which transmit his preference for pop forms of culture (serials, comics, etc.).[14]

Yet, the way Resnais makes film III function is quite ruthless, and this ruthlessness rubs off on the character of Bernard. It is clear that the function of Bernard's film is meant to be ruthless and house-cleaning in the sense that it uncovers truth. Its point is not to call attention to Bernard but to the contradictions of Alphonse, the film's mythomaniac and liar. The function of film III most importantly is not self-reference. Bernard is not a stand-in for director Resnais! Bernard is a camera.

Resnais, we can interject at this point, has always shied away from the New Wave's love of self-reference. He has never, for example, appeared in one of his own films. He has never used clichés which tend to be self-serving. He would rather educate or elucidate than draw attention to himself. Thus we must resist any notion of trying to equate Bernard with Resnais on the superficial evidence that both are 8mm movie camera buffs. Bernard, if anything, is Dziga Vertov's "The Man With the Movie Camera," wandering around within the film, who keeps reminding us it is a film we are watching.

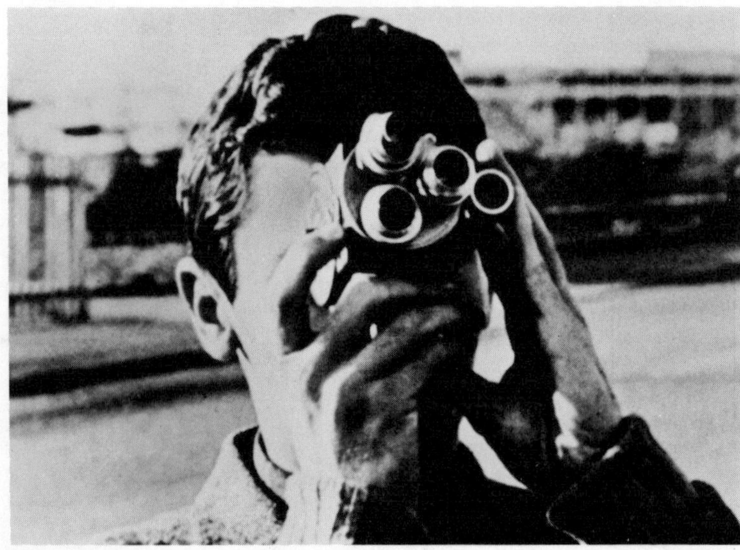

Bernard is "The Man With the Movie Camera."
Frame enlargement

Is *Muriel* Really a Difficult Film?

Muriel should not, for all its devices, be a hard film to like. Resnais has said it has a narrative that is "rigidly chronological"[15] but he admits that it is at the same time "not linear, maybe, because it passes from one character through another."[16] But is that not true in our daily lives? It is hard now to believe that this might have given audiences in 1963 trouble.

Another problem audiences had with Muriel was that it was so different from *Marienbad*. *Muriel* was surprising, because the characters in *Marienbad* behaved so passively the audience sensed the demand that they participate in order to complete an action. This feature of *Muriel* threw off many, including the aging Dean of New York film critics, the *New York Times'* Bosley Crowthers who declared,

> Perhaps there are those who can follow the scattered clues in the devious mystery that Alain Resnais has thrown together in his new French film, *Muriel.* But I am not one. I can see that he's giving us another of those wistful reflections upon the moods of a lonely woman who is trying to sort her memories and her present desires for the resumption of a past love . . . and that her stepson, who is just back from military service in Algeria, is having romantic troubles, too. And I detect that the stepson and the visitor [Alphonse] both know more than is explained about the death of a girl named Muriel back in Algeria. But that's as much as I can fathom.[17]

Crowthers then rejects *Muriel* because it is not "subliminally emotional.":

> . . . it strikes me that Mr. Resnais has carried intentional elusiveness so far, without any evident justification for it . . . [but while] he was opaque and elusive in *Marienbad* and he was psychologically esoteric and evasive in *Hiroshima* . . . his style was expressing the nature of subliminal emotions in both those films, and it also achieved a distinct poetic effect and harmony. I get none of that in this picture. All I get is stunning mise-en-scène . . . I get a feeling that Mr. Resnais is somehow pulling our legs and I don't find it amusing. He's too good with the camera for that.[18]

Resnais never could have made *Muriel* the way Crowthers would have wanted it, and still made it work. Resnais could never have supplied the missing information Crowthers wanted, and still addressed the spectator in a critical state of mind apart from the numbing job usually done by the Hollywood film.

I feel that Resnais' withholding of information about Bernard's affairs is justified. *We* hold some of that information. *We* can supply it from our reservoir of knowledge of Algeria and add it to the fragment called Bernard's film. Thus x plus y = s Ans. We supply x, Resnais supplies y.

There is no doubt then that Resnais wanted audience participation in *Muriel*. He did not intend that all the information he presented add up to one-hundred percent, or to corroborate all other bits of information to produce a neat program. *Muriel* is not an accidentally unclear film, but a deliberately unclear one. It *is* a mystery, but not of the mystery film genre.

At the end of Bernard's film, as much of the mystery is solved as is going to be, and the parent film blithely resumes its narrative and takes us to the end. Proceeding to an open-ended, less cluttered finale, disposing of its characters rather than resolving the narrative or plot line, the film passes into silence. Who was Alphonse? We never learn. Why did he run away? No comment from Resnais. It is all unneccesary to explain, for the impetus of the film should have passed to us. The parent film's last images are seen via a travelling shot where the director invites us to join him in the search. He, too, is still looking for Muriel.

EDI
OTES
ARS A
de la MAIRIE

7

La Guerre Est Finie: Resnais Changes Style

Resnais at a Crossroads: Which Direction?

AFTER WE BECAME ACCUSTOMED to the lack of a straightforward story in Resnais' cinema, his next film, *La Guerre Est Finie* (The War Is Over [1966]), came as a surprise. By 1966 people were much more prepared for involuted or skimpy narrative films and were not so dependent on narrative certainty as they were, even in 1960. The Beatles, and other socio-cultural phenomena had seen to that. To understand the difference between *Muriel* and *La Guerre Est Finie*, we must take into consideration—among other things—changes that had occurred in the political world and the artistic world in the three years between them.

Before we consider these, however, we must mention that the critical reaction to *Muriel* may have been something of a setback to Resnais. Never overly sensitive to critics, he still must have emerged a bit puzzled as to why critics were negative about what he, at that time, considered his finest film.

Ten years later, Win Sharples, Jr. asked Resnais a crucial question pertaining to *Muriel* that echoed a criticism made by Susan Sontag in her essay "Resnais' *Muriel*:" "Most critics seem to assume a compulsion on your part for the complex rendering of the narrative structure."[1] Sontag had said, "Resnais conscientiously avoids direct narration… Resnais had taken a story, which could be told quite straightforwardly and cut it against the grain. This 'against the grain' feeling—the sense of being shown the action at an angle—is the peculiar mark of *Muriel*."[2] "I have the compulsion, yes, that's clear,"[3] admitted Resnais. To Sharples' question "Why does one take a simple story and render it so complexly?" Resnais answered,

ves Montand as Diego Mora, an aging revolutionary, in La
'uerre Est Finie.
he Museum of Modern Art Film Stills Archive.

I can give you one answer, and maybe you will think it's a joke; but I don't know if it is. It could come from the fact that when I was a kid I was fascinated by Milton Caniff's cartoon "Terry and the Pirates" but it was an impossible task to find that story in France, because it would be published for two weeks and then disappear. Then I would find it in Italian, and then that would disappear too. And after that there was a war and so I had to read "Terry and the Pirates" in complete discontinuity. Well, I discovered that it gave the story a lot of emotion to know Terry when he was fourteen and then he was, say twenty-four, after which I would make up myself what had happened to him when he was twenty-two or seventeen maybe."[4]

Sharples, however added a disconcerting comment that led to Resnais' making an admission that—perhaps—something went wrong in the relationship of *Muriel* to the spectator. "My students," said Sharples, "who responded well to *Hiroshima*, had great trouble with *Muriel*, which is of course one of those two hour films you mentioned. [Sharples had earlier in the interview suggested that the short film is Resnais' *forte*] The class was disconcerted."[5] To which Resnais replied, "Yes, I can understand that. It is a two hour film, and I think there are some mistakes in that first reel—some things which should have been made clearer were not made clear enough. And I have a feeling that people lose track at the beginning and after that it is too late to establish contact with them. Especially with that kind of narrative structure, which is like a spider's web with at least three different subjects there, so it's not very easy to follow."[6]

There were many more criticisms of *Muriel* made, mostly decrying its obscurity. Bosley Crowthers, as we have seen, stated that *Muriel* was a waste for a man with Resnais' cinematographic talent.[7] The praise for *Muriel* was far from overabundant. However, film directors, in particular, understood it and admired it. Jean-Luc Godard was later to render homage to the film with his *Two or Three Things I Know About Her*, in which we see a poster for *Muriel*. Director Joseph Losey was unreserved in his praise. "I understood Muriel perfectly."[8]

Muriel did not find its audience. Perhaps this is not surprising if one considers how close the film was to an essay—a highly refined version of the "camera-pen" idea. The explanation may partially have been the *Zeitgeist*. Audiences were shifting their tastes in response to shifting times.

In 1963 French cinema and, to some extent, world cinema had reached a crossroads. The New Wave ended after having accomplished its purpose, which was to give new filmmakers a chance by letting directors try out a less expensive, more personal cinema, minus certain narrative conventions.

Leo Braudy has suggested an interesting definition of many of these *Nouvelle Vague* films, one which he applied to *Hiroshima* and *Marienbad*, among others, though whether Resnais is "New Wave" remains debatable. Braudy said that the basis of all the "revolutionary" films made in the late 50s and early 60s is that they used "open structured styles" to film "closed structured themes."[9] This definition, equally applicable to *Muriel* as to *Hiroshima*, shows the importance filmmakers were now granting to the spectator. Yet, one could only go so far with such an approach.

In 1963, Resnais, along with many other young directors, found the novelty of the approach exhausted. The average spectator had reached his or her limit as a participatory element in the structure of a film. Audiences now seemed to want a cinema of incarnated characters again, only these characters now had to be imbued with modernist folkways and mores. The "New Wave" suddenly seemed "old-fashioned"

François Truffaut, a New Wave director himself, but still wearing his old hat as a critic, succinctly summed up the progress of the New Wave. "The success of 1959 went to people's heads, and some of them went a bit too far. I don't think a film should try to be new in every aspect."[10] Truffaut was right. After the breakthrough, consolidation was needed at least until the arrival of fresh impetus. Truffaut himself made a tactical retreat to a genre film, *La Peau Douce* (The Soft Skin) in 1964, and did not try to go beyond *Jules and Jim*. Truffaut epitomizes the New Wave dilemma. There seemed to be two things he could have done at this point, but fortunately he did neither: to go more "American," i.e., to make a schlock story film based on the American B film plot, or to film a Balzac story such as *Père Goriot*. As it was, Truffaut never resolved this crisis completely, and *The Man Who Loved Women* (1977) telegraphs his desperation.

Alain Resnais was in an equally strange position after *Muriel*. As Jacques Rivette pointed out, *Muriel* was part of a "cinema of retreat,"[11] and the point of this cinema—its anti-American, anti-Soviet national cinemas—its French insularity—would no longer be so valid in the rapidly changing world after 1963.

France had changed. Algeria was independent. The hurt ended.

The world was changing. The Beatles had arrived. A new generation was moving in to take power as the old nineteenth century leaders were dying off. Cinema audiences, while temporarily shrinking, were getting younger.

Jean-Luc Godard appears to have been the first to have seen the way the wind was blowing and to have had far more concrete observations than "It's Blowing in the Wind," the title of Bob Dylan's popular American song of 1963. Godard had always been ahead. Resnais emphasized that, years later, when he said, "Oh, Godard was very important! Yes, because at that time [1959] everybody was always saying, 'No, the grammar of the film is complete; nothing new can be invented. Maybe we can change some things about the story or about the character, but from the point of view of form, of editing, everything has already been done—nothing new can ever be done.' And then Godard arrived and everything was changed."[12]

The same thing was true again in 1963. Godard not only had a whole new series of stages planned for his "multi-staged rocket" cinema, but he solved the problem of where to go by deciding what to be: "Today," he said in December, 1962, "I still think of myself as a critic, and in a sense I am, more than ever before. Instead of writing criticism, I make a film, but the critical dimension is subsumed. I think of myself as an essayist, producing essays in novel form, or novels in essay form...."[13]

Resnais, who never pretended to be a critic, nevertheless continued to use the cinema as a vehicle for essays on time-space. This is how we can readily explain the apparent "inconsistency" of his interest in both projects like "The Adventures of Harry Dickson" (narrative adventure) and *Je T'Aime, Je T'Aime* (non-linear narrative science fiction). Both projects were ideal subjects for further explorations with non-linear narrative, and from what we know of the screenplay for "Dickson," it would have been in no way just a *Count of Monte Cristo*.

Staying fascinated with the time-space problem will also partly help to explain Resnais' shift from the mysteriousness of *Hiroshima, Marienbad,* and *Muriel* to the flat realism of *La Guerre Est Finie*. If we keep in mind that the "Spain" of Resnais' *La Guerre Est Finie* is forgotten Spain, then the familiar theme of the presence of the absent is apparent, which links the film to all of Resnais' work.

After 1962 this exploration of what cinema could and could not do with time-space would be all that Resnais, Godard, Truffaut, and the other more film-as-film oriented directors (Rivette, later Alain Tanner, Rainer Werner, Fassbinder, Werner Herzog and Hans Jürgen Syberberg) would have in common. But, as of 1963, this seemed to be a complex and fruitful enough path to follow, enough to keep one busy for a lifetime.

Furthermore, a wind of optimism, starting in 1963, made it seem likely that the "public" was becoming more socially conscious and more adept at taking in life in a less linear way. Experiments in real life were interesting people more than films which merely obeyed clock time. Film had to compete. How else are we to explain that anyone at all would have been deeply interested in the films of Godard and Resnais?

"Harry Dickson" Abandonned; *Je T'Aime, Je T'Aime* Postponed

And what would Resnais do now? In 1962, while still working on *Muriel,* he had read Jacques Sternberg's novel, *Un Jour ouvrable.* The filming of *Muriel* ended in January 1963, and, after editing, was first screened in Paris on July 24, 1963. Without yet being aware (or without being very concerned) that the public would not acclaim *Muriel* as they had *Marienbad* or *Hiroshima,* Resnais began considering two new projects: filming a script, begun by Jacques Sternberg in 1963, to be called *Je T'Aime, Je T'Aime* (I Love You, I Love You), which was not finally shot until autumn, 1967, and filming a script already completed in 1959 by Frederic de Towarnicki, to be called *The Adventures of Harry Dickson,* which Resnais never completed. The latter film was to be based on a European author's version of an American pulp fiction detective hero in the mold of Phillip Marlowe—an homage to Dickson's creator, Jean Ray (the pseudonym used by Flemish writer Jean de Kremer), and at the same time, an homage to the serial detective silents of Louis Feuillade. Resnais never made this film.

Why Resnais really wanted to make it remains something of a mystery. Either his desire to make a Feuillade-like film continually fascinated him, and he did not want to introduce its elements into his serious feature films; or, it may have been intended to be his autobiographical film, the one in which he would reveal himself the most and indulge himself in the making of a strictly serio-comic film. In 1964, along with the death of Jean Ray, the Dickson project died, leaving only a script behind. Resnais returned to the *Je T'Aime, Je T'Aime* project.

After seeing *Je T'Aime, Je T'Aime* with its sparse plot it is hard to believe it was the result of three years work. However the intellectual science fiction writer, Jacques Sternberg, provided Resnais with "a little mountain of eight hundred pages" to cut down to make into a final *Je T'Aime, Je T'Aime* script. By the summer of 1965, Resnais had structured Sternberg's overworked script fragments into a master script. But while still working on *Je T'Aime, Je T'Aime* after he had also read and enjoyed Jorge Semprun's novel, *Le Grand Voyage*, Resnais contacted Semprun, an expatriate Spanish socialist living in France. They corresponded, and Resnais asked him if he wanted to do a film script for him. He offered Semprun two ideas, one about "a Greek political prisoner working on behalf of his comrades not yet released, or one dealing with the efforts of a committee for peace in Viet-nam or Algeria. It was Semprun who, realizing that the director wanted a specifically political film, insisted on Spain."[14]

La Guerre Est Finie
Resnais Changes Style

La Guerre Est Finie, Resnais' fourth feature, was understood, praised in its own time, and did not suffer from the lack of appreciation that characterized the critical reaction to Resnais' previous film, *Muriel*. This film appeared in 1966, a year when audiences seem to have been attracted to what we now, for lack of a better term, embarrassedly call "political aesthetics," which is now used to castigate a work which is neither art nor politics. But *La Guerre Est Finie* is about political aesthetics in the positive sense of the phrase—about politics and about sensibility, without either snuffing the other out. It is yet another Resnais story with two parallel narratives: Diego and Spain and Diego and Marianne.

The most striking thing about this film is Resnais' apparent shift in style to a kind of flat realism. It has disappointed many Resnais buffs, particularly those who had become accustomed to his nonlinearity. They felt cheated by the simplicity of *La Guerre Est Finie*. But it was intended for the mass audience; the buffs were simply caught off guard. It was as if they had tooled up for something complex and were then thrown a knuckle ball.

A brilliant answer to this second guessing and subsequent disappointment was given in a 1966 review of the film by *Cahiers* critic Michel Caen. It is worth quoting at length:

Besides, it is powerfully curious that *La Guerre Est Finie* has discontented so many Resnais-ians, those of the newly come variety who admired him, no doubt, for the wrong reasons. The lovers of *Hiroshima* were exchanging unlikely improbable litanies in bed, those of *Marienbad* were losing themselves in a Borgesian decade; thus but a monstrous reality led to the nothingness of the characters of *Muriel*. Each time, reality was sublimated or buckled. That was necessary, a kind of justification on the part of the author in facing his environment. That also was an excuse (an intelligent and elegant one) to keep a distance, to establish the proof—by this only aesthetic option—of a rare lucidity. Besides, everyone knows these days of Resnais' passion for comics. . . . *Marienbad* is falk plus Raymond [i.e., Falk plus "Flash Gordon"] and *Muriel* is Chester Gould ["Dick Tracy"]. Today [as Godard also noted in *Masculine-Feminine* (1965) some six months later] the times have changed, it is not enough anymore to be lucid and to show it. *La Guerre Est Finie* is thus an open work, but on the only path possible, one of action, stubbornness, and beyond doubt, *allegro*, in the sense of Bach. The European cinema and, most particularly, the French lack heroes, it seems. It's true, and more yet than the lack of heroes, we lack a sense of tragedy. Politics is the tragedy of our era. That is also the case in *La Guerre Est Finie*. The hero isn't called Mandrake or Dick Tracy or Guy the Flash [or Michel Poiccard] any more,"[15]

He is simply Diego, Diego Mora.

La Guerre Est Finie is the first Resnais film to have a full-fledged protagonist, Diego Mora (Yves Montand). It has a love story, Diego and his Scandinavian mistress, Marianne (Ingrid Thulin); it has an affair between Diego and a young political radical, Nadine (Geneviève Bujold, then a starlet, now a well–known actress); and it has its politics spelled out in clear discourses by Diego so that a middlebrow audience could understand them: old style Socialist personal revolution versus theoretic Leninist revolution practiced by young radicals who only learned it from books.

And who was Diego Mora? Did Resnais invent flat realism for *La Guerre Est Finie* because the nature of the film's chief character, Diego Mora, demanded it? Resnais apparently thought of it that way. The style of the film had to fit Diego. "Yes I think [that *La Guerre Est Finie* is an accessible film] but this comes from the character; it is always a matter of whether the character is simple or not. In *La Guerre Est Finie* Diego is a simple character; he has true motivations, but he is simple and it would have been stupid to superimpose an artificial structure on that character."[16]

It seems that some of the viewing public, as well as several critics, would not believe that the flat realism of the film was not just an end unto itself, but a means. Writing six years later, structuralist Annie Goldmann complained of a serious fault in *La Guerre Est Finie*, one I do not feel exists. Goldmann was disturbed that the film lacks structure and that Diego's political story does not link up with his personal story. It we grant the style of the film to be "flat realism," we would expect the two to link up. Two unlinked stories would give the film a depth through tension that would belie flatness; it would also make Diego into a complex character, which Resnais denied. Goldmann was obviously looking for a way to apply structuralism to the film so as to find its "deep structure"; not realizing that the deep structure is at the surface of the film, she seems to have gone to excessive pains to find fault with it, and, because it did not suit her model of a political film, she charged it with a fault which it does not have.

> The film is here and there subjective (metal images) and here and there objective (discussions with the party or with young people), but these two tendencies do not result in a unified synthesis: the external action goes on until the end, graced with the predominant intervention of his wife [Diego's mistress, Marianne] without that that be necessarily justified[17]

Somehow, Goldmann misses the structural parallels between Diego's political life and his sex life. *La Guerre Est Finie* was, along with Godard's *Masculine-Feminine*, one of the first films made about sexual politics, something that would dominate the rest of the decade's youth culture. In that sense, the film was prescient and predictive, even while documentary. Structurally, John Ward argued the exact opposite of Goldmann when he noted that

> the conflicts and confusions of myth and reality in Diego's political life are reproduced in his sexual life. His brief affair with Nadine [whom we shall discuss at greater length elsewhere] arises directly from his role as a professional revolutionary. He has used her father's passport . . . for his recent trip to Spain, and when he is close to being discovered she proves that she can play the spy game as well as anyone, and over the telephone, readily accepts the role of his daughter. She belongs to the unreal side of his life. In the course of making his contacts, dodging possible police tails and playing

the spy game generally, he begins to wonder what she could be like. Resnais accomplishes this piece of interior monologue by flashing on the screen images of different girls doing the kinds of things a student would.[18]

The fact that he knows the girl—or knows about her, that is—before he even meets her suggests that she is less a person for him than an idea. (Michel Caen suggested in his *Cahiers* review that this behavior is a pose.) Ward argues that Diego goes to Nadine's home ostensibly to see her father; but he does so, structurally, to show the spectator that he is getting bored with his role as revolutionary, for is the war not over? Here, the two strands, Annie Goldmann to the contrary, seem to synthesize perfectly into one structural whole. Ward adds that "the circumstances of this meeting thrust Diego into an immature sexual relationship and further bizarre political manoeuvres," since he makes love to her "almost by chance"; yet, we, the spectators, however, are invited to feel that she willed it. Ward concludes that

> in the treatment of the love scenes, Resnais makes Nadine exhibit all the coyly affected shyness that we associate with the sexual fantasies of Roger Vadim. . . . Like Bardot, she almost pouts over the top of the bedclothes. And in his extensive references to Godard's *Une Femme Mariée* [*The Married Woman*], Resnais' stylized shots of limbs pale against bedclothes take on some of the meaning Godard originally gave them; of a kind of ironic aestheticism rather than passion; of style rather than feeling.[19]

Nadine in *La Guerre Est Finie* and Madeline in Godard's *Masculine-Feminine* (the films opened within weeks of each other—*La Guerre* on May 11, 1966, and *Masculine-Feminine* on April 22, 1966) are cousins, as are the two films in a way I am surprised no one has ever noted. Resnais had—with a giant leap—caught up with Godard's stage of discourse, with the fast moving 60s, both films catching up with the *Zeitgeist* itself.

Godard, with *Les Carabiniers* (1963), had already done his "nostalgia film for Spain." Resnais was now to do his, with Godard's masculine/feminine theme employed whenever Nadine appears. The title of Resnais' film is, however, as ironic as Godard's is literal. The war is, of course, not over. But it could be for Diego, unless he finds the answers necessary to keep him going on with the struggle. In a sense the film could be called *No, The War Is not Over, Unless*. There is a conditional tense employed in Resnais' film. And there is

Genevieve Bujold, above, in *La Guerre Est Finie* and Chantal Goya, below, in Godard's *Masculine-Feminine* were "two of a kind." They represented the naive and willful college girls of 1965 who flocked to excitement, record contracts and radical student groups.

the issue of the hero who is falling slightly behind the times (as is Paul in *Masculine-Feminine*). As Godard noted in the latter film, "the times had changed. . . ."[20] It was 1965, the year that only the Beatles' *Rubber Soul* seemed advanced. But the Beatles would not get around to the theme of *La Guerre Est Finie*, the old versus the new revolutionaries, until their single, "Revolution," in 1968. And that would soon enough give way in the face of the further demands of the children of Marx and Coca Cola. The Monica Vitti heroine was now obsolete! She was unmasked as an aestheticized vision and transformed into the flighty, early "mod" Modesty Blaise. The Truffaut hero had already died with James Dean and Albert Camus. No one under forty could understand Sartre. A power vaccum existed that would not stay unfilled. The innocence of Modesty Blaise's veneer died with Mick Jagger's September, 1965, song, "I Can't Get No Satisfaction." In her place came the Mod girl as the heavy, Madeleine Zimmer, child of Coca Cola, and Nadine Sallanches, the superficial daughter of Marx. As Michel Caen described Nadine at the time in *Cahiers du Cinéma:* "She's called Nadine Sallanches but her real name is Geneviève Bujold. She is a Canadian girl. Twenty years old, five feet, four and one half inches, one hundred pounds, stubborn, ironic, falsely, phonily adult, egotistical about her own accomplishments, realistic, seductive, Geneviève-Nadine exists. She is a girl cousin, a distant cousin of Monique Zimmer [whose name was changed to Madeleine Zimmer and played by Chantal Goya in Godard's *Masculine-Feminine*] signed Jean-Luc Godard; the expression of her countenance (or the ostentatiousness of how she displays herself, if one prefers), she is a carbon copy of that of any fifteen other girls, known from the park benches of the college campus, somewhat full of nervous energy and, often, nuisance-like, but lively, and not without charm."[21]

To which we can add: Godard also calls her Madeleine Zimmer, but her real name is Chantal Goya. A real *yé-yé* singer, (*yé-yé* comes from the Beatles' line: "She loves you, *ye*ah, *ye*ah, *ye*ah," and describes the French version of the 1963–1965 pop singer). Chantal existed as much as Madeleine did; her pop narcissism made her cruel without her meaning to be. She would not make Paul (Jean-Pierre Leaud) happy; but she was not without her charm.

One sees the documentary care with which both the Resnais characters and the Godard character have been drawn. Resnais, following his concept of flat realism, makes Nadine a carbon copy,

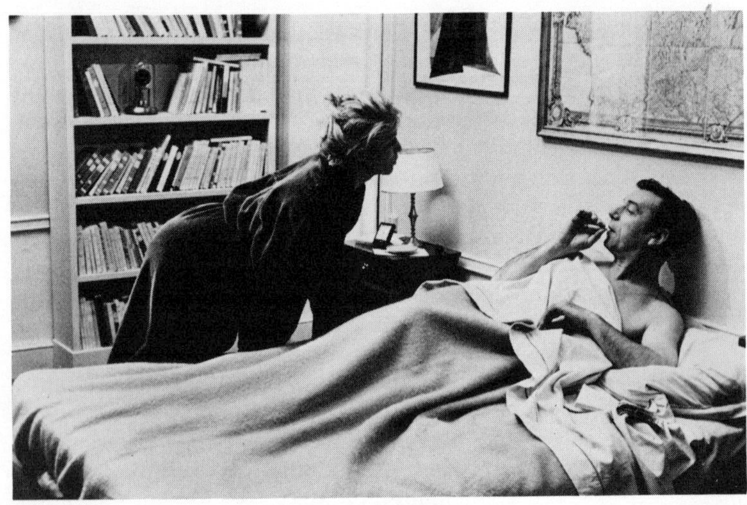

Ingrid Thulin and Yves Montand in *La Guerre Est Finie*.
The Museum of Modern Art Film Stills Archive

an index, of fifteen other girls. Godard makes Madeleine authentic by allowing Madeleine to keep most of Chantal Goya's identity.

The other female relationship Diego has is with Marianne, who, fifteen years older, belongs to the era of the fifties—the time, Jorge Semprun explains, when Diego would have met her while leading a more bourgeois life as he was building up his cover, his false identity for Spain as a technical representative of UNESCO. At least this is what Semprun replied when one of the critics of the Marxist magazine, *Positif* (which took a strong interest in *La Guerre Est Finie*), asked how it was that Diego became involved with a woman who is a "model, that is to say a woman with an 'independent profession' who earns enough to be independent and who seems completely cut off from class struggle and most indifferent to Revolution?"[22]

Other questions were put to Semprun by the *Positif* critics. Semprun answered them well, without appearing to be on the defensive. Take for example this question: "The word 'communist' is never pronounced. Is it clear that it is the Communist party that you show in action?" Semprun: "If one ennunciates neither the word party nor the word Communist it is the workings of the Communist part and not about it, or the exterior of it. Amongst themselves, they don't have to refer to things with their names and say 'we are Communists,' they speak about their work; they have their vocabulary, their references. It is the interior that we wanted to show."[23] This is what also distinguishes the militants from Nadine, who says to Diego: "Formidable! You're a professional."

When asked where Diego's motto, "Patience and irony are the principle virtues of the Bolshevik" came from, he replied, "No it is not historic. It is an extract from a poem I wrote when I was eighteen years old and which was an imitation of a poem by Mayakovsky. It came back to me as a memory at that moment in the film."[25]

Semprun defended the Leninist student group's confrontation with Diego as based on fact, but he also stressed that it was used to show the militant's dilemma when he disagrees with a policy set up by the central committee (Diego is not in favor of the general strike for Spain) and yet has to defend it against the young Leninists who endorse plastic bombing in Spain. He also defended the lack of proletarians in the film (only Ramon is a worker) by pointing out that the story dealt with the leadership.

To the serious question of Jean-Louis Pays, who asked, "To Resnais, who is considered to be a 'non-committed' filmmaker, I would like to say, to show Communists for two hours in a revolutionary action is audacious in view of its non-committment. If all the 'non-committed' cinéastes were like him, the term 'committed filmmaker' would lose all its interest and significance. For you, what does the fact of having made this film represent?" Semprun answered, "For me, evidently, it is a committed film and Resnais is a committed filmmaker, but he has a very exacting, hard to please notion of 'committment' and there is the modesty of his attitude. [In plain English, Resnais dislikes bullshit committment.] Perhaps he has a slightly puritan idea of what 'commitment' is."[26]

That about sums up the factographic quality of *La Guerre Est Finie*, its approach to telling the story, in a Kantian fashion, from the inside, and its integration of Diego's political problem with the two women. In the script, the "second act" of the film which features two long love sequences, first with Nadine and then Marianne, is appropriately entitled, "The Truths of the Lie," referring to two points at which Diego must level with their demands that he reveal his true identity.

Diego never totally reveals his identity, although he does reveal more to Marianne than to Nadine whom he playfully tells that his name is Domingo (Sunday), as if they were children playing a game of spies. Marianne finally discovers his true identity in the last sequence when she joins the Party and goes to Barcelona to rescue him from certain arrest. Marianne and Diego achieve solidarity only when she joins him in the Party, the most important part of his life. The shot Resnais uses of Diego's head dissolving to Marianne's head is formally justified by cinematic convention as well as thematically justified by the interlocking of the two narratives of Diego's life.

John Ward has challenged this sequence, however:

> This turn about . . . that the group at last trusts Marianne, the breaking down of the mystique that only Spaniards have a part to play in Spanish politics . . . is perhaps the only unconvincing feature of the whole film. It is hard to believe that such men would be changed suddenly, by a single truth [the recognition that Diego is in danger]. It is quite easy to accept something as true and even act on it, without experiencing its force. [i.e. why is Resnais' film suddenly so passionate at the end?] And on a practical level, of all people, why send Marianne?"[27]

Why not send Marianne, one could ask. The reservoir of Spanish spies in Paris was not infinite, and Marianne does fit the M.O. of professional revolutionaries in that the prime goal of a professional spy is not to look like one, but to go unrecognized. Also, one has sensed throughout the film that the Spanish revolutionaries were running out of manpower. They needed a new recruit. However, it is true that it gives the film a pat ending. But I think this can be forgiven because the film is not actually about Spain as a literal country at all. Of all the *Positif* critic's specific factographic questions to Resnais and Semprun, Semprun's answer to Jean-Louis Pays as to the relationship between France and Spain in the film is most illuminating. "Alain asked himself this question from the start. If you seek your inspiration in the Spanish emgrés, it is most easy then to [use them] to speak of equivalent things in France."[28] *La Guerre Est Finie* then is not what we can call a factographic film. Whether incidents seem fictitious or factual on the level of the total film is less relevant than whether they could have happened.

Resnais and Semprun's concern over factography is clearly expressed in two statements they each made. After admitting that Diego in the Party is to some degree, a privileged character (but to go into that more heavily, would be "another film"), Resnais also admitted that "it is possible that the young people [Nadine and the Leninist group] are more the young people of 1964. [The film was shot August-November 1965] There is, there, a shift and that scene in 1965 should have been, without a doubt, done differently."[29] But it was extremely important to include Nadine in the film. She is the youngest major character Resnais has used thus far. Without her, would the more sexist critics have reacted so well to the film, would the more socio-politically oriented *Cahiers* have given it such a good review, would twenty-year-old girls have gone to see the film? Jorge Semprun stresses, "Besides everything else, for Resnais and myself, one of the most important problems was to see if we could reach young people."[30]

The criticism that the personal love story and the political discourse in *La Guerre Est Finie* never merge can be refuted on several levels. To Annie Goldmann's charge that the mental images and discussions with the party or with youth "do not result in a unified synthesis," we can point out that she has not noticed, as John Ward has, that the conflicts and confusions of myth and reality in Diego's political life are reproduced in his sexual life. And we can also counter with Bosley Crowthers' (who is not notably sympathetic to Resnais' concerns in film) review in *The New York Times.*

> The drama is on two levels—first, that of the intrigue and peril of the man getting over the border and avoiding detection in France, and then that of his indecision toward his mistresses and toward his work. He is getting on, he is disillusioned and he is bored. Perhaps he should give up being a revolutionary and settle down with his mistress and a job. Mr. Resnais blends the drama of both these levels, most artfully moving with sure fluidity from the realistic tensions of his man's political contacts and his activities into the sweet and wistful areas of his own feelings.[31]

In the sense that the film is both about sex and politics, *La Guerre Est Finie* could almost be a Godard film.

The fundamental distinction between Godard and Resnais, however (and we can see it most clearly in *La Guerre Est Finie)* is that Resnais does not trust us to take our information system just from him, rather, he invites us to bring our own perceptions to the film viewing process. Godard, like Emile, has faith in himself as a teacher to such an extent that he invites us to trust his cinema totally. Godard can thus be seen to have produced a cinema which is characterized by a poetic self-trust, such as Mayakovsky had about his own role in being a people's poet, and which is intellectually characterized by recognition of Wittgenstein's postulate that the word is a representation, neither entirely literal nor entirely metaphoric. (Mitry's claim that cinema is not metaphoric because it is itself is nonsense. Cinema is both language and discourse. That is why it is complicated.) Godard's tactic is thus Wittgensteinian, Mayakovskian, Vertovian. Resnais' cinema is much more austere, a cinema of distancing (rather than of aloofness), one where he wishes not to interfere with our perceptions (he assumes we like to make the discovery rather than have the discovery made for us; *we* are to have the "aha!" reaction). Resnais' cinema, from a political aesthetic standpoint demands more activity on our part than Godard's. As of 1966, it is completely understandable why the Left activists in general, whether political or social, would find more to recommend in Resnais' cinema than in Godard's.

Yet, what is most important, both Godard and Resnais are working in their area of strengths. Aside from its cinematic qualities, *Masculine-Feminine* by Godard is brilliant tragic poetry, superb sociology. Philosophically, it is but a clumsy reiteration of Heisenberg's Uncertainty Principle. Resnais' *La Guerre Est Finie,* on the other hand, is a good discourse in political philosophy, a good example of how to use cinema to philosophize, as opposed to having a character in a film do the philosophizing as Eric Rohmer does.

Godard, then, is obviously to be commended for not trying to be like Resnais and vice versa. The net result was that two films appeared in the spring of 1966, *Masculine-Feminine* and *La Guerre Est Finie,* that again suggested through the medium and agency of the cinema that the world had changed and become more complex. Like *Hiroshima* and *L'Avventura,* which announced that a new higher order of narrative film was here to stay, the 1966 pair of films hit at the same problems from different angles, namely, how cinema could be used to tell people about their own lives, quickly enough and on time, so they could still be the shapers of their own destiny. That a Resnais film was present twice, at historic moments in the history of cinema, is indeed an indication of Resnais' breadth of powers as a cinéaste, for merely to have made either *Hiroshima* or *La Guerre Est Finie* would have been sufficient to rank him in some film pantheon. As it was, the critics of *Positif* had every right to be satisfied in that Resnais had done his Marxist homework for *La Guerre Est Finie* (along with Jorge Semprun, who is a socialist and naturally knew Marxism). Those who merely went to see the film to "see something new," certainly got to see something new when they encountered Geneviève Bujold as Nadine. If flat realism is what *La Guerre Est Finie* represents, we should realize that Resnais did not pick this style in order to foist it upon us, but to signal that we should see Diego's simple meanderings—the surface of the film—the flat real surface of Diego's life—as, in fact, the deep structure of the film, something that we should arrive at with our own perception.

8

Je T'Aime, Je T'Aime

CONCEIVED AS AN IDEA BY JACQUES STERNBERG and suggested to Resnais as early as 1962 as a science fiction narrative to film, *Je T'Aime, Je T'Aime* [*I Love You, I Love You*] is a time travel story about a man who—after reliving certain moments of his life—seems to learn nothing more than a conviction that if he had to live his life again, he would do it much the same way. A fated view of existence, *Je T'Aime, Je T'Aime* is told lethargically. Only the image flow redeems a film paced so slowly that it threatens to provoke boredom and self-consciousness in the viewer. Sternberg bears the responsibility for the narrative, and one can find little that Resnais might have changed. Of all Resnais films, it is the least "Resnais like."

The film, shot in and around Brussels, Belgium, follows the principle of *Muriel*: its locale is neutral. It begins as a *série noir* B film, almost like a Samuel Fuller parody of the genre. Claude Rich (who plays Claude Ridder, the lethargic hero) has the right type of face for his role, but the banality of the plot requires considerable audience patience. In a strange way, the film, shot in the spring of 1967 ("Sergeant Pepper" time), seems to defy the frenetic spirit of that youth-enlivened era. As with most Resnais films, it is entirely peopled with adults. Its purpose is only and partially slowly revealed. In fact, it would be difficult to explain why Resnais made this film at all, were it not for its theme of time.

Yet even here, there remains a mystery. The theme of time has always been approached indirectly by Resnais. All of his other films contain the tension of the tenses. This film is directly about them, is a study of them. The spectator is thus made a party to the experi-

cene from Je T'Aime, Je T'Aime. *The multiple allusions of* riel *again surface in this film whose hero is forced to live* *ugh the same love affair twice.*

ment in progress. All subtlety is thrown to the winds on the narrative level. Only the splendid use of images attracts.

The film is not highly entertaining even then. It lacks, quite bluntly, cinematic innovation. The imagery is so straightforwardly edited as to come close to producing a banal film instead of a film about banality (i.e., *Muriel*).

But, *Je T'Aime, Je T'Aime* (the double title refers to the fact that Claude, the hero, lives his love life out twice) may be seen as an experiment in the philosophy of our thought processes. It demonstrates the way we arrange and reorganize nonlinear narrative in our minds, and thus it approximates some of the pioneering efforts made in modern Czechoslovakian novels in the late 1920s and 1930s to produce a clear logical story despite apparent shifts in narrator. In this chapter, I shall try to corroborate, with a simple experiment, this theory first by describing a segment of the film as it runs achronologically, and then by showing how efficiently we can rearrange it into chronological order, even to the point where the pure chronological rendering becomes boring. Although two shots that are visually contiguous may turn out not to be syntagmatically sequential, Ridder's story is never hard to follow.

He appears, for example, in 1950s costume in an office; with Catrine, his mistress/lover/companion, being happy; lying in bed with Catrine; without Catrine, but talking to a girl who looks like her; in the orange time capsule; or with the scientists. From this, we can read the film as follows, regardless of its shot order a happy-go-lucky bachelor, Claude Ridder, bored with office work in the late 1950s, meets a sexy girl, Catrine, in the early 1960s, with whom he, at first, has a happy affair. They spend much time in bed together. Eventually they quarrel. Catrine, an insomniac, dies, or commits suicide, or disappears. Ridder lies in a bed and tells a new girl the story of Catrine. Ridder tries unsuccessfully to shoot himself. He survives. Listlessly, he signs up for a scientific experiment on time travel. This reading is based on a mental reconstruction of the film which we can do while watching it, regardless of its scrambled order.

The film contains (approximately) thirteen discernible time sets, twelve of them corresponding to times (years) in Ridder's past. The film is divided into 164 shots, according to the published screenplay.[1] It begins with twenty-one shots of in the filmic present tense (September, 1967) of Claude Ridder letting himself be taken to a science research center, a "night club" of the mind, where

This still from *Je T'Aime, Je T'Aime* shows how Resnais uses a formal device, two mirror images to illustrate how everything in the film seems to happen twice.
The Museum of Modern Art Film Stills Archive

"anything can happen." (The film unfortunately takes place in one of the most boring cities in Europe, Brussels, taking the Resnais tendency towards neutral setting a bit too far.) In an opening that resembles a *série noir* crime film the victim-protagonist, Claude, is taken away to a new fate. During bits of conversation, we piece together that he has just tried suicide and doesn't much care what happens to him. The scientists plan to send him back in time, for one year, to relive one minute of his life. They have already done this successfully with a mouse (Mouse B), and now they hope to accomplish the same with a human being.

But as Ridder returns to his past, the time machine goes out of control, causing him to travel erratically from year to year, which gives Resnais a marvelous excuse to present us with well-executed flicker cuts. Never do more than two successive shots ever occur in the same time frame from then on.

Resnais' experiment should give a license to all filmmakers to make their films as non-linear as they dare, as long as they narrate something. The way to prove this point is first to take the film as it is, reading the scrambled narrative in the achronological order Resnais has produced, showing how well we understand it. Then, we can compare the scrambled narrative with a strictly chronological sequence that we can produce by cutting up the film and respIicing it in properly chronological order. When we then make the comparison, we will find the chronological reconstruction superfluous, for our mind has already done it for us. So clear is the film already that my experiment will prove that nothing is gained by having the narrative unfold in straight historical time order.

As we shall see, not only is our ability to organize sets good, but also our memory for parallel narratives can accomodate up to nine or ten of them without any difficulty. (Whether two different narratives are characterized by two completely different persons narrating them, or by one person in two different costumes recognizably representing two different years of history in his own life, is immaterial.) We take each recognizably different narrated shot of Claude Ridder's past/present/future as soon as we have seen it once and assign it to a special narrative set: "mid-1950s," "later than that," "after he has met Catrine," etc.

If we continue this process to the end of the film, we will get the same result we got through using set theory. Our original reading will be fleshed out with more detail, more nuance, more philosophic certainty. But it will be the same in all essentials. *Je T'Aime, Je T'Aime* proved its point that a film can let us build a para-logic to it, even while we watch its images. Resnais had already examined this point with *Marienbad*, but *Je T'Aime, Je T'Aime* proved that while we watch a film we can construct a story different from the one we are literally shown. Susan Sontag's contention that *Muriel*,[2] was deliberately cut across the grain, fails metaphorically to apply the *Muriel;* but it perfectly fits *Je T'Aime, Je T'Aime*. Syntagmatically glued together, the latter film gives us the whole piece of wood glued together again as it was before it was creatively jigsawed.

Yet, despite its noble experimental effort, *Je T'Aime, Je T'Aime* lacks the balance a full-length film needs; it lacks cinematic integration. Only, perhaps, as a dress rehearsal for *Providence* eight years later is the film interesting for the general viewer. (The film is rarely ever to be seen, anyway; only on French television does it occasionally surface.) But, for the specialized viewer or film student, or student of narrative, *Je T'Aime, Je T'Aime* is a "must," for it suggests, by actually being made, that the way we perceive a film counts more than the film itself. Whereas Godard used his *Masculine-Feminine*, *Pierrot le fou*, *Two or Three Things . . .* , and *La Chinoise* to harry people into discussing language and its formal structure, as from a lectern, *Je T'Aime, Je T'Aime* expresses the idea that a film is not a unit of clock time but itself a series of spatial-temporal intervals.

Je T'Aime, Je T'Aime, Blow-up, and 1967.

The year 1967 was a milestone for Resnais, as well as for Godard and Antonioni, whose *Two or Three Things I Know About Her* and *Blow-Up* I briefly want to compare to *Je T'Aime, Je T'Aime.* The temptation at this stage of the careers of these directors was to make a different, newer form of film. If the Zeitgeist films of 1962–1963 (*Muriel, Marienbad, The Eclipse,* even Fellini's *8½*) of these three directors seemed like deeply pessimistic statements at the time, in the middle of an era on a plateau of prosperity, these films also could be seen as critical of society because of a secret confidence in society's ability to progress by reform or self-reform via the process of the artistic depiction of an ill and the pin-pointing of its cause. If we are alienated or we fear war, those are effects which have causes, and which the cinema can tackle.

In 1967, these three films all seemed to question the very existence of causality. Resnais' *Je T'Aime, Je T'Aime,* aimed at showing a time experiment. As I have suggested, the title refers not to the hero, Claude Ridder telling Catrine that he loves her twice in a row, but to his telling her the same thing in two time existences. Certainly, the film is pessimistic: neither in the present nor the flashbacked present, does Ridder's declaration of love provide enough meaning for the chronically sleepless Catrine to keep her from suicide.

Blow-Up, in turn, shows another filmmaker's loss of confidence in a world of cause and effect. By forcing us into a photographer's over-causal point of view, it asks whether it may not be dangerous to cling to nonexistent causal relationships in life. In his story of Thomas the photographer, Antonioni only "fakes" an interest in developing a mystery story. *Blow-Up* is an epistemological quest, impossible to solve, for certain causality, the near zero probability of Thomas' ever arriving at meaning by his clock-time photographic blow-ups being made tragic by the uselessness Antonioni consigns to them in solving a real quest for the audience to see. So we are forced—and all three films are very forceful in this sense, to share in Thomas' fall in face of his disbelief in relativity.

Godard, in *Two or Three Things,* also manipulates. He insists, like

Hegel, upon a system for solving a sociological problem; but, after establishing a complex, mathematically sound search grid for the way urban dislocation causes social prostitution on many levels (housewives prostituting themselves to pay highrise rent), he seems to show us, as in the film's coffee cup sequence, that causality has eluded even him, at least this time around.

Perhaps an object like this [a coffee cup with coffee bubbling, like galactic entropy] will make it possible to link up . . . to move from one subject to another, from living in society to being together. But then [Godard admits] since social relationships [like Claude and Catrine's] are always ambiguous, since my thought is only a unit, . . . since an immense moat separates the subjective certitude I have for myself from the objective truth I am for others, since I can never stop finding myself guilty even though I feel myself innocent, since every event transforms daily life, since I always seem to fail to communicate. . . .

But where to begin? But where to begin with what? We could say that the limits of language are the limits of the world. [But, Godard, after finishing his setting up of the problem, despairs] . . . And when mysterious death finally abolishes these limits. . . .[3]

These words of Godard express equally well what Resnais' Claude and Antonioni's Thomas were also saying; it is horrible to run up against the feeling (after having been trained in a Newtonian world) that there is no real causality.

One essential difference separates Resnais' film, though, from its counterparts. Resnais, who did not seem to care philosophically to manipulate as much as Godard or Antonioni in order to make points—and perhaps who doesn't understand his own films as well as they do theirs—did not want to manipulate *Je T'Aime, Je T'Aime*.

On paper, Jacques Sternberg's screenplay for *Je T'Aime, Je T'Aime* contains all the weaknesses of the final film. As I have mentioned in the Preface, Resnais can not transcend a weak script. In *Je T'Aime, Je T'Aime* he follows the script faithfully, and his innovation is mainly to rely on the film to relay its content through each image functioning as a mental point space in a scrambled narrative. The shots are very beautiful, but there is virtually no movement within them. We experience a corpse-like mise-en-scène. The cutting does not establish any aural rhythm. One even gets the feeling of an excessive number of shots, as in a film that is poorly edited by an amateur. The message of the narrative is intellectually excellent if one can use one's intelligence to play with it. But the film is cinematically flat. Can this be justified in cinema, an art of motion? Flat is flat, but there is perhaps one possible justification for this experiment, albeit a far fetched one.

This has to do with the theory of relativity. It could be that Resnais has tried to show how a film using relativity would appear to our consciousness. (And the film "proves" that our mind just does not enjoy the implications of relativity as an *experience* if they are literally spelled out.) Why? What proof is there of this?

According to the Dutch physicist, A. D. Fokker, time-space does not exist (though movie critics will continue to write about it in relation to what discrete images suggest) except as a consciousness in relation to events. There are no pieces of time or space. Events predicate time-space, not the other way around. Given an event, you then construct time-space. In *Je T'Aime, Je T'Aime*, Resnais needed a far stronger narrative presence to create a sense of time-space. Too little happens. But, the real problem may be more that Resnais should not have cut up time-space into things, shots, whatever. What then is reconstructable (and we have shown it is easily done) is the narrative continuity and the narrative chronology. But, from doing this, we do not gain back a new sense of time-space. The literal assemblage in the scrambled order is what we use to derive our notion of space-time vis-à-vis the film. Note, also, that it is our own sense of psychological time, and not one we can assign to Claude Ridder, the film's protagonist. In a sense, Resnais has nullified filmic time, and replaced it with our own sense of a slow, boring psychological duration. *Je T'Aime, Je T'Aime* does prove something. I fear it is, however, the opposite of what Resnais might have wished. And that is that we perceive our sense of duration about a film not from what we reconstruct but from what we see and experience while we are watching it. We can not bottle Ridder's time and relate it back to him. Indirectly, we can see how futile it would be for him to try to do it, for we cannot. Thus, the film itself proves the impossibility of its narrative's time capsule experiment.

In *Je T'Aime, Je T'Aime*, Resnais has also profoundly violated his own style of associationism. What we see are not associated shots, but *concurrences*. In physicist A. D. Fokker's words,

New concepts require new terms. People with a visually inclined intellect tend to think of visual pictures. Such pictures arouse associations, which are no longer conscious; the majority are useful, but some may be obstructive or even deceptive. If we use the word "space," we imply something unique and permanent, in fact we imply the totality of "enduring points," even if we disregard this "duration." Yet we need a term for a set of point events, which is flat, three dimensional, and without "duration." Such a set I call a *concurrence*. There are many concurrences, they may intersect and the intersection of two concurrences must be a plane.[4]

If this is so, then the fundamental weakness of *Je T'Aime, Je T'Aime* is that it did not recognize the limitations of its structure. Its concurrences do not interrelate, as in *Muriel*, to suggest duration. *Muriel* is successful as a Bergsonian film, an evocation of time-space. *Je T'Aime, Je T'Aime*, in attacking the same problem more directly, ends up with nothing but air.

I am tempted to agree with Roger Greenspun, who described the ending to *Je T'Aime, Je T'Aime* succinctly:

I am disturbed by that mouse [Claude Ridder is found at the end of the film, returned in time to the present, with a bullet in his gut, having relived his botched suicide, but his time-travelling companion, Mouse B, returned from time unharmed] not only for the bathos of the image but also because his situation so ludicrously (and, I think, intentionally) recalls that of the wife, Simone, looking for her husband, already light years away, inside another woman's deserted apartment at the end of *Muriel*. For *Je T'Aime, Je T'Aime* resembles *Muriel* in so many close ways that the success of the older film stands almost in total reproach to the general banality of the newer one.[5]

Yet, in the final analysis, the serious student of Resnais' cinema should not be driven away even by the more obvious flaws of *Je T'Aime, Je T'Aime*. Every Resnais film is interesting paradigmatically in terms of the way it elucidates his other films.

9

Stavisky

RESNAIS MADE *STAVISKY* BY ACCIDENT. Successive projects had fallen through. In 1969, Resnais had gone to New York City and began to work with Richard Seaver, an American scholar whose speciality was the Marquis de Sade, on a film which was to be made in England, starring Dirk Bogarde and to be called "Deliver Us From Good." The collapse of the British economy apparently wrecked their plans. The "Red" Ryder project and "The Inmates" project, both involving Marvel Comic's Stan Lee, never made it to celluloid because Martin ("King Lear") Ranshohoff failed to come up with enough money to produce them. Another project with William Friedkin on H. P. Lovecraft fell by the wayside when Friedkin lost interest and took up, instead, *The Exorcist*. During 1972 Resnais and his wife Florence spent weeks travelling around New England doing research, following Lovecraft's trail which led them ultimately to Providence, Rhode Island. The name, Providence, will come up again as the title of Resnais' most recent film and the evidence suggests that a touch of the collapsed Lovecraft project found its way into Resnais' *Providence*. While in New England, Resnais wrote a revealing postcard to Jorge Semprun in Paris.

Springfield, Massachusetts, March 25 1972
Photographed the post office here yesterday while submerged in a pea soup fog. . . . It was the Post Office for Deerfield, Massachusetts, a building in wood, of spruce, and looking very pioneer-like, surrounded by large trees, under a dappled cloudy sky, from where these words have been mailed. I'm very impressed by the beginning of this pilgrimage over the Lovecraft territory. In a few days, we climbed Morse Hill in search of the "Grand Antel defying all descriptions." Then we traversed the spurs of Mineral Mountain, splendidly recalling the mysterious megaliths of Pelham, the flagstones of Lake Quabbin, the conical stones of Cthulu, the

nny Duperey, who plays Arlette Stavisky in Stavisky.
Jnifrance Film

angular crypts of the Goshen cemetary. . . . Later, we will get to Salem Arkham, Marblehead, *Providence*. . . . [my emphasis][1]

Resnais, apparently had excitedly explored all of ancient New England and was thinking about filming it as the Lovecraftian city of Arkham, one of those composite cities Resnais so loves to use as the backdrop in his films. No one backed this project either. When it fell through, Resnais retained not only his intent to show comic book narrative on the screen—ideas remaining from "The Inmates" and "The Red Ryder" projects—but also the theme of death and obscurity from the Lovecraft project.

In *Stavisky*, the theme of death haunts the entire film, one he was fortunate to make at all. Resnais' sixth feature film tells the story of a real person, one Alexander Stavisky alias Serge Alexandre, born in Russia, resident in France, a swindler whose exposure for fraud, Watergate style, caused the French government to fall and provoked rightist-inspired, Fascistic, anti-decadence oriented riots known to history as the Stavisky Affair (1934).

Why Resnais decided to make *this* film is not crystal clear. It seems as if he had no other choice. Eager to work again after six long years, Resnais chose to make the film in the style of the elegant 1930s, using CinemaScope and Saulnier sets, the same winning combination that made *Marienbad* a superb spectacle. Yet, it was not the fun of making an elegant period film, but the chance to replay the mysterious biography of Stavisky that fascinated Alain Resnais.

A scare that almost halted production occurred when a relative of Stavisky threatened to sue for the besmirching of Stavisky's honor, not realizing that Resnais meant to produce quite a sympathetic portrait. These apprehensions were needless, for as Jean-Paul Belmondo, who played Stavisky and also backed the production with his own money, plays him, Stavisky is but a charming rogue, not a political demon.

The question as to why Stavisky fascinated Resnais is perhaps best answered by viewing the film. *Stavisky* is Resnais' only biographical film. But, on careful scrutiny, one sees that it is no ordinary biography. As Frederic Vitoux observed, "*Stavisky* is not a portrait of Stavisky but of the person he pretends to play."[2] Thus *Stavisky*, we can see, fits nicely within that Resnais theme, "the presence of the absent." The Russian refugee, Stavisky, does not dare be himself. The Stavisky France knew was an imposter, and the police investigation into his career reopens the question of memory. We are on familiar ground once again.

Even more than *La Guerre Est Finie*, *Stavisky* favors truth over drama. Yet its style avoids epic distancing and thus lacks the punch of *Muriel*. In its place comes a kind of trust that the viewer will become absorbed in a theatrical tragedy that is kept realistic, however, by Resnais' decision to run a parallel narrative of Leon Trotsky's stay in France. Trotsky's stay was a fact, and since the police commisioner detailed to watch Stavisky was also told to watch Trotsky, Resnais, for the first time in his career, begins to trust the documentary.

Yet, the film stays highly dramatic because the Stavisky-Trotsky parallels (they are both Jews, Russian born, and foreigners), while well intercut cinematically, do not join each other sociologically. Resnais the structuralist has in a way tripped up Resnais the documentarist. However, the great beauty of the film lies in its use of comic book minimalism in presenting a period and costume narrative and in its bravura acting.

Perhaps the very finest sequence in *Stavisky* has the least structural connection to the film at all, except in that it has yet another refugee motif at its core. This is the sequence where we see a play within the film, when Erna Wolfgang, a Jewish refugee girl (it is 1933), gets up on stage (she is an experienced actress, perhaps from the Berlin stage) to read for a part in a play to be produced in a Stavisky-owned theater. (Resnais, who is outspoken against anti-Semitism, once declared, when a relative told him, if he went into film, he would have to deal with all of those Jews: "Thank God for all of those Jews.")[3]

For her audition piece, she chooses Giradoux's *Intermezzo*. She needs a partner to read, and Stavisky, sitting placidly in the theater, suddenly feels energetic and volunteers to go up and read the other part. Something touching emerges, for they form a duet. While the two refugees read the otherworldly lines of Giradoux, we, the audience, are brought close to them and their point of view even though the camera keeps them in an objective point of view, never giving us a countershot of their point of view looking at us like Welles's Susan Alexander in *Citizen Kane*. The camera catches them seemingly unaware. We feel we are eavesdropping, intruders. Resnais' play within a film emerges as nothing less than a personal homage to his old love, the legitimate theater. Perhaps he meant this sequence to be ironic: "illegitimate people" superbly performing roles in the "legitimate" theater.

The entire film is more slowly paced than any of Resnais' previous efforts with the exception of *Je T'Aime, Je T'Aime,* but it is fluid and flows even more than *Marienbad.* It is one of the best examples in cinema of effortless narrative. *Stavisky's* sense of period is also remarkable, and superior to *The Great Gatsby, The Day of the Locust, The Last Tycoon,* or even *Borsalino.* Its low key "by candlelight" shots are more majestic than those of *Barry Lyndon* shot through a Zeiss lens at *f*0.8. Yet, as in those films, one senses time, and slowness of pace. Fortunately, *Stavisky* is minimal, uncluttered. It does not come across as overblown, for its little moments count. *Stavisky* is one of those "little themes" Claude Chabrol would approve and that macrocosmic film nationalist Vsevolod Pudovkin would deplore. *Stavisky,* to be liked, must be seen as a film with a limited objective.

The versimilitude of the film is nicely extended by Resnais' choice of actors. Belmondo, as Serge Alexander Stavisky, is type cast, almost repeating his portrayal of the jolly gangster, Capella, in *Borsalino.* Yet, beyond being *Stavisky's* Stavisky, Belmondo gives the film a charlatan charm, a star presence which *Stavisky* must have to sustain our interest. Annie Duperey, who plays Arlette Stavisky, his wife, like Belmondo, began on the stage, and graduated to the screen. We all remember her taking off her blouse in Godard's *Two or Three Things I Know About Her,* but in *Stavisky* she plays a very chaste role. Charles Boyer, who plays Baron Raoul, functions as a sort of narrator, an authorial presence of Resnais, and ends the film with a soliloquy on Stavisky and the mystery of death.

The theatrical talents of this cast enabled Resnais to use to advantage a more theatrical type of dialogue than usual in his films. *Stavisky* thus emerges as a film similar to the Hollywood nostalgia films of the early 1970s, but with a deeper, crisper narrative. What the film may lack in mise-en-scène, it makes up for in acting and execution of dialogue. Belmondo's Stavisky versus Robert Redford's Gatsby shows the advantage of the Resnais touch even in the lighter moments.

Stavisky is, perhaps, a bit too melodramatic. It is, seen against all the other Resnais films, the one Resnais film where he seems almost to beg the audience to accept the film's naïeveté. The film, at moments, cries out to be seen as a *Beau Geste,* a film of lost honor, manners and causes, and invites the psychologically oriented critic to point to something in Resnais' personal life that may have caused all this. Coming to audiences at the height of the graceless 1970s, this, however was not seen by anyone as a flaw. To most, the film, taken by itself, seemed not Resnais' "hottest" film, but rather a cool film; and critics referred to its cool elegance, its icy Art Deco sets, its superb decor its nostalgic evocation of a bygone era, with the adjectives normally reserved for Frigidare commercials.

The Stavisky legend, perhaps, was too obscure for the American audience. But even in France, where it is well-known, the film was not popular; audiences in Paris were less than pleased. Only in New York City did the film seem to succeed.

As a period narrative, *Stavisky's* photographic beauty was sufficiently evocative of the 1930s as rendered by modern color techniques to win a cinematography award. The critical reaction to the film centered more on its plastic beauty than its narrative. As a consequence, the film has fallen into critical limbo, which is unfortunate for anyone who wishes to experience the totality of Resnais' cinema.

Stavisky, for the first time in Resnais' cinematic history, uses flashforwards (the film's narrative occurs in 1933, the flashforwards are to the inquest in 1935). Instead of flattening the flashforwards to merge them with 1933, Resnais lets them formally stand out. We see Arlette, Raoul, the police inspector who shadowed Stavisky all face forward in *Dick Tracy*-like close up, wearing distinguishably more modern clothes than they wore in the main narrative in 1933. In these flashforwards, they face an inquisitor, and us, the audience. This point of view makes us the inquisitor, a stylistic device Resnais first introduced in *Muriel*. These close ups however are something new for Resnais; for they work ingeniously to depress us with Stavisky's fate largely through their being isolated, in Bressonian fashion, from his accusors. Stavisky's death is constantly foreshadowed by these flashforwards, as in the Hollywood film. Why is it then that we never become totally interested in Stavisky, as we would if this were a Hollywood product? Perhaps the answer lies in that Resnais makes the film jump intermittently between Stavisky, France and Trotsky, and like an alternating current, asks us not to sympathize with one victim but with many victims: Stavisky, Trotsky, Erna Wolfgang (who curiously, bears as her last name, Mozart's first name, one of the only instances in which Resnais has stooped to use a Godardian reference.)

For the first half of the film, Stavisky/Belmondo shows a lot of the

Jean Paul Belmondo as Stavisky.
Cinemation Industries, Inc.

old chutzpah that was once known as *Belmondisme*; Jean-Paul Belmondo seems to be continuously running out of the frame on errands. Almost as in a Hollywood film of the 1950s we hear from the minor characters what a great guy Stavisky is from all sides. Had Resnais stooped for the first time in his history to creating a live character for us so as to conquer our hearts? Was he testing out a new way for himself to film narrative, a more conventional way? Or, was he just being extraordinarily loyal to Semprun's script?

Jorge Semprun, who wrote the sçreenplay for *La Guerre Est Finie* as well, must now be called to account. Semprun's script for *Stavisky* was in many respects different from *La Guerre Est Finie*. In *Stavisky*, the problems of writing a famous man's biography come up. In *La Guerre Est Finie*, the invention of "Diego Mora" made things much simpler. Diego could be made an index of a man like Semprun himself; he could even symbolize Spain in exile. But what was Stavisky to stand for besides Stavisky? Resnais and Semprun get caught in the paradox of biographical fiction as it relates, for example, to the folkloric bad man, the bad man of the epic Western film, if you will. Stavisky, like Wild Bill Hickock, Billy the Kid, Jesse James, etc., exists both as fact and as legend. There were several alternatives. One could show the fact, one could show the legend's falseness, one could have the fact confront the legend. But, as Frederic Vitoux noted, what Resnais seems to have done is to have made "*Stavisky* not a portrait of Stavisky but of the person he pretends to play." Here we have a strange renunciation by Resnais of his theme of "the impossibility of documenting." In *Stavisky* we have an art of documentation, but on the fictive level of the Western movie documentation, where the heroes are given a motive to reconfront their pursuers, and in a reversal of history, history is replayed. Stavisky in *Stavisky* is retried by Resnais. A new jury is there. As in *The Legend of Tom Dooley*, as sung by Doc Watson, a new version of Stavisky emerges. On what basis did Resnais make a claim, then, for this new Stavisky? The real Stavisky, after all, was a guilty swindler. Did Resnais decide that the tragedy of Stavisky was that he could never be himself? Apparently, here, we have the conflict of two Resnais themes, and "the presence of the absent" overrides "the impossibility of documenting." In *Stavisky*, we get a documentation of "the presence of the absent."

What Semprun seems to have done is to have repeated the theme of Diego Mora, the man with a false identity. (The older you get, the less fun it is to have one.) Stavisky begs our indulgence and asks that we give the same sympathy we did to the worthy Diego to the blustering Stavisky. The world Stavisky lost—the fields of the Ukraine, perhaps—now seems to be the world of the bourgeois individualist—and we do not feel as sorry for his loss of wealth, as for the loss of the man he could never be. Yet we do not feel for him as we do for Diego, who lost Spain. There is no demand in *La Guerre Est Finie* that we identify with Diego; Stravisky demands identification. *Stavisky*, in so doing, succumbs to its own nostalgia.

At the risk of being overinterpretive, I would like to suggest that Resnais' best films are those where he is tight and manipulative in the extreme. *Stavisky* for all of its correct chords of nostalgia, its admirable score by Stephen Sondheim, teaches us almost nothing verbally, tells us nothing literally. It is Resnais' most ambiguous film.

Stavisky's best lines have to do with death, something unusual for a Resnais film, which is generally equally devoid of both animal sex and epiphanies. When Baron Raoul sums up Stavisky in a closing soliloquy, these lines could have been meant for anyman and everyman, a sort of epitaph in the manner of Gray's "Elegy Written in a Country Churchyard." Here we have a fine moment, a metaphoric one though, almost apart from the narrative. In *Stavisky*, Resnais breaks away from metonymy and moves towards metaphor.

Thus, I conclude that the lack of manipulation in the film has a purpose and that Resnais' deviation toward telling a narrative through character rather than metonymic displacement forced *Stavisky* into a competition—an unfavorable one, in my opinion—with other conventional narrative films, unmasking the fact that it is not a very singular film.

Before leaving *Stavisky*, a stronger recapitulation has to be made on the subject of its parallel narratives. These are the narratives drawing links between Stavisky and Trotsky. The insistence upon filming this way undoubtedly came from Resnais, who was delighted to find such things as that the same detective was assigned by Paris to shadow both men. Here again we see Resnais mixing illusion and factographic documentation—both men were, after all, fugitives from Russia—in order to aim for some kind of abstraction. Rather than film this via the psychological narrative of a Joseph Losey in *Mr. Klein* (1977), Resnais was wise to stay with his technique of parallel narrative.

Stavisky gains thereby in abstraction, but the narrative occasionally tends to get clumsy and is only rescued by cinematography. The interweaving of the two narratives—normally Resnais does it exquisitely—is generally the clumsiest in all of the Resnais films. Only one shot, depicting both stories, is marvellously rendered, however, as a pan suddenly shows us the other group, the other story. This is perhaps one of the finest shots in Resnais cinema. But is mostly made beautiful by the fact that no words are uttered. Cinematography, however, can not alone glue everything together, and we can fault the script of *Stavisky*, perhaps, more than that of the other Resnais films, for not providing very much good material to film. What we realize about *Stavisky* is that the best parts of it approximate in quality the silent films of the 1920s by Marcel L'Herbier, a hero of Resnais'.

Perhaps, after *Marienbad*, the viewer is just not prepared for low key Resnais, the relative unmanipulatedness of *Stavisky*, which is neither as didactic or as heavily open structured as *Muriel* or *Providence*, and by no means as seductive as *Marienbad* or the more *Marienbad*-like sequences of *Providence*.

Seen historically, then, *Stavisky* is the beginning film of Resnais' second period—a period forced into being by financial problems rather than artistic intent. It is his *Touch of Evil,* not in the sense of the closed structure of Orson Welles' film, but in the nature of its handling: like Welles', it suggests a "comeback," a nervous desire to make good and regain public attention. Historically, *Stavisky* now looks like a redefining film for Resnais and a dress rehearsal for the more open structured and more successfully seductive *Providence.* Also, there is another important feature of Resnais' filmmaking that, in its redefinition of his style, *Stavisky* highlights: Resnais has developed most clearly in *Stavisky* a narrative style based on the technique of comic book panels.

Stavisky, Resnais and the Comics

Alain Resnais, as I have tried to show, is like no other film director. His is a difficult mind to understand. Yet his seemingly surprising love of the serio-comic strip is, perhaps an easy quirk to explain. *Stavisky* makes perfectly clear that Resnais' love of comics is not "slumming" but one facet of his purism in style, a purism that can only allow itself to take ideas and building blocks from high art and from simplicity, and not from middlebrow culture or masscult love of one-dimensionality.

The ellipsis of the comic book style also fits well with Resnais' personal metonymy and his desire not to become pinned down. In addition, as Resnais himself explained, comics were quite logically the means by which he, a precocious child of the 1930s learned, before he had the money and a 35mm camera crew, how to play film director.

Comics, well beyond the function of creative play, showed Resnais how to solve the problems of camera setup and cutting; for the comics were developed in parallel with the Hollywood school of continuity cutting and non-montage editing of the 1930s. In Resnais' own words: "The rules of shooting-script and editing are the same in the comics as in the cinema. What I know about the cinema, I have learned as much through comics as through the cinema.[4]

We have already pointed out the enormous influence of comics on Resnais from 1934 to 1940. We can add that this period was also the High Renaissance of the comic book in America, and this linkage with (indirect as it was) the American national cinema would be as close as Resnais would ever come to professing the pro-Hollywood Hawksish classic cinema mania of many of his French directorial colleagues. (Truffaut and Godard have never publicly admitted to any fascination with comics, though Godard seems to be quite taken with posters.) Sociologically, this is very interesting because it means that even in an out of the way place like the Depression-days Vannes railway kiosk, French comics, and sometimes Italian and American ones, were available for purchase.

Resnais tells the amusing story that his cinematic style was influenced by the appearance and disappearance of certain strips, creating a mystery as to what had happened to them, a case of narrative getting lost—something which certainly occurs in all his films. Resnais later defined this pleasurable sensation of mystery: "I like films where I lose a sense of what is going on for ten minutes, and then, suddenly, I catch on again."[5] This always happens—in a minor way—in comics on a panel-to-panel basis, and Resnais has made this sensation a major event in all of his feature films. (There are invariably a few shots in all of Resnais' films which evoke an "aha!" reaction. See "Dick Tracy" strips for similar moments, usually vocalized by italicized words in the balloon spoken by Tracy or an assistant!)

Roy Armes has analyzed what he thinks the influence of comics on Resnais is: "The importance of comics to Resnais' work is twofold. First, they represent a non-realistic method of narrative, using such processes as distortion, isolation of a character from his setting [especially in *La Guerre Est Finie*] and violent color contrast for dramatic ends [especially in *Muriel*]."[6] This fits with Resnais' statement: "The realist cinema, the reconstruction of daily life, the reproduction of gestures, all that does not interest me at all.[7]

Second, comics techniques apply to a Resnais film because they frequently have commentary quite separate from the visual flow of the panels, narrating a different pace, in a line or two of print underneath the panel, or in Armes' words "they frequently have a 'commentary' quite separately narrating the events. . . ."[8] But Armes did not relate this accurate description of comics to Resnais' use of it. It seems the possibility of separate rhythms of narrative and image in comics intrigued Resnais, for in *Muriel* in particular, he quite often uses separate, contrapuntally related rhythms of narrative and image, one often in advance or retardation of another, creating, in the narration/image flow relationship, a sense of—as in music—ritardando or accelerando, a sense of dragging or speeding up of time due to tempo manipulation. Thus Resnais' use of comics is deep and important to understand if we want to understand the structure of his films, and, at the same time to find a lighter entrée into the often heavy works of Resnais.

Resnais' interest in the comic strip first began in 1934, when he was a twelve year old boy in Vannes. "He was fascinated by the evocative quality of the Nick Carter (the great American detective) series and the dynamism of the attitudes depicted on them, immutable though they were. A fascination which left its mark on the hieratic composition of certain scenes [i.e., sequences] in *Last Year at Marienbad* which are quite immaterial to the action but very revealing of the director's preoccupations. But a discovery made quite by chance and resulting as Resnais himself put it, in love at first sight, completely eclipsed [Sherlock] Holmes and his derivatives."[9]

As Resnais told Francis Lacassin, "In June or July of 1934 at the newspaper kiosk in the Vannes railway station, I noticed for the first time a publication very similar in appearance to the Nick Carter series. The rather old fashioned wrappers bore an alluring title, *The Phantom of the Red Ruins.* It was No. 67 of the fortnightly series, 'Harry Dickson, the American Sherlock Holmes.' I was to remain a devoted reader until the series ceased publication in May, 1940. . . ."[10] One of Resnais' life-long projects has been to make a film entitled "The Adventures of Harry Dickson."

Despite the emergence of formidable rivals after 1936 in Mandrake the Magician, Flash Gordon, Dick Tracy and other American comic strip heroes—whose adventures Resnais insists taught him the principles of filmmaking long before he held a camera—Harry Dickson never lost his pride of place in Resnais' affection.[11]

That Resnais' interest in comic strips centered on the "advanced" American comic strip is no surprise ("Dick Tracy," Resnais' favorite American comic, was already in full bloom in 1934!) for at the time of Resnais' initial interest in them (1934–1936) the American strips had already developed the unique narrative aspects of their style (the graphics revolution was to come in the late 1930s). Resnais would be the first to admit that the comics, as a blatant graphic art form, were, perhaps, uniquely an American invention, part of the escape literature of the Great Depression that still flavors the daily strips (and their inferior analogs, the TV soaps) and which fits well with Resnais' wish to get away from "the reconstruction of daily life, the reproduction of gesture."

Resnais' absorption of American comic strips continued into their real heyday. After 1938, several American strips were already into a heavy use of tilts, pans, and crosscutting, even before Hollywood unleashed Orson Welles' *Citizen Kane* (1940). The comics learned narrative innovation faster than film did.

"If the screen were vertical, I'd make a film about New York City," quipped Michelangel Antonioni in 1975.[12] In the comics, the screen already was vertical. Beginning in the early 1940s, *Batman* comic books specialized in quickcutting, zooms, telephoto shots, inserts, angle shots galore, and the occasional vertical panel or screen. *Spiderman* used "conventional" shots when Spidy was Peter Parker, but when Parker became Spiderman, the "camera" went "crazy." One saw low angle shots, narrow depth of field shots which exaggerated Spiderman's feet, tilts, pans, high angle zooms, all leading to a more fluid pace than of *Batman*, whose "Pow" condemned it to a jerkier style.

In 1940 the panels of urban comic strips were already very cinematic. Greg Toland's deep focus and linking graphics in *Citizen Kane* only used cinematic elements that already existed in the comics. By the late 1950s, when Jim Steranko, whom Resnais was to meet in 1971, took over drawing *Captain America*, the cinematic nature of the comic strip was so evident that even the highly cinema oriented Steranko could only take the cinematicity of the strip a little bit further and mainly through a refinement of choice of "camera angles" that would propel the narrative toward suspension of disbelief. This is the reason Resnais became so fascinated with Steranko's work and paid him a visit in his New York apartment in 1971, the point at which Resnais was most fascinated with directly linking comic book panel style with the format of a film he wished to make.

By the end of the 1940s, the comics had already reached their maximum point of urbanization—film would catch up in the late 1940s thanks to *film noirs* and crime films. These comics were urban rather than urbane or sophisticated. One could say there was something comically primitive about them. They still belonged to escape fiction. But, as with any pop art form, the best has a singular quality. Here lies the "secret" of Resnais' love affair with Chester Gould's *Dick Tracy* for *Dick Tracy* had been well ahead of its time—Gould was the Howard Hawks of the comic strip world—and that is why Dick Tracy has worn so well.

Batman and Superman, like *Dick Tracy*, became specialized vehicles for a "big city" type of narrative. It was the form rather than the content of urban comics, epitomized by the Marvel Comics Group in the 1950s, which we shall discover in *Stavisky* (and in *Muriel*) that intrigued Resnais. It was not for nothing that he had Dick Tracy airmailed to his office in Paris all through the 1950s and 1960s.

Resnais' use of strip style in his films really begins with *Muriel*, a highly urban film with an episodic narrative eminently suited to the jump cutting options of panel narrating. In *Muriel*, color is used in the same way as the inked-in solid colors surrounding comic characters, such as when we first see Ernest. Why else is Ernest surrounded by solid orange? In *Muriel* Resnais uses a color scheme reminiscent of *Flash Gordon*, with lush greens and reds throughout. Ernest's first appearance almost mimics the cheap process color used in comics on newsprint. Everyday reality in *Muriel* has the coloration of the everyday reality of the internal logic of the comic strip. (Resnais thus invites us to "see through" his "documentation" of Boulogne.) Finally, *Muriel* is deliberately shot and specially exposed so as to draw the most out of the potential garrishness of Eastmancolor, a film stock that, during its early history, gave some serious color control problems.

In his next film (and second color film), *Je T'Aime, Je T'Aime*, the panel style appears again in full force. Virtually the entire film is shot in medium shot, and I would argue that this is a comics influence rather than a Bressonian option. This, along with a claustrophobic mise-en-scène, highlights the isolation of Claude Ridder and Catrine. In the intervening black and white *La Guerre Est Finie*, Resnais uses only one comics device, but he uses it unashamedly: that of a character—usually Diego—being too tightly cropped, with part of his head running over the frame line, a style normally accepted in comics but not in cinema. This style is illustrated by *Rex Morgan, M.D.*, where all but the essentials of face and torso are removed. When applied to the screen, it creates a sense of mystery.

In Search of the Masters of Comics Narrative

After making *Je T'Aime, Je T'Aime* and failing to get "The Adventures of Harry Dickson" off the ground, Resnais went to New York City several times, where he stayed for long periods of time and

Jim Steranko
John Francis Kreidl

toyed with the idea of doing a film based on the cartoonist *Red Ryder* comic strip (Red Ryder, with his sidekick, Little Beaver, an Indian, had been a beautifully drawn, minimal—like *Dick Tracy*—comic strip of the 1930s which vanished, after the 1950s, from the daily newspapers). Nothing ever came of this project. But it heightened Resnais' curiosity about the masters of the comics. Finally, on one of his visits to New York City, Resnais decided to hunt down urban comics artist, one time amateur jazz musician and ex-*Captain America* illustrator Jim Steranko and find out what Steranko was about.

By 1970, Resnais—like all the rest of us—had experienced the bombardment of experimental techniques of the sixties, and had become increasingly interested in going back to working with the minimally composed shot as the basic unit of film rather than the long, extended sequence, as in *La Guerre Est Finie*. This decision is perhaps what drew him instinctively and strongly to the urban comic style of which Steranko was a practitioner—to the comics of action (the Marvel Group) and away from the French 1960s erotic-decorative style of strips, as exemplified by Jean-Claude Forrest's *Barbarella* (a poor imitation of *Flash Gordon*, ersatz and sloppily drawn and, a very literary-pretentious noncinematic strip that was even improved upon by the mediocre film version of it made by Roger Vadim in 1968.

Thus, dropping in on Steranko was not only fun for Resnais but an interesting visit to one of his sources. Since Steranko is as interesting a character as Jean Ray, the creator of *Harry Dickson*, it is worth telling the tale of the Resnais-Steranko encounter in some detail.

Jim Steranko, a Pennsylvanian from the Wilkes-Barre region, had gone to New York in the mid 1950s, where he joined the Marvel Comics Group of Stan Lee, as an illustrator. He eventually designed and illustrated his own version of *Captain America*, bringing to it a unique style, one somewhat different and more "Gregg Toland-like" than the other Marvel Comic strips. In 1973, he came to Boston as a speaker at a comics convention, and for the first time, told of his encounter with Resnais. "Marvel Comics originally gave me about five dollars a panel for drawing. I worked in a New York City jazz band at night to support myself. Eventually, I also worked in an ad agency."[13] For years Steranko lived in the intense milieu of Marvel Comic books. Stan Lee comes across as a nineteenth century printing plant Scrooge, and Marvel Comics as a modern day blacking factory. Marvel seems to have meant hard work and quick deadlines, a place where only a Hotshot Charlie with great stamina could survive.

Steranko continued: "After the illustrator would draw the page, including captions, an inker would then finish the page." Color would come next and Steranko would go nuts when they colored his chrome machines pink. So he left more and more detailed instructions as to what colors to use. Stan Lee almost fired him, he says, when he left a note saying, "color each Hydraman individually!" in a panel where three thousand Hydramen gaped at a "trapped" Captain America. (Normally, comics coloring is done in "sectors.")

"Every machine that you see in my comics, works," says Steranko. "I design the machines and weaponry of the future."

"In 1971, I was telephoned in the middle of the night by French film director, Alain Resnais," "Resnais," says Steranko "adored the Tarzan strip of the 30s, applied comics techniques to *Last Year At Marienbad* when he abolished the lap dissolve, which was customary in movies [up until then] when you changed clock time on the screen and wanted to move on to another time period.

"Anyway, I heard this voice on the telephone: 'Iz zis Mr. Jim Seranko? Zis is Alain Resnais. Eye vude lak to meet you sumtime. How about tomorrow?' "

Soon, Resnais was in Steranko's Manhattan apartment asking him about every panel he had lying around. "Why do you use this angle shot, and not another one?" the intellectual, urbane, and charming Resnais kept asking, pointing to each panel.

Comics, being a visual art, share the exact montage, type-of-shot, and angle problems, as film. Comics are a two-dimensional art form, not so much concerned with apparent motion but with narrative containing a lot of ellipsis. Every panel has to count. Much must go on, in comics, "off screen." So, Resnais, first of all, milked Steranko for his shot vocabulary.

"My drawing dynamics go like this. My characters and action aim to the right, leading the eye onwards. I use geometry to create effect. To create glory and power, I use symmetry." Steranko cites a panel where Captain America towers above twelve villains trying to kill him. The characters all together form the letter "A," with the head of Captain America at the apex of the subliminally perceived A, at the top of a full page panel.

Also, Steranko loves to draw his covers and full page panels using the principle of "deep space." "Greg Toland," Steranko says, "invented a lens with a very large depth of field at relatively low light for *Citizen Kane.* By this technique, everything from three to one hundred feet is in focus; so you see objects behind each other, and behind and in front of the horizontal plane defining the key object of interest in the panel, all in focus, and clearly defined and resolved. This gives the panel a science fiction look of deep-space, of looking far but seeing much detail, in the fashion of later films such as Kubrick's 2001: *A Space Odyssey.*"

All this Steranko pointed out to Resnais, who kept pointing to panels, asking him again and again: "Why zis? Why not that?"

Reading *Stavisky* through its Panels

By the time the *Stavisky* project surfaced, so much time had elasped between it and his last film (eight years!), that Resnais had to rethink his style. *Stavisky* is a return to the uncluttered minimalism of his early documentaries; and while it does not have an overall comic book panel style, parts of it are totally set up as panels. The flashforwards of Arlette and the police inspector testifying at Stavisky's post-mortem parliamentary inquest are straight out of *Rex Morgan, M.D.* or *Mary Worth* in their coloration and flat focus, and *Dick Tracy* in their way of having their characters facing forward to address the spectator.

This stylistic use of the panel in *Stavisky* is formally justified. Serge Alexandre Stavisky is designed as an off-screen character—he is, for a character at the center of the film, rarely seen—a certain indication that the film is not about Stavisky but about something else: France in the 1930s? Time? Death? The character, Stavisky, is often just talked about, is dealt with by ellipsis. The characters who speak about him, are then brought forward—as in the device of the inquest—to narrate his story in comic strip frontal fashion, facing the screen audience in the inoffensive, traditional soap-opera panel style of *Rex Morgan*, whose permanent medium close-up image statically lingers all through his daily adventures, as an icon who speaks, with little change in his position ever occurring.

When Rex Morgan deigns to speak to June Gale, R.N., he is really speaking to us, the eavesdroppers on his world. In *Stavisky*, Resnais likewise intends his strip-like characters to provoke our eavesdropping. In medium close-up admittedly these characters look a bit stiff on the screen. They never move anything but their lips (Resnais' admixture of comic panel and Bressonian style). They are formal in attire and speech, but no more, no less formal than Dick Tracy, who never takes his hat off. (And we don't care.) No more static than the handsome costumes that speak out at us from *Terry and the Pirates*, *the* pin-up comic of the late 1930s-early 1940s. (In fact, Charles Boyer's Baron is more of a Colonel Flip Corkin than a Baron Charlus, Stavisky is a Terry Lee-Hotshot Charlie, and Arlette is all of Terry's girls rolled into one.)

If we see that the testifiers, the witnesses to the life of Stavisky, are all in panel form, we can see Resnais' use of the comic strip's method of handling time; often fast ellipsis takes the place of dissolves.

This technique helps Resnais get the pseudo-plot out of the way very quickly. He can then concentrate on the second and third elements of the narrative, a more typical interest.

The second element of narrative interest in *Stavisky* is Resnais' comics-like use of Belmondo, the actor who plays Stavisky. Belmondo comes out of elevators, runs out of doors. Belmondo bursts into a group, as if a cartoonist threw him there, and he runs off like a Captain America. (That is, when he is shown at all, in the present tense of the film. He is never seen in the flashforwards, for he is already then dead.) The contrast between the dynamic Belmondo/

Stavisky alive, and the static panels informs us that when we see the static panels Stavisky must be dead.

The third narrative element in *Stavisky* worth considering is how Resnais connects Stavisky and his friends with the parallel story of Trotsky, the fellow exile. No comic panelling is related to the story of Trotsky, a serious subject. The one time these two stories intersect, they are connected by a pan from one grouping to the other grouping, and where these two space-time located point spaces meet is shown with pictorial reality and classically fluid camera movement, not in comic strip fashion at all.

It seems Resnais intentionally structurally differentiated the three interrelated themes of *Stavisky:* Stavisky live, Stavisky legend, and Stavisky's parallel, Trotsky. Stavisky live is cut quickly, as is comic strip action. Stavisky legend is shown in isolated comic panels speaking back to us down the corridors of time. The Trotsky story is shown in fluid camera movement with documentary-like pictographic realism. Resnais, we could speculate, lent the comic panel to the most tragic aspect of Stavisky, again showing us his amazing eclecticism in style.

All of his use of the panel format in *Stavisky* is economical, displaying a minimalism that makes sense and redeems a film with what would otherwise be too slow a pace, a film that often threatens to use pictorialism for imagery's sake. By using the highly abbreviated panel style, Resnais changes the punctuation of the film. He also heightens the tragedy of the short, abbreviated life of Stavisky, the formal elements of the composition and the narrative intent of the film here becoming delightfully fused into one statement.

Resnais put in ideas from the urban comics—ideas he could have culled from Steranko, especially his constant use of the ascent and descent of his main character on the Hotel Claridge elevator—and *Stavisky* shows aspects of Steranko's verticality in *Captain America*. Yet reviewers, especially in the United States, rarely if ever note the comic book connection with Resnais. Critics overconcentrated on the sets in *Stavisky*, for example, for they felt it safe to peg him as being interested in things and not in people.

Stavisky is the first of Resnais' films to show his advancing age. It is peopled with a coterie of human and accessible characters, it abounds in chance conversations, with eavesdropping, and the characters' essences of the moment. *Stavisky* seems not to have been made from an existential or Marxist urge, but simply to show life out there. Stavisky's quest was his continual seeking of the answer to a question Resnais never lets him ask outloud, but which he transfers on to us. This question is: "to be or not to be?" That Stavisky is suicide ends the film shows that Resnais felt Stavisky's life was made tragic, that he died because there was never a chance for him to achieve an identity. The refugee's tragedy is that he often is denied the nobility of even posing Hamlet's question.

Resnais and the Comic Imagination

In Wittgenstein's words, as recently quoted by director Michelangelo Antonioni relative to the closing sequence of his film, *The Passenger*, "to be is to be out in the world."[14] Comics not only have their being out there in the world (like movies) as a mass art, but they are also one of the least corrupted (and corruptible) methods of reaching both educated and uneducated people alike. Comics suspend disbelief and provide "cinematic authenticity," as good films should. And they can communicate while staying "pure." So this relationship of Resnais and the comics should not be interpreted narrowly. The way Resnais used panels in *Stavisky* is only one of his styles.

Resnais uses his comic panel style in many other ways. The panel structure is the key for him to a kind of minimalism in cinema where one can simplify form so one can concentrate one's attention on narrative. Comic panel style also goes well with film music, for example, shown in the film's nickelodian origins. The fluid panel style of Resnais' *Muriel* goes well with the sung soprano notes of Rita Streich. The lush music of Stephen Sondheim goes equally well with the staid close-up panels of *Stavisky*, as its composer broke it up into many brief, personally evocative themes. The panel style fits into Resnais' larger, "operatic" style, as it were. It creates mood rather than distracts from it. It helps create tragedy in *Stavisky's* inquest sequences, an aura of mystery in all of *Muriel*.

So, to sum up, it is not just for their pseudo-cinematic nature (i.e., they use angle shots, cuts, etc. even more daringly than film) that Resnais liked the serio-comic strips. Rather in the case of the better ones he likes their suppression of arbitrariness through strong stylization even while remaining open to the viewer's narrative imagination. In short: their certainty of touch through insistence that a certain panel follow a certain panel, thus by definition, creating style. That fascinated Alain Resnais, as style (suppression of the arbitrary) and Resnais are synonymous. Any serious student of Resnais' cinema will have to take this into account, especially in dealing with *Muriel*, *Stavisky*, and *Providence*.

10

Providence

Who ever has tried, one day, to write a scenario wouldn't be able to deny that comedy is by far the most difficult genre, the one that demands the most work, the most talent, also the most humility.[1]

WITH *PROVIDENCE*, RESNAIS' SEVENTH FEATURE FILM, we finally see him try his hand at comedy. After making *Stavisky*, Resnais was faced with a simple choice. In *Stavisky*, he had, in effect remade *La Guerre Est Finie:* again a political subject subjectively filmed: again, realist images filmed to give a flat, two-dimensional, point-space imaginative "reality":

It seems to me that one has never treated the imaginary side in the ordinary, the banal side of imagination. Because the dream . . . we all live to dream, but because there was, maybe [in *La Guerre Est Finie*] also the effect of taking from fact, since the imagination often lies beneath reality. In any case, I feel obliged to have the imaginary intervene in the moments where the character is caught in between places and if I think: I will go to place X in an hour, I do not come to see myself leave for there, go down to take a taxi, arrive, go up the elevator, and ring the bell, no! I find myself already in the apartment and then later I search out the way I got there.[2]

Stavisky was Resnais attempt at re-finding himself, not an advance. It differed filmically from *La Guerre Est Finie* only in that it used static frontal close ups and contained legitimate flashforwards. The close ups were done in Chester Gould comic panel fashion and suggested that Resnais had had just about enough of true documentary reality. *Stavisky*, further, structurally repeated the blocked out, theatrically divided into acts type of study of a life in transit that characterized the eight years older *La Guerre Est Finie*. As Resnais

John Gielgud in Providence.
ma 5

himself would be the first to admit, none of his films had as yet been very daring in any other way than in treating time.

The choices Resnais now faced were either to do something new, or to repeat *Marienbad,* recapitalizing on its success, or to make a structural repeat in a slightly different version of his emotional favorite (among all his films), *Muriel.* With *Providence,* fortunately for him and us, Resnais opted to try something new: to make a comedy. There are obvious visual stylistic hangovers from *Muriel,* centered mainly on the depiction of the character, Claud, who is written by screenwriter David Mercer as an analog of Bernard Aughain, and whose part is intentionally tailored for Dirk Bogarde. But *Providence* looks more like a *Marienbad* in Eastmancolor. Resnais has again eschewed Technicolor in favor of the "washed out" watercolor look of the less expensive Kodak stock. *Marienbad's* art director, Jacques Saulnier, is back again; and we have changes of backdrops outside the same door, characters repeating encounters, overlapping montage. But the structural use of these details seems now to be different. The first clue is that the aspect ratio of the film is now 1:1.33 and not CinemaScope, an aspect ratio more suitable for cutting than for naturistic mise-en-scène.

Note Resnais' eclecticity: while the surface structure is like *Marienbad* the deep structure is like *Muriel.* This is quite clever: *Muriel* "subverts" *Marienbad.* The result is an intramural tension, based on a clash within the director's own approach. It is also an elegant compromise; Resnais can do something new, while relying on a tried and true structure.

Providence opens with a travelling shot more reminiscent of Hitchcock's opening to *Rebecca* (1940), with its narrator's voice indicating to us that we are dealing with a first person narration, than of Welles' series of travels to the mansion of *Citizen Kane,* Xanadu. *Providence's* mansion is also, perhaps, closer to *Rebecca's* Manderley than Kane's Xanadu, for another reason. It is a house of fiction, a place where fiction is going to be created. The creator of this fiction will be Clive Langham, perhaps Resnais' most memorable character.

Providence quickly shows its true colors as a film evocative of the mysteries of fiction because of a quick shot of the state capitol building in Providence, Rhode Island—a pun on the word "Providence" which Resnais uses to destroy any illusions that we are in a literal place. "Providence" is a mansion in a "town" situated somewhere in the Western world.

If we want to "read" the meaning of *Providence*, we are soon compelled to choose between two opposed possibilities. *Providence* is about a man writing a novel and the problems he has with it. Or, on the other hand *Providence* is a dream and has a dream structure. Like Fellini's *8½*, it plays with itself. I cannot reconcile these two readings. Either it is one or the other. I shall argue that *Providence* is the former.

Let me first present the two arguments as others have stated them. *Providence* is "about the creative process," goes the first argument, about

> how a novelist twists reality to create a story. On the evening before his seventy-eighth birthday, Clive Langham [played by Sir John Gielgud], a well-known author, is writing feverishly. In the story he is writing, an author—the narrator's alter ego—is dying. He is obsessed by the slow degradation of his body and the insidious progress towards death. He is working on his latest work, a novel in which he will explore several aspects of himself through his son, Claud (Dirk Bogarde) and several other characters of major importance in Claud's life.[3]

Langham's nightmares and his novel occasionally merge, but we are always told this when it happens. "At the moment when the characters are arrested and when the doors close behind them, Claud and his wife Sonia are discovered in the garden of the narrator's country house . . . in his real world. At the end of the film, one witnesses on the narrative level, the confrontation between Claud and his wife with author Langham. The writer lies cocooned in a covering of books, papers, wine and food at the close of a sunny afternoon. The old man is about to be taken to a home for medical care. But he refuses, energetically, violently, and the responsibility of his son in the matter will become the final area of dènouement between the two men."[4]

Marsha Kinder, writing in *Film Quarterly*, seems to have a completely different interpretation of *Providence*, one I think is fallacious. Kinder opens her argument by claiming that Robert Altman's *Three Women* and Resnais-Mercer's *Providence* use similar structures, "structures of the self," according to the title of the article, a term evoking French psychologist Francis Lacan. "Both films use dream structures that contain inset dreams [certainly true of *Three Women*] but which move fluidly into conscious artistic creation—

painting in *Three Women* and writing in *Providence*."[5] I disagree. *Three Women* is not about the conscious artistic process. It is about the unconscious effect of art on a sick girl. *Providence* is about the creative process in the hands of an artist in full possession of his faculties. Kinder continues: "In contrast [with Bergman's *Persona*] *Providence* is more like Fellini's *8½* in its focus on a narcissistic artist who is obsessed with his own creative process as a means of fighting pain and death." What Kinder misses here is that *Providence* is open structured and Fellini's *8½* is close structured. While *8½* doubles back on itself, *Providence* ends with us. Kinder adds, "Drawing his art from his memories, dreams, fantasies and immediate sensory experience, he projects himself onto those around him, forcing them to play roles and deliver lines that he has spun out of his own psyche." Kinder sums up by insisting on the Fellini-Resnais comparison. "Resnais and Mercer follow Fellini's narrative movement, which goes in circles and ends with a positive acceptance of life's multiple realities and contradictions." This remark may fit Fellini, but it does not seem to fit Resnais. As Antonioni once told me, "I work from the outside, Fellini from the inside." And Antonioni considers himself and Resnais to be similar.

Resnais, who likewise acknowledges his similarity to Antonioni, sees the ending of *Providence* not as a "positive acceptance" but merely a neutral acknowledgement of life's multiple realities and contradictions. Kinder pays too much attention to the fact that one sees Langham wake up from an occasional dream. I am not denying that Langham may dream, but these "dreams" shown on the screen are too explicit and uncoded to function like dreams. Dreams according to Freud must be decoded to reveal meaning, and that means they must be coded messages to be dreams in the first place. The so-called "dreams" Langham cites function like daydreams and can be interpreted as hallucinations or visualizations of the author's reveries at his desk while he is writing his novel. If Kinder had posited a daydream structure of *Providence*, I would agree. A major bit of comparative evidence, perhaps, is sufficient to dismiss the argument of *Providence* having a "dream structure." This is that *Providence's* complete structural similarity to Resnais' hero's major work, Marcel Proust's *Rememberance of Things Past*, a novel about a narrator named Marcel, who narrates that he is about to write a novel. Resnais' film is about a narrator named Clive Langham who narrates that he is about to write a novel. I therefore favor reading

Providence as if it were the story of a creation, not a study of the characters themselves.

Other factors favor this interpretation. There is a strong use of Brechtian distancing in *Providence* which itself is very much a Brechtian comedy about the folly of taking oneself too seriously during the act of creation. There is much evidence to support this. Consider the distancing devices in *Muriel* that Resnais had used earlier. Bernard's contradictory yes-no articulations, the authorial camera looking around, the 8mm film of Bernard's counterpointed against Bernard's narration, the smiling-soldiers/torturing-soldiers visual/aural disjunction. Claud, with his bifurcated dialogue, serves the same function again in *Providence*. Claud in *Providence*, like Bernard in *Muriel*, is a Brechtian device to drive the viewer to laugh and cry. Even though seventy-eight year old Clive Langham ostensibly seems to be the leading character of *Providence*, structurally he is no more important to *Providence* than Alphonse is to *Muriel* or X is to *Marienbad*. (The point here is that it would have sufficed to show Langham or Alphonse or X mute, and for Resnais to have narrated their parts via voice over.) Langham, from the viewpoint of character—from the point of view of who he is, filmically, to the spectator—is just a tease.

The subtle beauty of Resnais' cinema is that it disguises his own narration by launching a surrogate narrator; reviewers do the rest, writing about "Langham's narrative," "X's narrative." Resnais, always a secretive man, could ask for nothing better to protect his metonymy. But the cleverness of Resnais' cinema involves a simple fact: the length of time a character appears on the screen bears no direct relation to his or her structural importance in the Resnais film. Consider the same case in Brecht's plays, the exciting function of the secondary character. For example: Kattrin vis-à-vis Mother Courage in *Mother Courage*. Courage in *Mother Courage*, Langham in *Providence*, Hélène Aughain in *Muriel* all narrate the epoch, and give the historical setting. But Kattrin, Bernard, and Claud are the daggers, the activating agents. Mute Kattrin does it with the sound of her drum; Bernard and Claud do it with the biting commentary of their voices. Kattrin is Bernard is Claud, structurally. Thus, Claud is the key activating character, the key activity awakening player of *Providence*.

As laid down by screenwriter, David Mercer (British absurdist playwright, television and movie writer, and author of the script for

Karel Reisz' *Morgan,* made in 1967) and Resnais, *Providence,* I propose, is a Brechtian comedy based on the humorous distance of us, the audience, from the *I* of an author. Mercer, apparently, finds the Freudian *I,* the ego aspect of it, funny because of the self-importance we attach to it. If life is absurd, reasons Mercer, surely this is the reason. Resnais and Mercer also make Langham's *I* a totally bourgeois *I* and thus they forestall our speculation as to what he is really like as with Brecht's Macheath in *The Threepenny Opera.* Brecht intended him to be a bourgeois type, but the bourgeois audience saw him as a proletarian. Furthermore, Resnais and Mercer do not pretend to be other than bourgeois; they distance the characters but do not attack the bourgeoisie. There is no shocking the bourgeoisie in *Providence.*

When we view *Providence,* we see this emergent structure; we also hear it: we see "first person" shots, seemingly the consiousness of somebody, some *I*. But which *I*? (Listening here, gives us a better clue than watching.) Resnais' or Langham—the character's *I*? Langham's dream state *I*? His waking state *I*? (Is the film paralogical or metalogical?) We see so many *I*'s (Resnais' imagined analogs to Mercer's script, then rendered by him in pictorial fashion) they start to compete with one another, to run amok. (I shall leave it to the reader to decide whether this is a metaphor for bourgeois society built into the script, but something Resnais himself did not consciously understand as being there.)

Perhaps if one were to view *Providence* as a comedy based on the *I*'s of an author and were to think of it less, if at all, as an intellectual presentation of the function of an authorial *I* in making up a narrative (do we even learn the name of the book Langham is writing?) then, the film's confusion of narratives (which I think is deliberate and not meant to be "sorted out") will make the best sense. This means we should think of the film as giving us Mercer's and Resnais' narratives in the plural form: *their* many narratives, their many "I's" and not Langham's story about Langham's filmic novel in progress, as we would most certainly expect, had the film been made in 1940.

Thus after introducing Langham's disjunctions as the "shot vocabulary" of the film, the film's self-description of how it should be taken by the audience, i.e., Langham as a vehicle, Resnais and Mercer next need another character to harangue the audience, e.g., the Brechtian distancing character. This role they assigned, as we have already suggested, to Claud, Langham's son, who addresses the spectator primarily by the pretense of haranguing Woodford, his step-brother and Sonia, his wife.

In the final analysis, however, our postulate about the comic/comedy structure of *Providence* has to stand up to the following scrutiny. Does a supposed comedy structure for *Providence* yield up an information system that enables us better to "read" the film in this way? Does screening *Providence* for a comedy structure better teach us *how* to look at seventy-eight year old Clive Langham, the writer with the "I," and to explain more congruently the entire film than, say, taking Langham more seriously as a character and postulating *Providence* as a tragedy about the decline of the novel?

We must find out if the methodology of *Providence* lets us see "I's" which are all fictive, or whether it makes one "I" more real than the others. The first would indicate there is nothing to understand besides accepting the totality of a disguised authorial presence; the second would mean we should "listen" more to what Langham has to say. (We are, analytically speaking, asking the question that should already have been phrased about Resnais' work at the time of *Marienbad.*) A narrator narrates; but are we supposed to believe (1) he is the narrator of the film, or (2) he is the dupe of "his" own "narration"? And there is in *Providence*, as in *Marienbad*, a clue to the answer. The authorial presence of the director strongly appears at the end of both films. In *Marienbad*, dialogue informs the spectator that X is alone and will vanish; near the end of *Providence*, a 360 degree pan begins as Langham's point of view but concludes as Resnais'. Langham is then found alone by Resnais' camera, as it completes the pan and the narrative or story ends at this moment slightly before the film ends; that is, the character again vanishes. (*Muriel*, by the way, ends the same way.) Having "used" Langham, Resnais returns to inform us that he—after all—is and was the director.

Providence as a Brechtian Comedy

In citing *Providence* as a Brechtian comedy, we hope not only to assign a structure to the film but to make a case for Resnais' and not just Mercer's authorship of the film. It is Resnais who has repeatedly given evidence of preferring this structure. We still need to clarify more fully what we mean by a Brechtian comedy. What we mean by a Brechtian comedy (which is more Brechtian than comic, if one wants to get philosophical about it, for sadness lurks beneath

Resnais' *Muriel*, a repressed comedy, one that never develops.
Frame enlargement

Brecht's Hegelian humor) is that it is epic rather than dramatic. Brecht really did not distinguish much between "comedy" and "tragedy," as his *Dreigroschenoper* shows. Just as *The Threepenny Opera* was intended by Brecht not to involve the audience but to give them a "world view" of life, so does *Providence* try to give us a similar all-encompassing Western world view. I disagree with Daniel Yakir that "the film is a retreat from life because it is not set in an actual locale."[6] There is a "ubiquity" rather than a "fictitiousness" about the setting of *Providence* analogous to the composite castle of "Marienbad" Resnais built out of shots of three separate German castles. *Providence*, analogously, shows Providence, Rhode Island, as well as shots of Castle "Providence," France.

What epic theater does is to discourage "nostalgia of place," say, a depiction of Paris in 1977 as it is, because it fosters illusion. Epic theater, whether on stage or transferred to film form (for which Resnais seems to have a gift) entails telling/discoursing, not the engaging/arresting, as in dramatic theater or cinema. The crux of epic as opposed to dramatic theater is that epic "distances the viewer but awakens his activity, his active energy," while dramatic "involves the viewer but uses up his active energy."[7] This is not only a qualitative difference, but, according to Brecht, a quantitative one, if we could only measure it.

Jerry Lewis ordering a "reheated Alaskan Polar bear" in the Purple Pit sequence of *The Nutty Professor*.
Jerry Lewis Productions

What *Providence* becomes, almost immediately after the title is flashed on the screen, is a distancing comedy that awakens the viewer and gives him or her a world view of society.

Resnais (the reader will recall Resnais' half-hearted attempt to make his *Muriel* function like Jerry Lewis' *The Nutty Professor* [1963]), had yearned to make a comedy ever since his days as a theater student in 1942. He always had the impish sense of humor for it. He had *tried* to put traces of comedy into *Muriel*, but nobody laughed; so that perhaps scared him off for awhile. The kind of comedy Resnais admired at that time, however, was not Brechtian but Hollywoodian, an offshoot of the Jerry Lewis film, one which contained comic/tragic *Doppelgängers*. The Lewis film, further, was enormously popular in France at the time of the New Wave, and it was considered a role model. Jerry Lewis *was* funnier than French film comedy (which often went into or fell into the ludicrous, and was consequently rightly feared as a film genre by many French directors: *vide* the horrendous Jacques Tati films, etc.), which of course did not have the schizoid American way of life to draw on.

The French, Resnais included, also had a curious way of being impressed by particular (peculiar?) facets of the Jerry Lewis films—facets, I believe, that were the hardest for a Frenchman to synthesize by himself. And yet, these were the universally funny gag scenes. So the French, not given the ability to make them, put double their energy into praising them.

Claude Ollier, the *Cahiers du Cinéma* critic who wrote what Ron Gottesman considers the best essay ever written on *King Kong* (1933), had written about *Muriel* in 1963 in terms of its "banal universe," apropos of Hitchcock, which Resnais translates, "develops," and as a film which is "a pretext to discover new logical structures, where the psychological universe is as simple as possible."[8] Ollier, writing a year later, described Jerry Lewis' *The Nutty Professor* (called *Doctor Jerry and Mr. Love* in France) in similar terms, noting that it is located in a psychological universe that is "as simple as possible" in order to let its structure inform its narrative. Ollier wrote that *The Nutty Professor* displayed a

> dazzling alternated narrative [which] is precisely picked, the weight of which is felt, put into place, in the holding and keeping up of a compatibility of two doubles, where all the scripting of all the jobs and stationings exactly correspond to each other: looks, visceral movements, bearing, walk, gestures, clothing, hairstyles, vocabulary, syntax, pitch, delivery of lines, hesitations, intonations—all rock and swing, so much as to gulp down the repugnant liquid of the most ineffectual comic fumble, the most veiled of sleights of hand, those which bring us back to an asceptic "Old Black Magic," craftily distilled out of an eyedropper in the coolest of realistic surroundings: the Purple Pit, where the being, disinherited in the optics of a crushing, overwhelming revenge, exercises his technique of Seduction."[9]

But Ollier, talented as he is in generalizing on American film comedy, shows his lack of savvy of its fine points. In his review of *The Nutty Professor*, Ollier was particularly impressed by the scene where Lewis as Buddy Love sits at the bar of the hideaway night club, The Purple Pit, where he is romancing Miss Stella Purdy, and asks the bartender to make him a "reheated Alaskan Polar Bear," a special drink. (It was "hip" in the late 1950s for "swingers" to drink *only* special cocktails in order to impress people with the idea that they were "unique.") The bartender tells Lewis he never heard of it. Lewis, with gangster authority, tells the bartender what it is, with mock erudition and sophistication, with the bartender repeating after him the whole list of alcoholic ingredients, something building up to a Molotov cocktail in potency. Ollier, misunderstanding this scene, writes, "It is necessary to see Buddy Love murmuring there [to Miss Purdy in the Passion Pit] after having given the bartender a lesson in *diction*" (my italics).[10]

Ollier saw the same funny scene as the American audiences. But, not being an American child of the late 50s, he missed what Lewis was so ably mocking. Yet, he realized how effective such comedy was, how universal, how releasing. It is a similar urge to make American comedy that undoubtedly stirred several French directors to try to move in that direction. However, Resnais (and also Francois Truffaut) wisely restrained themselves from jumping in when they knew they had no skills. Resnais thus took his time in going towards comedy, and finally picked a British screenwriter to do the script for *Providence*.

Another aspect of the comedy in *Providence* is its Anglo-Saxon character, due quite obviously to its Anglo-Saxon screenwriter, David Mercer, a trait which pushes *Providence* ever so slightly towards being a Hollywood comedy. Just as Claude Ollier was impressed by Hollywood comedy, so too was Resnais, which was a major factor in his hiring Mercer to do *Providence's* screenplay.

Resnais, I should like to suggest, made *Providence* as a kind of homage to a uniquely American type of film comedy. Originating in the 1930s, the screwball comedy—its characters in tuxedos in drawing rooms—is Hawksian comedy, best illustrated by *20th Century* with Barrymore, for example. It is not the comedy of Chaplin or Harold Lloyd.

For a French director to translate this American subgenre, showing the world through comedy (the screwball comedy actually expressed an ontology: a laughing, self-confident response to the Great Depression involves problems; for the type must be true to its American form, or it becomes a parody of a parody. It must be shorn of any quasi-sociological pretensions. It must simply be very witty and very funny to a mass audience.

In this regard, Resnais' choice of Mercer was a good one. Mercer had written the script for *Morgan* (1966), a film of the British nonlinear absurdist school of the early 1960s. David Warner played the title role; so Mercer must have had him already in mind when writing the part of Kevin Woodford for *Providence*. Despite flaws in Karel Reisz's direction of *Morgan*, Warner's mouthing of Mercer's lines was good. The pairing was to prove equally delightful in *Providence*. Would it then be too much to suggest that *Providence* is but a French remake of *Morgan*? Perhaps. But one should bear in mind that *Providence* represents the British, not the French, absurdist strain, and that it belongs partially to the British Modernist genre of film comedy that flourished during the era of the early Beatles.

We can be sure of one generalization: Resnais was always attracted to the vein in Western European-American culture that saw the way out of man's existential dilemma through laughter. No devotee of the black turtleneck crowd, Alain Resnais seems to have cast longing looks all his life towards the membership of the small elite circle of film comedy writers who were most productive in the 1950s and 1960s, hoping one day to use one of them in a film.

Why Resnais waited until 1976 to make his first comedy film is a subject of pure speculation. Reticence? Lack of financing? The most probable reason was the lack of contact with and support of the right screenwriter.

In fact, the *Providence* project was offered to Resnais by its producers, whose objective was not so much to have him make a comedy as to "break" him in America. Given the requirements that the project had to be filmed in English with English speaking actors, Resnais needed an English screenwriter. It was his inspiration to find Mercer.

He was also offered Ellen Burstyn and Dirk Bogarde (who was to have played Harry Dickson), with whom Resnais had always wanted to work. The rest of the cast of *Providence* was cast before the script was written, as well. As a consequence, Resnais and Mercer could write a special script with that particular cast in mind. (Imagine Margaret Mitchell's having written *Gone With The Wind* with Gable, Howard, de Haviland and Leigh in mind. She would certainly have written it differently.)

What is bizarre in *Providence* is that the script was written by an absurdist and that Resnais had never (consciously) been one. One might ask whether the result was that with *Providence*, Resnais had made a film he did not himself completely understand. In an interview in *Les nouvelles litteraires*, Resnais just about admitted as much. He told Marc Terasse, "Besides, it's difficult for me to have a rapport with the film. In a month, in two years, maybe."[11]

Hence, for *Providence* we can posit a wider gulf between image and narrative than is normal for a Resnais film. How does this affect *Providence*? The surety of the images, the editing, the sense that it is a film shot by a director who knew exactly what he was doing, make it seem as though the narrative filmed was on another level altogether, giving the latter a surreal touch, the glassine transparency of a Katherine Mansfield short story. At times, as with two-shots of Bogarde and Burstyn, Resnais' camera seems to direct a play, pushing around the mise-en-scène as if on a revolving stage. At other times, especially in Clive Langham's monologues, one has the sensation that a heavy-handed script has assigned to Sir John Gielgud a series of in-jokes about authors: Maugham, Waugh, the Oxbridge type, etc., that poor Resnais could hardly be expected to understand.

There is thus much evidence for arguing that Resnais filmed a Mercer script with little interference on his part at the script level. The structure of *Providence*, then, it can be argued, owes inordinately (for a Resnais film) much to its screenwriter. Whether Langham's "I" is to be taken as more real than that of any of the other characters is then dependent on Mercer's fancy; but we could not have figured this out readily from our previous knowledge of Resnais films.

What I believe we are seeing in *Providence* (up to the point of Resnais' photographic shift to more versimiltude at the film's climax—very obviously announced by a Resnais trademark, a montage sequence of nine documentary-like shots) is Mercer playing the "very fictive" and the "less fictive" against each other with the hope of amusing or confusing the spectator. The last fifth of the film, if one applies an authorship analysis to Resnais' films, shows much more the Resnais touch. Thus the so-called realistic frame to the film, which shows all the characters behaving differently than they did during eighty percent of the film, is very much a signature by Resnais of his own film as well as the resolution to the plot of *Providence*. How else are we to account for a new dimension to the film: a shift from somber to bright colors, as if the film stock had been changed (was it?), and a shift from playing with fictions to the making of a toast to the bourgeoisie? Is not this last section of *Providence* a summing up by Resnais?

No doubt it is. The rest of the film requires a more thorough search to find where Resnais is a co-author of its structure.

One way to look at *Providence* is to take Resnais' "documentary" ending as a disjuntion, as just another of *Providence's* many disjunctions, and assume, with it, that Resnais is again showing us "the impossibility of documenting." And, as *Providence* plays upon its own Proustian theme, Resnais makes his own film ironically com-

Resnais' *Providence,* a wide open comedy, one that mocks the almighty authorial "I."
Cinema 5

ment upon itself. Many critics, however, felt differently and thought the "real" ending to *Providence* was to give a surprise summation to its "plot": the wicked characters are, after all, sheep. There is no certain answer which of these two interpretations is correct. Arguments can be made for both.

Providence thus ends, like *Marienbad,* by throwing a curtain upon itself. What we are left with is the urge to contemplate all the subsets of articulation of the valiant, struggling author, Langham. What we make of these subsets of Langham's articulation is in part influenced by the way Resnais has filmed them. Here, Resnais' influence on *Providence* becomes marked, if not paramount.

A set of Langham's articulations (Langham-the-novelist's activities in his own novel) is opposed to a set of Langham (Langham-the-liver) alive in Providence Manor. Resnais' camera does not seem to ask us to bother to differentiate these clearly as he makes them flow into each other. Only, on a semantic level, do we know they are separate. Thus, Resnais approximates Proust's novel, which is, after all, about the narrative of a writer named Marcel who is about to write a novel; Marcel the narrator is equivalent to Langham. Also parallel to *Remembrance of Things Past* is the fact that Marcel the narrator is not Proust the author of the piece; so also it is a fact that

Resnais used a device from *The Nutty Professor* (shown above), that of showing the same event twice, in *Marienbad* (seriously) and in *Providence* (comically).
Jerry Lewis Productions

the narrator of *Providence,* Langham, is not synonymous with the authors of *Providence,* Resnais and Mercer. Thus it seems that *Providence* is about the structuring of a fiction, the author's trial and error as he begins to write a novel.

The basic structure of *Providence* is not so unlike that of *Muriel,* if we examine it carefully. There is a "suspension-of-disbelief" set of information, designed to make us believe there is a Clive Langham. This is accomplished by Resnais' showing us how much Langham loves to mix up fact and fiction. In the concentration camp sequences, for example, Resnais' visuals make Langham's thoughts seem vivid, as if Langham were really believing these fictions of his. Then, there is a "distancing" set, which occurs off and on, when the real members of Langham's family come and visit him and interrupt his casting of them into various roles in his novel. These are embarrassing moments for Langham because we see through his fictions: the very character we have seen just dramatized through his fantasy suddenly appears again, a second later, looking different, acting differently, saying something quite apart from what he was saying in the last shot. These disjunctions—like the films within the film *Muriel*—should give us the structure of *Providence* and tell us how to read it.

Neither set of information—Langham's novel's set and Langham's life's set—is developed syntagmatically in *Providence*, and this is what gives it its peculiar screwball character—makes it a screwball comedy, but a screwball comedy of a different structural type than those of the 1930s. It is a tribute to the success of this screwball style that, after the passing of the realism boundary of the film four-fifths of the way through the narrative, Molly Haskell, reacting to Langham on the plot level, remarked of his not yet having died of cancer: "I [can not account for] the emotional power that it had as the camera recedes to show us his entire body, beautifully attired in beige, a smile on his lips, wine glass in his hand. Is there no justice in the world, he is quite alive."[12] Haskell here has obviously misread Resnais' intention and mixed up the sets. She describes Langham in his life as if he had been one of the evil, diabolical versions of himself he had made up for his novel. Haskell, by putting both Langhams on the same level, reduces *Providence's* structure to its plot, an all too American thing to do. It shows how badly the public is still attuned to the *Rashomon* plot. It wants a summation for every disjunctive story. It wants to be told the answer.

If we, however, appreciate *Providence's* structure as Resnais intended it, we find that he and Mercer have taught us what fiction is. (Possibly Mercer has taught us what absurdity is as well.) Mercer and Resnais have taught us the linguistics of comedy. We can place *Providence* in the Jerry Lewis tradition of Jekyl-Hyde comedy. We can find some Gallic parallels to the bartender sequence in *The Nutty Professor* in Claud's confrontations with his wife in the kitchen of Providence Manor. We know Lewis was having fun; we should see that in *Providence*, Resnais was having fun. Mercer's peculiar Anglo-Saxon boffo humor filtered through Resnais' camera lens is especially amusing and transcends the Franco-English linguistic gap, plummetting *Providence* more genuinely into company with the Jerry Lewis films that Resnais so ardently admired.

Providence as a Comedy

What is a comedy anyway, we might ask? In film, a comedy is based on situations, as on stage; but even more a film comedy is based on distortions of meaning. If we distort we can have a comedy; if we don't then we cannot. For a comedy begins when we are given two articulations that contradict. Then we need in addition a character who does not so much try to resolve the conflict as he/she alternates between falling in with and working against the false structure. The results are comic. For example, Ginger Rogers says to Fred Astaire, "Come here" and "go away." When she repeats "go away," however, her facial expression says "come here," Fred comes. Ginger says, "Why did you come." Fred says, "Because you asked me to." She says, "No I didn't." The audience, by this time sees through the structure of the farce and laughs.

Sir John Gielgud as Clive Langham has a "come here"; "go away" relationship in his own lines. Dirk Bogarde as Claud has it with David Warner as Woodford. The city one sees in the background, at moments being attacked by barbarians with artillery, at other moments totally calm and rural French, is also a funny double articulation. And Resnais' use of the werewolf figure in *Providence* is so preposterous as to recall *I Was a Teenage Werewolf.* Who are these "wolves"? Langham's metaphors? Resnais'? Are they a threat? If so, then to whom? Are they a product of delirium tremens, too much chablis for Langham? But even more important is the fact that Resnais makes us care about this funny family, as in *My Man Godfrey.* Again, Resnais has wisely given us a flat-out phony (Gielgud is Alphonse again), reminiscent of the fictions in *Muriel;* and carried over from the same film is the accuser, Claud as prosecutor, redoing what Bernard the inquisitor did in *Muriel.*

Bogarde, as Claude in *Providence*, functions much like the Carole Lombard character in *My Man Godfrey.* Like Lombard, Bogarde's function in *Providence* is to point at things, shake an accusing finger (all on the level of Langham's fiction, of course). "This family is ridiculous," he is saying. And he points this out by rearranging his wife and Woodford in all sorts of situations, causing them to commit adultery, etc., disjuncting each scene with another equally hilarious scene, all in such a *Kammerspiel* style that we feel Bogarde is directing a play within a film. At these moments, the Brechtian distancing awakens our activity and we feel the relationships of all these false articulations and see the transparency of the "narrative."

Ultimately, then, comedy is based not only on a relation of false articulations but also on the transparency of them to the audience. (Comedy is a form of privileged information.) The audience then goes along with the fiction, laughing at the characters for still believing it. *Providence* can be seen as a comedy, and the laughter I heard during many screenings of the film is a witness to the fact that Americans, at least, found the film funny.

Resnais' talent in filming *Providence* was to make Mercer's script visibly transparent. *Muriel* had its comic moments, but they were a bit opaque. In *Providence,* Resnais shifts over to a transparent style: the third stylistic change in his career. (The other two are Brechtian-fluid, i.e., *Hiroshima, Marienbad, Muriel,* and flat-realistic, *La Guerre Est Finie, Je T'Aime, Je T'Aime,* and *Stavisky.)*

So in *Providence,* we are seeing Resnais attempt a new type of film and not just a repeat. Of course, there are reused devices, familiar characteristics, and overdone moments. But the latent ability for Resnais to make comedy of a zany type, I have argued, was always there. He had seen enough plays, understood the acting style of comedy, but he needed Mercer as a catalyst to draw it out of him. With hindsight, it seems Mercer suggested to Resnais the film style he uses in *Providence,* one which is reminiscent of the style of another writer Resnais had long admired, Katherine Mansfield. *Providence* is the film equivalent of a Katherine Mansfield story. It is transparent, and if any one word could be used to describe the stories of Katherine Mansfield, it would be "transparent."[13]

Once again we have the old familiar Resnais pattern in creating a film. He wants a transparent narrative. He gets Mercer to write a transparent script. Then he films it transparently.

Transparent: from the Latin *transparere,* "having the property of transmitting light without appreciable scattering so that bodies lying beyond are entirely visible," almost a definition of film itself, and "easily detected, or seen through," "readily understood." *Providence* is almost a play on the word "transparent"; it is all three meanings which dance around each other in constant surreptitious interplay.

The interplay of narrative in *Providence* is surreptitious, clandestine because Mercer thinks that is how life is if it is shown naked. It is an absurdist's garden, a personal bourgeois view, and as much of a personal *Welt* as Fritz Lang's Berlin, Bertolucci's Parma in *Before the Revolution,* or Antonioni's Ferrara in *The Red Desert.* Resnais then reinforces this notion that we are in a mind garden (but we are awake there and never dreaming) full of filmic points of view. The camera of *Night and Fog* now reverses its tactic and serves deception. The camera style is fluid, smooth, lugubrious.

To sum up: the comedy plays heavily on the level of dialogue. Meanwhile, the camera serves the dialogue by setting up props. All this is done with magician-like rapidity. Never has a Resnais film been so speedily talky. On the level of the image, disjunction reigns supreme. The integration between disjuncting images and comic punch lines is superb and combines the best of the continental and Hollywood styles. *Providence* is a masterpiece of comic timing. Resnais learned his Jerry Lewis well.

But what is the justification for giving so much of the floor to Langham's son, Claud? Is he so important to Langham's narrative? Or, is he a Brechtian distancing device Resnais has inserted, the director within the film, the Bernard of *Muriel*, who rearranges events and mise-en-scène for us before our very eyes? One thing is sure: he is not there because Resnais wishes to create more illusion as mystery, as with Fritz Lang's Sandor Weltmann and other Mabuse figures in *Dr. Mabuse, Der Spieler* (1922). Claud plays a key epic role in the film, one designed to destroy our involvement with any one illusion we see on the screen. In its unique way, *Providence* is not an arty film. Its sets and images are not there so much for beauty's sake as for the sake of illustrating the narrative.

The characters of Langham's little family are—as the film progresses—easily seen through. The narrative, unlike the narratives in most of Resnais' films, seems to care about its characters. We begin to believe they exist, to enjoy them. But this is done just enough to set us up, enough to make them lambs for the slaughter. They are devices with voices, and their voices reveal them as devices. In fact, the script gives them more life than Langham does; for the characters in his novel are filaments and figments of his burning bulb imagination. But, for all their surface charm, they act like zombies. It is almost as if Mercer were saying that the characters of modern English literature do not live much, that English literature is dying on its feet, that the modern novel is bankrupt.

Yet, there is suspense to the film, not just presentation. The suspense caused by the fact that Langham is dying of rectal cancer and, at the end of the film, is still alive, alive after one senses all the time that he is writing because he knows he will not survive. Yet, on another level, this statement can be interpreted to mean that Langham is a pain in the ass. This is the beauty of the idea of interplay between author and author of the narrative within the film. We now can sense the purpose of the film. It seems to ask whether authors die after giving birth to fictions because they, the authors, cannot live in the fictive worlds they have created. Are authors abandoned mothers?

Are Mercer and Resnais soliloquizing on an author's death or on the death sensation an author feels after he is delivered of a novel? Are artists lonely by definition? Resnais' camera shows Langham mostly alone. At the end of the film, he is shown alone. Is *Providence* to the writer what *Blow-Up* was to the photographer: a study of limits?

Given the above, Resnais' self-appointed task in *Providence* was to get us to care about this world with loaded dice, this noncausal world. *Providence* in this sense approximates the pseudoclosed world of *Citizen Kane*, a favorite Resnais film, a film where just as one door seems to close on the findings about Kane, another door opens. Resnais' device in *Providence* seems to get us to care about its plot, not through Wellesian pathos but through Brechtian comic devices, giving us bursts of laughter. The "closed structure" of *Providence* is again and again interrupted by openings, with high humor, giving us an open structure in our mind. The enclosure of the film breaks open the more we see what we see isn't so. By the end of the film we realize *sic transit gloria* Xanadu. We can transcend it all.

What are we to make of the film's ridiculous backdrops? In the light of the above, they seem now to be not gratuituous at all but a vital part of serving the narrative. Throughout the film, backdrops switch rapidly. We are both in the countryside near Limoges, France, and in a war. It looks at times as if the Goths are defeating the Romans in the distant city. But they have modern artillery. The Goths are also establishing modern concentration camps for Romans (the patrician Langham is definitely one of the Romans), the last decadents of the Western world. We are in the fictive *Castle* of Kafka. We are invited to blend *Providence*, Xanadu, Manderley, and Kafka's *Castle*. A careful semiotic reading of *Providence*, however, will show, as in Antonioni's *Blow-Up*, a film that Resnais likes, that Providence contains an absurd (i.e., meaningless) information system on the level of its passively observable narrative, from the illusion we see on the screen before we have acted upon it ourselves. *Providence*'s story is absurd but its message is not. What we decide counts. The basic mode of articulation of *Providence* is an epic narrative—a Brechtian one—as in *Muriel*. What we make of it must be in our thoughts, not gleaned from its narrative through code deciphering. *Providence* is a paralogical film, as in *Marienbad*, constructed by us.

Open Structure in *Providence*

However, unlike those in *Muriel*, the Brechtian devices in *Providence* which invite us to make a search for an answer to life, do not lead us to any definite conclusions. *Providence*, from its Hitchcockian, *Rebecca*-like opening shot on, which shows the camera travelling in to investigate, informs us that we the spectators are going to have to participate. *Providence* tries in its final soliloquy to make this quest a bit easier for us, summing it up, and giving us some additional information almost as a sort of consolation prize for the film's not leading us to a firm answer. Compared, say, to most Godard films—*Pierrot le fou*, for example—*Providence*, for all its Brechtian devices (normally used for didactic reasons), remains a curiously undidactic film. So much of its speedily presented information system remains, after analysis, mere bluff.

One can interpret the last twelve minute segment of *Providence* in several fashions. One interpretation that I favor is that it is a discourse on the rest of the film, much like the last seven minute sequence of Antonioni's *The Passenger* (1975). As with the concluding sequence to *The Passenger*, the final sequence of *Providence* is not a retort to *Providence*'s *Welt* but a soliloquy to us.

The last twelve minutes or so of *Providence* I read as Resnais' message to his film constituents, the faithful in the screening room. Whereas Antonioni's message at the end of *The Passenger* (and I am comparing Antonioni with Resnais for important cultural reasons) was "life is out there, not with the dead man"[14] (i.e., the Jack Nicholson character who is killed mid-sequence as the camera moves on, stating that nature moves inexorably on). Antonioni asks, what is the value of only *one* man's life, etc? Resnais' message seems to be the opposite: it is nice to survive, to have seen the face of death, the farce of life, its disjunctions temporarily resolved, even though it is just a lull in the storm. Whereas Antonioni's character in *The Passenger* lies dead on the bed after telling a terrible story about life, Resnais and Mercer's Clive Langham is very much alive after telling terrible stories about death.

How does *Providence* inform us that we are to take with us an authorial "I," first person ending, a literal summation by Resnais? The only evidence is the literality (its non-metaphorical use) of the 360 degree pan the camera takes, a circular pan that begins as Langham's point of view and ends as Resnais' point of view showing

Langham still sitting there, mute. Why, here, for example, did Resnais not have Langham disappear before the shot returned to him? That could have been the end. The answer is probably that Resnais not only wanted to empty out of the film all its characters but one (just as at the end of *Muriel*) but also that he wanted the last word. Resnais, by usurpation of the point of view hints that he, too, is just glad to be alive; and he wants to share this feeling with us.

The ending to *Providence* is not comic. The comedy is over. The comic first four-fifths of the film is life; the last fifth or less, only a quiet moment amidst life. Resnais at fifty-five has realized life is a lot of fun at the nodes amongst the chaos. Also, like Thomas Mann, who tried to be very liberal in his youth and ended as a bourgeois individualist, Resnais, too, admits to and celebrates his middle class origins.

11

The Resnais Style Continues: Resnais' Legacy to the New German Cinema

The Nature of the Legacies

MOST NOTEWORTHY ARTISTS, INCLUDING FILMMAKERS, leave legacies which can take several forms. A film director can become the acknowledged leader of a new movement during his active career and lifetime, transmitting a living legacy that others may draw on when tackling their own problems and use as a guideline in making their films. In this case, the filmmaker acquires "students" who follow the form of the "master." Alfred Hitchcock is a good example here: his film style, one that emphasizes suspense rather than surprise, has been widely revered and imitated during his lifetime. Hitchcock's *Vertigo* (1958) has been remade in part by many others, all "Vertigos" having in common their incorporation of Hitchcock's device of keeping the audience in suspense rather than surprising it with privileged information. In Hitchcockian narrative the audience's attention is also held by a heavy exposition of the human interest of the characters: connecting a victim's liking of certain food, for example, with the fact that the murderer is a butcher.

But there is also a second kind of legacy in film. Here a director becomes respected by another filmmaker (or movement) without inspiring cinematic imitations, chiefly because of the appeal of the coded effects his films contain. In plain English, his legacy is the result of social influence or popularity. In drawing on the older or model filmmaker, the younger filmmaker (or movement of filmmakers) pays homage to an attitude, a recurring stance, of the earlier filmmaker. The students (or movement) respect and refeature his style in the sense that they replicate some part of his cultural code. For example, they may copy his naturalistic use of actors, they may reuse John Wayne in depicting violence, they may reflect the gen-

ain Resnais in 1967.
: Museum of Modern Art Film Stills Archive

eral vitality of his themes, his treatment of social class, his attitude towards myth and history, etc. (These code replications are often noticed by critics and then further broadcast to younger filmmakers.)

Given this second kind of legacy, the younger filmmaker uses the known filmmaker as a sourcebook (asking himself, for example, how Renoir might have shown some point). The French, in particular, have derived beneficial legacies from their earlier filmmakers in this fashion, Truffaut rephrasing Jean Renoir, Resnais recreating Feuillade's sense of mystery, Godard codifying the opposition of styles of Lumière and Méliès—all without, however, there being any specific shot in a Truffaut, Resnais, or Godard film that looks as if it had been lifted from Renoir, Feuillade, Lumière, or Méliès. Eric Rohmer has succinctly commented on the way Hollywood cinematography acted as such a sourcebook for him.

> There are good and bad American movies, but there is a cinematographic quality about them that you could not find anywhere else—action, movement. But this admiration I had did not entice me to imitate the American cinema. On the contrary, I have done just the opposite. Instead of showing action, I try to show ideas.[1]

But there is another phenomenon altogether. In this case a filmmaker—especially if he has been ahead of his time—can anticipate a new movement that is not, strictly speaking, a linear continuum of his own career, but rather an eruption of similar purpose later in time (and even in another country). One might call this a deferred legacy, one which has been delayed by an unfavorable climate, lack of interest, or the inhibitions of the socio-cultural *Zeitgeist*. This has been Resnais' contribution. Alain Resnais has no students probably because he is just too difficult to imitate; but he has become a sourcebook for the future.

This point can be demonstrated. Direct imitations of Resnais films have almost never been attempted on a full scale, and the attempts that were made were failures. Examples of failure are some of the sequences from Truffaut's *La Peau douce* (1964)[2] or the films of Liane de Kermadec such as *Ariane* (1973), which starred Delphine Seyrig going through the motions of *Marienbad*. Less direct paraphrases of Resnais, notably *Paris nous appartient* (1960) and several other Jacques Rivette films, have been slightly more successful in respect both to architectonic photography of Paris and to narrative quality. One could say Resnais has had a strong but more indirect extracinematic influence on his New Wave colleagues, perhaps as some kind of symbol of quality or purity, especially from 1959 to 1964; but one could work overtime without finding much evidence that Resnais exercised any direct cinematic influence on the films of the New Wave. In fact Truffaut summed it up when he suggested that "Resnais would help people if he emphasized the difficulties he encountered (in making his films) instead of giving them the impression that they should make anything that comes into their head."[3] But Truffaut further corroborates my point that no one did try to imitate Resnais when he says, "Well, some young people see Resnais' films as an example of courage instead of an example of skill."[4]

One reason no one thought to imitate Resnais could have been that Resnais' successes, *Hiroshima* and *Marienbad*, would have been too obvious to imitate. But what is more instructive, it seems that Resnais imparted enthusiasm to his colleagues more than he gave them good, easy formulas to imitate. The New Wave formula, as has been well documented, came from another direction anyway: a congeries of Renoir sensibility and Hollywood cinematography, of documentary camera work and cheap, independent production.

Resnais' style, then, it can safely be said, was in no way advanced because others imitated his "big hits" and thereby crystallized them more solidly in the cultural code. There was no "Resnaismania." There was nothing like the burst of Belmondisme after Godard's *Breathless*. Rather, the Resnais film is more in vogue today than when it first appeared because the times have changed. In the same way that public acceptance of relativity made the public come to regard Einstein as "normal," Resnais' cinematic innovations have now largely come to be seen as obvious. What was once regarded as innovative in *Hiroshima* (i.e., making sound/image disjunctions in dialogue or changing tenses without flashbacks) seems now like old hat. The same is true for *Marienbad*, where Resnais shows several levels of narrative pretension with no single one emerging as truer than any other, a method that transcended the earlier form introduced by *Rashomon*. In *Rashomon* there were three versions of the same story, but the syntax of the film made the final statement seem more true than the first two. *Hiroshima* and *Marienbad* are now regarded as having normal film forms; they are no longer considered freaky stylistic quirks.

Resnais himself has commented on this change in attitude: "I recall the violence of the reactions [to *Marienbad*] with a certain surprise, for the film was mostly rejected by the gentlemen who were brought up on a lot of cultural baggage, while those who weren't liked it. But even though *Marienbad* utilized a means a bit different from that of some other films, it was not such a big rupture with traditional cinema or narrative."[5]

Resnais' cinematic style is now in vogue, then, for the most part because the times have changed; his premonitions in 1959 about the future (now) were correct. What was once his own personal *Geist* has since become the *Zeitgeist*. History offers many examples (and Resnais' case is one) to suggest that this phenomenon is nothing but an artist's belated vindication.

Several years ago I saw a film by a new German director, Ottakar Runze, that could have been made by Resnais himself. *Messer im Rücken* searches the points of view of ten witnesses to a stabbing; it uses the method of *Muriel* to demonstrate the inadequacies of all the viewpoints. Here was a perfect example of Resnais' vision and the vindication of his method of dealing with time in film. Here was a highly narrative and entertaining film probing deeply into a social issue through an exquisitely honest cinematic handling and rendering of time. (The movie is deeply ontological, probing into the essence of reality by adopting Resnais' techniques and eschewing the outmoded tradition of mise-en-scène and the long take.) Furthermore, here was Resnais' technique being used by someone a generation later, not even a Frenchman and certainly not someone much concerned with Resnais.

Putting Resnais into this third category is my attempt at identifying historiographically not only Resnais' accomplishment, but also the manner in which a new style seems to come about in the world of film. (It is also a validation of the method of historiography when actual examples of a *topos* are found after a theoretical *topos* is proposed.) We owe the groundbreaking French *Cahiers* critics a debt here. They first realized the importance of assessing the present position of cinema in order to decide where it could or could not go. Their *politique d'auteurs* was an attempt to "read" films in order to establish film history. Trying to establish a director's position accurately has thus become an important business of film criticism, and the best method seems to be historiography. Thus we are warned never to try to evaluate a filmmaker outside of history. Why? Because if we do, we have no way of telling whether a director is an original or worth our time.

In other words, another reason for attempting to establish a director's position as precisely as possible, and to do so historiographically, is that a purely formal analysis of his films could reveal him as simply an eccentric. A historic evaluation of Resnais' film productivity (and all three categories are historically verifiable), on the other hand, yields a vital revelation of Resnais' full worth, the specifically humanistic merit of his artistry.

Despite its errors, the *Cahiers du Cinéma* seminar, "Les Malheurs du *Muriel*,"[6] held in 1963, was superb example of an attempt at locating Resnais in a humanistic-historic context. Admittedly, the attempt goes beyond simple film criticism. But it is necessary to transcend subjective, egotistic film criticism if we really wish to see what a film is.

The humanistic information yielded by a Resnais film is important. As we have seen, no Resnais film ever wanders totally away from the locus of the Western middle class, particularly the upper middle class. In focusing on it, the class which most sees films with a critical eye, whether in New York or Paris, and which writes most film criticism, Resnais reveals himself to be just as bourgeois as Godard or Chabrol or his average spectator. It is no coincidence that the seven Resnais feature films that this book deals with were made during what Hilton Kramer calls the last age of the avant-garde (1956–1972),[7] an age during which the bourgeoisie asked its artists to criticize it and, somewhat masochistically, paid the price in both psychic pain and admission tickets to hear and see what they said, hoping for some kind of verdict.

It is to Resnais' credit that his films did not fall completely into this trap. Philosophically at least, they remained above the level of the middle class message that the middle class cinemagoer wanted. For this merit, Resnais paid the price of obscurity with all his films, particularly with *Muriel*, his least popular but best film. *Marienbad*, by the way, was only saved from this popular neglect because it was a success in the art houses; its uncompromising nature was veiled by what looked to be commercial success.

Ironically, unlike the movies of many more popular directors, all Resnais' feature films and major shorts have, with the exception of *Je T'Aime, Je T'Aime*, won prizes. In 1977, with *Providence*, Resnais became a little more popular, especially in France. But he still has not stooped to conquer the mass audience.

Although *Providence* shows that Resnais wishes that audiences would come to him, it is surprising that, while confirming his bourgeois leanings, it demonstrates at the same time his refusal to pander, his continuing to take an ironic and philosophical view of the plight and fate of his class. It is as if Resnais were too honest to attempt to separate himself from his own middle class origins (in spite of his occasional use of Marxist terminology); he seems willing to rise or fall with that class identification. When Daniel Yakir asked him whether *Providence* contains an anti-bourgeois message, Resnais replied that it was "entertainment" and "not specifically" intended to be anti-bourgeois.[8]

At the same time, Resnais' lack of hypocrisy is the quality that, despite his philosophical detachment, makes his films accessible. They may not always count as true documents of the *Zeitgeist*; but, like Freud's work, as a documentation of the middle class's avant-garde hopes and fears about itself, they are second to no one's. He makes his narratives universal, using all the while new angles to gain new perspectives. His method of presenting his narratives through "tricky" schemes is what the public had first to grasp. Now in 1978 the public is closer in spirit to Resnais' approach to narrative; and Resnais' vision, regardless of the exact popularity of any one film he might still make, is safely confirmed.

Resnais to the New German Cinema

My strong belief is that Resnais' innovations in cinema will be seen as even greater and more important as time passes. My feeling is based on the fact that already filmmakers in Europe have emerged, particularly in West Germany, whose movies display many of the same strategies as Resnais'. Many filmmakers under forty (Resnais is fifty-five, Truffaut is forty-five) are now using such characteristically Resnaisian devices as associationism, metonymy, irony, a more fluid form of Brechtian distancing than is to be found in epic theater, and music that gives the movie the structure of a ballad. More young directors now use this style (if such a melange of devices can be called a style) than Godard's binary opposition of image and narration or Truffaut's brand of Franco-Hollywoodisms. Godard and Truffaut may be better known than Alain Resnais, but his style seems now to prevail.

The cinema of the new German directors vitally and viably continues Resnais' movement towards a cinema that represents the raw material of action without allowing the filmmaker to predicate the action itself. It should not be surprising that this approach has gained more favor in Germany than in France. The new West German cinema, with less tradition to fight, is, at present, highly socially conscious and self-reflective. Besides, national boundaries in Europe have ceased to mean much since 1968. Werner Herzog, for example, could just as well be French as Bavarian. Witness the cases of Eric Rohmer, who is German on both sides of his family and who has made his most recent film *(The Marquise of O)* in German, and Jean-Marie Straub, who is French but is considered in film books as a German filmmaker of the avant-garde.

But let us examine Werner Herzog. No one can deny that Herzog relies almost exclusively on visual associationism (what used to be called "associational montage"). Born in September, 1942, he is twenty years younger than the white-haired Resnais; but he is making "Resnais films." What Andrew Sarris wrote about Herzog's *Stroszek* (1977) describes just about any film made by Resnais: "*Stroszek* makes little sense as narrative, as drama, or as psychological portraiture, with its beat-up, mixed up characters drifting with antic aimlessness from Berlin to Northern Wisconsin to North Carolina."[9] Or take a Thomas Elsaesser comment about Herzog's *Aguirre, Wrath of God* (1972).

> Unique to contemporary filmmaking is that distrust of spectacle—nagging doubts about presenting as a logic a purely aesthetic causality has produced misgivings about the status and function of fictions (their ontology and their ideology: what reality and especially whose reality do they codify as verisimilitude?). Films that have any claims to truth have to battle with the difficulty of not assuming any kind of *a priori* correspondence between the universe of fiction (in which a film necessarily moves) and the world (of which it necessarily represents the external appearances).

Could this remark not also be applied to the narrative reticence of Resnais' triad?

All of Herzog's films have come after Godard, after the hippie era. They are a minimalist revolt against the excess ego and "license-to-kill" of the filmmaker. They reject the self-consciousness of focusing on the self, the self-conscious stance that, as Elsaesser emphasized,

> owed so much to the Godard of the 1960s and reminded the spectator of just how contrived and fragile a construct he was watching. Filmmakers now tend to draw attention to their labour, their own intervention in the [act of]

signifying and [in the] representational act by rather indirect means; in almost all cases the stance is one of ironic "as if": holding the fiction at arm's length.

When I say irony, it has to be understood not only in its limited sense of puncturing inflated pretensions and making assertions tongue in cheek, but also in a more technical sense. It names all the strategies of displacement, distancing, detachment—verbal, visual, structural—whereby a statement, a message, a communication, image or action may be qualified, put into question, subverted, parodied or indeed wholly negated while preserving visible that to which it refers itself ironically. As such, irony is dialectical in intention and invariably points out a potentially significant gap between the signifier and signified.[10]

This cinema of irony transcends generation gaps and could as well include Resnais as Werner Herzog. It merely formalizes our sense of the vanishing from the world of the logic of causality that we once felt pervaded it. Completely closed systems of any type—hip, Godardian, self-conscious, karmic, Hollywood classic—are now "out." In such a structure, film certainties or absolutes are refuted by the film itself, perhaps as an act of Marcusian refusal to become hypocritical. It seems clear that the same attempts that we found in the movies of Resnais (avoiding a cinema of system as far as possible, avoiding ego, avoiding hypocrisy) have taken root now in Germany.

At this point it might be instructive to compare in detail *Hiroshima* and *Aguirre, Wrath of God.* Simply on a visual level they are very much alike, for they both present splendid images that are beautiful both in their own right and in the syntax of the finished film. But they are also similar in terms of their handling of authorship. The disguised authorship that we have been at some pains to explore in the works of Resnais, what I chose to call his "metonymy," is characteristic of the films of Herzog as well. In *Aquirre*, for example, the pretended author of the adventures along the Amazon that the movie presents to us is a diary. In *Stroszek* Herzog could be justifiably equated to all three of the main characters not just to Brunos. The two directors are similar in the way they use music. Both films have an almost operatic quality, their conversations taking on the style of recitative, while the music presents what can only be likened to *Leitmotif*. A theme, for example, is used to cue the audience into a particular emotion. Visual images then powerfully render the emotions that have previously been felt only as premonitions. This technique makes nonsense of Andrew Sarris' statement in respect to narrative in Herzog's cinema that "there are times even in *Stroszek* when an image is too suddenly beautiful."[11] All the images have been foretold by the musical themes and follow a musical logic.

Both directors reveal a fondness for minimalism, too. Their dialogue is always spare, and very often key statements are made once and once only. "I am the wrath of God," says Aguirre; he never repeats it. "I can't remember [my German lover]," the actress in *Hiroshima* tells the Japanese, but only once.

I have saved the most important similarity, however, until last; for it is the most complex. Stated simply, the films of both Resnais and Herzog are not discursive. Whatever messages their films convey come to us, not through the usual method of film discourse, but through a language of cinematic glyphs. They depart radically in this respect from the schools of both Godard and Truffaut. Godard is known for his paradoxically Apollonian passionate discourse; Truffaut represents the intelligence of the literate man expressed verbally. (Thus we might say that the films of Swiss director Alain Tanner are discursive in the style of Godard.)

But as Elsaesser notes, the cinema of irony

> in practice . . . covers a very wide range. It may be carefully embedded in a neutral delivery [as in *Hiroshima* and *Aguirre*] and underplayed to the point where it becomes a slow burn verging on oblique ambiguity. . . . [Or] it may even embrace two totally opposite kinds of cinema—say, that of Werner Herzog, where the fiction (not in the form of a plot, but as a series of "what happens if" propositions) only intermittently rises from a documentary flow—and Chabrol's cinema where the plot [as in *Muriel*] foregrounds itself into almost operatic theatricality. What unites the extremes is a radical de-dramatization of naturalistic action, an intellectualization of montage which lets the image in its immediate presence hover, as it were, over the possibilities of precise or remote signification.[12]

We are not being presented with a set of symbols that conveys visually an exact intellectual point. Rather we are given the freedom to take this concrete but subjunctive tense and to make up from it our own stories. Thus Elsaessar continues

> in the work of Herzog the scenes are dissolved into "moments," discrete, suspended, before they become opaque and solidify into blocks, harsh and unaccommodating in their un-metaphoric, un-symbolic facticity; they are actually material without the action.[12]

Let me stop here for a moment to reemphasize the special case that we are considering when we discuss similarities between Resnais and Herzog. My point is not that Herzog has absorbed the style of Resnais in any direct way nor even that Resnais' techniques have spread to form a directorial "climate" which Herzog has imbibed unconsciously. Rather, what I hope to have demonstrated is that Resnais was ahead of his time when he developed the methods that found their best expression in *Muriel*. These methods, now standard practice for younger directors, have since emerged in their work independently of Resnais as an expression of our present *Zeitgeist*. The link, then, is historical rather than a matter of influence.

In spite of many similarities between Resnais and Herzog, whom I have singled out for the comparison because I believe him to be the best and most unusual—and the least malevolent—of the young German directors, Herzog's cinema is not as complex as Resnais'. One aspect of Resnais' method has not yet become characteristic of the Germans: his obsession with time. No other filmmaker has yet cared to experiment as extensively as Resnais with cinema time.

If we turn to Herzog's most advanced film, *Stroszek*, we find a totally traditional method for handling time and duration. We never once find in Herzog's work anything similar to Resnais' "concurrence" shot (which we examined in detail when considering *Muriel*). There is no single shot (or group of shots) that can function simultaneously for each of several plausible narrative subsets in the film. There are no shots with double and triple meanings that emerge as the result of different associative relationships. Although Herzog relies heavily on jump-cut associations, the treatment of time is always conventional.

In Herzog's cinema there are not even any flashbacks or flashforwards. It is true that he occasionally tempers the time-space dimension of his films with hallucinatory images. But these serve the same purpose as similar images in the films of Resnais: they are intended to manipulate our memory, not the narrative proper. It is characteristic of our uncritical times, that Herzog's movies, with an average of only about ten such shots in each one, and without any of Resnais' devices for distorting time and space, have become known as hallucinogenic. In fact, most of Herzog's hallucinogenic shots are just beautiful, beautifully composed. It is Resnais' cinema, at its best, that truly defies the temporal order and lets us "travel."

Judging, then, from Herzog's cinema and that of others, Resnais' more purely visual associational achievements, we can now safely say, were the most "passed on" aspects of his cinema rather than his temporal approach to the narrative of a film. (With the exception of Nic Roeg—*The Man Who Fell to Earth*–who, today, films Resnais narratives besides Resnais?) It is not, then, Resnais' most drastic innovation, his successful use of time-distortion techniques to widen out the way narrative can function in film, that has been widely imitated, but rather his abnormally high standard of editing a film. His complex editing system that seems so easy ("leopard-linking montage") has set new standards, even for Hollywood, where editing has notably improved in the 1970s since the 1960s. Further, Resnais can also be said to have helped—in a minor way—to set the tone on how to use actresses. That Alsatian wonderwoman, Delphine Seyrig, while being starred, was never used by Resnais like a plastic Marilyn Monroe. Resnais' prescient knowledge of how cinema most successfully must deal with star iconography, method acting, even sex appeal—in short, with the problem of using the actor well, is another part of Resnais' legacy. Far from thinking of his actors as tools, Resnais loves and respects them. "I have a great respect, a great love for the actor. He has a very difficult and delicate task and enormous demands are made on him."[13]

Yet, as contributions to the development of the cinema, these achievements are considerably less important than Resnais' refinement of the craft of associationism—whereby two shots are linked together in the spectator's mind merely by what they suggest to each other. (Two shots of men drinking wine can suggest alcoholism, whereas a shot-countershot of the two might not so much suggest alcoholism as that there are two men drinking together.) Resnais' associationism and how it is combined with open structured narrative is one of the miracles of the cinema. (Most associationism in the cinema has occurred in dream sequences and other closed structured narratives, most notably, the Expressionistic films of Fritz Lang.) The resulting combination of power and openness, memorability and exposition of existential behavior by dwelling upon it, particularly in *Hiroshima* and *Muriel*, was designed by Resnais as a subtler way to keep the fires of meaning burning than by the kind of use of primary correspondences that made Hollywood films accessible even to morons. A Resnais film does convey messages, but always through secondary correspondences, through the kind of secondary associations Baudelaire made famous in poetry. Resnais' films thus deliver messages even while appearing to be innocent of them. Resnais' number one achievement is his having raised the craft of metonymy to the level of high art. In so doing, he invented a new variation of narrative form that we could persuasively call open-structured manipulation.

In *Hiroshima,* Resnais had already shown how to discard a narrative securely anchored to image and use instead a non-linear narrative based on incidental and occasional integration of iconic images with an emphatically recited narrative: that very *operatic* style that Resnais always talks about, employing, at the same time, a fearlessly honest presentation that is almost documentary on the subject of how little causality there is actually to be found in our lives. As *Hiroshima* was about the impossibility of documenting the effect of the atomic bomb, so Werner Herzog's *Stroszek* is about the impossibility of documenting what exactly immigration to the United States means. (It means different things for different people: some fail, some succeed.) But the film that is parent to the *Stroszek* style seems to me to be *Hiroshima,* where we have already found that a good nonlinear narrative *can* be made to reach the average audience. In *Hiroshima* the actress and the architect were not one character in the mind of its screenwriter, Duras, but were two different causalities. Resnais commingled them, and proved that the cinema can go much further than the point at which even the new German cinema of associationism has arrived. How? New German cinema seems to have stuck to a more careful, conservative use of association that mainly represents the main characters' imaginings than to have points of view of all the characters copresent and functioning to make up a non-linear narrative. It uses associationism to produce "intellectual montage"; Resnais used it to create a higher order of association: "overtonal montage." The man who invented these categories, Sergei Eisenstein, considered the latter far more daring.

Throughout his seven open-structured feature films, Resnais showed us, furthermore, a way to deal with the increasing inauthenticity of the time we live in, i. e., through trying to free us from propaganda by separating authorship from meaning, as Bob Dylan would have said, if he had dared, through metonymy. (Why else does "Diego" in *Le Guerre Est Finie* try to hide his true name, even from himself?) The form Resnais used to accomplish this, obviously, could not have adopted Hollywood shooting and cutting; for that yields a closed system that is too code-susceptible. The form (associationism) he used instead and the way he constructed narrative with this approach constitute Resnais' best and brightest contribution not only to film but also to the larger, on-going, lately somewhat faltering tradition of Western humanism. One can trace direct lines from Resnais, in this respect, to many contemporary filmmakers in particular, to one of the most narratologically experimental members of the New German Cinema, Wim Wenders, a thirty-two year old Dusseldorfer who has continued to deal with the same kind of inauthenticity of perception that plagues our society in all of his recent films.

Wim Wenders and his writer colleague Peter Handke's preoccupations, as seen, for example, in Handke's novel, and Wender's 1972 film of it, *The Goalie's Fear of the Penalty Kick,* are Resnais-like preoccupations in narrative filmmaking and at the same time, aesthetic responses to the grass-roots demands of the *Zeitgeist.*

Films such as *Hiroshima* and *Muriel,* and Wender's *The Goalie's Fear of the Penalty Kick,* and *Alice in the Cities* operate as concrete statements about inauthenticity in life, without forcing a particular point of view on the viewer, since the films are all open structured. They depict a particularly urban, middle-class, Western World, "life-as-it-is," as "changeable, as flexible, as threatened."[14] This is particularly true of Wender's *The American Friend,* which shows our landscape twenty years after Resnais' *Hiroshima* showed it pockmarked with memory, even more discombobulated.

The same can be said of Werner Herzog's *Stroszek,* even though it purports to be more metaphysical, because it uses Resnais-like associationism superbly to show how three people in Berlin and then in Wisconsin escape one treadmill only to find another. (Escape is thus inauthentic.) The themes of these new German films are modernist—they concern how to reconcile technology with feeling within time flow, what do we change, what can we not change as time passes on in a society which has committed itself to momentum at all costs? These are no longer clean-cut stories of alienation of the kind that were so existentially popular in the late 1950s and early 1960s. These are the types of films Resnais has been producing all along.

One can cite generational differences between Resnais and the new German cinema, but these mostly deal with film dialogue and pet themes not with the structure of the narrative. Thus Resnais and the new German cinema are similar in their structural route towards authenticity. One should recall that Resnais never used stories of lost adults in inauthentic environments as "facts of life" which are irreversible, given the tiny individual and the big megalopolis and Chinese hugeness. When this same theme (the landscape of Hiroshima and Nevers recurs as the city landscapes of Wender's *Alice in the Cities*), one sees that Wenders has fought for a modicum of authenticity even while spinning a fictive narrative.

One could argue that the new German cinema faces life squarely and has an even more pessimistic outlook than Resnais, but its very uncompromisingness—just as was so in the case of the Resnais film—indirectly produces a kind of guarded optimism.

What Resnais thus seems to have helped accomplish is preventing cinema from going down a blind alley—such as the one Abstract Expressionism went down in the 1950s. Coming into cinema in 1955, he foresaw how it could be both breathtaking and concrete, and, leaving his characters iconic and concrete, he chose to make his images breathtaking. Resnais should be proud of this achievement. It is a great legacy, to have combined such an unlikely pair of words as "breathtakingly" and "concrete."

Resnais' Lasting Reputation

What I have called the third fashion of legacy formation is clearly shown in the New German cinema's continuation of Resnais' pursuit (but for other historical reasons) of newer ways of narrative elucidation. It is Resnais' approach to irony and not Godard's, with its passionate predictions of whispered voice-overs, that has been swallowed up by the new German cinema movement. This is especially evident in the associative cinema of Werner Herzog and Wim Wenders, for in the socially oriented cinema of comment desired by the new German filmmakers, the form of the film must be neutral and unbiased (an obvious reaction against Hitler!) so as to allow the audience to examine society via an uncoded film.

Perhaps what I have said in praise of Resnais' approach will seem to the reader as some kind of harrowing assumption. Yet, there it stands in his films. As Joseph Losey said, "I'm *sure* I understood *Muriel* perfectly" (my emphasis). Are Resnais' films not obvious? Will Resnais' reputation have to be fought out in print? I hope not. But, perhaps due to a lack of any serious book on the narrative in film since 1959, Resnais will need some American champion to introduce him in print to the mass audience.

Resnais' reputation will not fade, I believe, for one important reason. He never overspecialized in one genre. He remained a generalist of the arts. Such men are valuable. Their concerns are large; their insights, broad. Such filmmakers survive those who are too narrow, for no one gives a damn about cinematic specificity, cinema as the seventh art, any more. There are, we know, many filmmakers whos legacies interest no one, and they are dropped, abandoned, like Sidney Franklin's, they are ignored and become "lost legacies," simply because their creators were *only* filmmakers.

But, for the most part, some directors fail to leave a legacy because they are too singular, too un-mass oriented. (This, of course, is a media question, strictly a function of the size of the audience; a director in Switzerland only has to please one-fiftieth of the number of people to be an absolute success in Switzerland, as in the United States; perhaps this is the secret of success of the Swiss filmmaker Alain Tanner.) In short, the United States will probably leave a legacy that will interest people. The label of oversingularity applies rather to filmmakers like Jean-Marie Straub (don't be ashamed if you've never heard of him) and Eric Rohmer. It applies as well to Resnais' ex-partner, Alain Robbe-Grillet, whose films have not survived, because they were too singular, too narrow, too experimentally remote from the flow of progress of the film as measured by time and determined by the world.

Resnais' films on the other hand, seem to be destined to last. The reason is that the public wants to keep them available—"on the shelf," in the manner of classic novels, and because the public likes and will always like genuine avant garde films that accurately predicted developments in life style and behavior. It makes one feel happy to be associated with such prophetic films for they prove that humanism of progress we so often doubt, a humanism that shows us someone besides ourselves has cared to struggle with the problems we perceived that the future would bring. In this way, Resnais' collected work of seven major films has the same value to us as Marshall McLuhan's *The Medium Is the Message.* In Resnais' case, his films informed us of progress in cinema, which we selfishly interpreted as our progress, towards thinking accurately in visual, non-linear terms. While watching a Resnais film, we can congratulate ourselves on how far *we* have come towards perfectly receiving a communication from the motion picture screen.

Notes and References

Preface

1. Alain Resnais, interviewed by Sylvain Roumette, *Clarté* No. 33 (February 1961) as quoted by Roy Armes, *The Cinema of Alain Resnais,* p. 27.
2. Ulrich Kurowski, *Film Lexicon,* 2nd ed., entry under "Neue Sachlichkeit" (Goldmann Sachbücher, Carl Hanser Verlag, Munich, 1973) p. 104. My translation.

Chapter One

1. Alain Resnais, interviewed by Jean Carta and Michel Mesnil, *Esprit,* No. 6 (June 1960) as quoted by Roy Armes, *The Cinema of Alain Resnais,* p. 17.
2. Resnais, after critics described *Hiroshima* in terms of its *oubli* or forgotten memories, and began to find it a recurrent theme, repeatedly stressed that it was imagination and not the fetish of memory that characterized his films.
3. Georges Hilleret, as quoted by Gaston Bounoure, *Alain Resnais.* p. 187. My translation.
4. Resnais has always loved authors; so his inclination to document their achievements goes a bit beyond being just an art groupie. By 1948, Resnais had evolved beyond this homage stage.
5. Jorge Semprun, in the introduction to *Reperages* (Paris, Editions du Chêne, 1974).
6. *Ibid.*
7. Alain Resnais in *Filmkritik*, Heft 10, (1965), pp. 510-511, as quoted by Wolfgang Gersch in *Film bei Brecht,* p. 307.
8. Jean-Paul Belmondo, *20 Films et 30 Ans,* (Union generale d'editions, Paris: 1963) p. 35.
9. François Truffaut, interviewed February 25, 1974, by Peter Michel Ladiges in *François Truffaut, Reihe Film 1,* (Munich: Carl Hanser Verlag, 1975) pp. 39–49.
10. Resnais has repeatedly, in his earlier interviews, denied the impor-

tance of whether he is an *auteur* or a *metteur en scene*. He prefers to be considered the *realisateur*.

11. Resnais' metonymy and modesty went to their extreme around the time of the making of *Muriel*. In the credits to this film, he calls himself the *realisateur* and not the *metteur en scene* which makes it seem as if he were the producer of the film and not its director at all.

12. Alain Resnais interviewed by Max Egly, *Image et Son*, No. 128, (February 1960), as quoted in Armes, p. 7. Resnais could have meant this literally or metaphorically.

13. Alain Resnais, *Les Nouvelles Littéraires*, No. 2571 (February 10–17, 1977), p. 11

14. Julia Rowe, "*Hiroshima mon amour*," unpublished paper, Harvard University (1976), p. 2. In the possession of the author.

15. See Jean-Luc Godard interview in *Cahiers du Cinéma* No. 194 (October 1967) p. 13–26, 66–70.

16. Alain Resnais, interviewed by Jean Carta and Michel Mesnil, *Esprit* No. 6 (June 1960) as quoted by Armes, p. 28.

17. Alain Resnais, interviewed by Max Egly, as quoted in Armes, p. 23.

18. See Alain Resnais, interviewed in *Cahiers du Cinéma* No. 123 (September 1961) pp. 1–18.

19. Danièle Delorme, quoted in Bounoure, pp. 190–191.

20. Alain Resnais, quoted in Armes, pp. 13–14.

21. This is why this book stresses that the New Wave and the Algerian War be considered as concurrent events, and not as separate situations.

22. Alain Resnais, interviewed by Eugene Archer, *The New York Times*, March 18, 1962.

23. François Truffaut, introduction to Andre Bazin, *Cinema de la Resistance et sur l'Occupation*.

24. Peter Cowie, *Antonioni, Bergman, Resnais*, p. 124.

25. Eric Rhode, *A History of Cinema* p. 424.

26. Rhode, pp. 425–426.

27. Danièle Delorme, quoted in Bounoure, pp. 190–191.

28. Alain Resnais, "Une Experience," *Ciné-Club* No. 3, (December 1948) (pamphlet). My translation.

29. John F. Kreidl, "Eric Rohmer," The Quincy *Patriot-Ledger*, (October 1, 1973).

30. François Truffaut interviewed by Ladiges, *François Truffant, Reihe Film I*, pp. 39–40.

31. *Ibid.*

32. *Ibid.*

33. François Truffaut, *Arts* (February 20, 1956) p. 7.

34. Alain Resnais, interviewed by Sylvain Roumette, *Clarté* No. 33 (February 1961) as quoted in Armes, p. 47.

35. Belmondo, p. 45.

36. Belmondo, p. 47.
37. Editions du Seuil publicity release for Jean Cayrol.
38. Dominic Benechetti, private communication to the author.
39. Many critics, to their credit, however, pick up on the notion that the film was saying that the heroes of Auschwitz were unknowable to the present generation.
40. Richard Wagner, *Das Rheingold,* Operbuch No. 5641, Phillip Reclam Jr., (Leipzig: Leipzig Verlag 1931), p. 62.
41. Jean-Luc Godard, "Chacun Son Tour," *Cahiers du Cinéma* No. 92 (February, 1959). The first theoretically incisive discussion of a Resnais film, i.e. *Chante du Styrène.*
42. Alain Resnais interviewed in *Tu n'as rien vu à Hiroshima,* Raymond Ravar, ed., Free University of Brussels, 1962.
43. Armes, p. 65.

Chapter Two

1. Alfred Cismaru, *Marguerite Duras* (New York: Twayne Publishers, 1971) p. 5.
2. See Alain Resnais, interview in *Cahiers du Cinéma* No. 123, pp. 1–18.
3. Alain Resnais interviewed by Richard Roud, *Sight and Sound* (Winter, 1959).
4. See published script of *Hiroshima* by Marguerite Duras, (New York: Grove Press 1961).
5. A. H. Weiler, *The New York Times* (May 17, 1960), reprinted in *The New York Times Film Reviews 1913–1970* (The N.Y. Times, New York, 1970) pp. 336–338.
6. The main evidence for this point is that the documentary-within-the-film is never made. We see film equipment and unmanned sets. Resnais is obviously referring here to the fact that the documentary of Hiroshima can never be made, as well as more directly showing that *Hiroshima* is not a documentary about Hiroshima. Another attempt to make a documentary about Hiroshima failed when the Japanese government in 1962 successfully opposed the filming of a script by Nedrick Young called "The Flowers of Hiroshima," based on a novel by Edita Morris.
7. See also Henri Bergson's PhD. dissertation, "Essais sur le donné et la memoire," 1889, The University of Paris, first translated into English as *Time and Free Will* (1913), available in paperback from Muirhead Library of Philosophy (1971).
8. Rhode, p. 534.
9. Rhode, p. 534.
10. Rudolf Arnheim, *Vusual Thinking* (University of CALIFORNIA Press, Berkeley, 1969), p. 89.
11. Gaston Bounoure, *Alain Resnais,* as quoted in translation by Peter Cowie in *Antonioni, Bergman, Resnais,* p. 128.

Chapter Three

1. Alain Robbe-Grillet, seminar on *Marienbad* and the new novel held June 28-July 8, 1975 at the Centre Culturel International de Cerisy-la-Salle, France. Reprinted in *Alain Robbe-Grillet: Colloque du Serisy* (Paris: Editions 10/18, 1976), p. 68.
2. See Alain Resnais interview in *Cahiers du Cinéma* No. 123 pp. 1–18.
3. Most of Robbe-Grillet's novels feature the destruction of the narrator.
4. Armes, *The Cinema of Alain Resnais*, p. 100.
5. Resnais, in particular, emphasized that he wanted to do just what Robbe-Grillet independently had come up with as a script. Resnais also said that of the four versions of *Marienbad* Robbe-Grillet offered him, he picked the most austere. Resnais was also too polite to mention that he did a little restructuring of the Robbe-Grillet script before it was published.
6. Alain Resnais interviewed by Sylvain Roumette, *Clarté* No. 33 (February 1961), as quoted by Armes, p. 27.
7. *loc. cit.*
8. Alain Resnais, *Les nouvelles littéraires*, No. 2571 (February 10-17, 1977), p. 11.
9. I once saw *Marienbad* screened where the projectionist left out reel two and the film became reel one followed by reel three. The result was a one-hour version of Marienbad which was quite satisfactory.
10. Henri Colpi, *Hiroshima's* editor, referred to the film's editing pattern as "leopard-linking" montage, "Editing *Hiroshima mon amour*," *Sight and Sound*, 29, No. 1 (Winter 1959-1960).
11. There is a real castle Marienbad, but it is not seen in the film. What we see is a composite made up of bits of two different castles, Amalienburg and Nymphenburg.
12. Armes, *The Cinema of Alain Resnais*, p. 110.
13. Rhode, *A History of the Cinema*, p. 537.
14. John Willet, "Expressionism," as quoted in Rhode, p. 181.
15. See Ian Cameron, *Film Quarterly* (Fall, 1962), pp. *1–15*, for discussion of *DE L'Avventura*.
16. Cowie, *Antonioni, Bergman, Resnais*, p. 40.
17. Resnais interviewed by Eugene Archer, *The New York Times*, (March 18, 1962).
18. Ward, *Resnais*, p. 57.
19. Resnais, interviewed by Gilbert Guez, *Cinemonde*, (March 14, 1961).
20. Resnais interviewed by Eugene Archer, *loc. cit.*
21. Armes, *The Cinema of Alain Resnais*, p. 115.

Chapter Four

1. Yvonne Baby, "Entretien avec Alain Resnais," *Le Monde* (August 29, 1961).
2. See Alain Resnais, interview in *Cahiers du Cinéma* No. 123, pp. 1–18.

3. Alain Robbe-Grillet, Interview with Brad Burke, *The New York Journal of the Arts,* No. 1 (1976). Interview conducted December 1975.
4. Noel Burch, "Ou est-ce que la Nouvelle Vague?" (translated into English) *Film Quarterly,* (Winter 1959–60) p. 16.
5. *Ibid.*
6. Anonymous, *International Film Guide,* Peter Cowie, ed. (*Tantivy London* 1963) p. 23.
7. *loc. cit.*
8. See François Truffaut interview, *Cahiers du Cinéma* No. 138, (December 1962).
9. Alain Resnais, *Lettres françaises* as quoted in *L'Avant-Scene,* translated and quoted by Armes, *The Cinema of Resnais,* p. 46.
10. Susan Sontag, "Resnais' *Muriel,*" *Film Quarterly* Vol XVII, No. 2, pp. 23, 27. Reprinted in *Against Interpretation* (New York: Delta, Dell Publishing) pp. 232, 241.
11. Alain Resnais, interviewed by Eugene Archer, *The New York Times,* (March 18, 1962).
12. *Ibid.*
13. Robert Benayoun, review of *Muriel, Positif,* (October, 1963).

Chapter Five

1. François Truffaut in *Films de ma vie,* "Muriel" (Paris: Flammarion, 1975), p. 263.
2. Alain Resnais, *L'Avant-Scene* No. 61–62 (special Resnais double issue) (July–September, 1966), p. 33.
3. Alain Resnais and Jean Cayrol, from the printed program notes to *Muriel.*
4. Wolfgang Kort, *AlfrediDoblin* (New York: Twayne Publishers, 1974), p. 103.
5. *Ibid.*
6. Döblin, a committed socialist, tried to show a collective and not an individual experience.
7. There are numerous connections between Resnais and Surrealism. French literary critic François Mizrachi for example considers *Muriel* an example of "negative Mallarmean surrealism."
8. Pierre Kast et al., "Les Malheurs du Muriel," *Cahiers du Cinéma* No. 149 (November 1963), p. 29.
9. Armes, *The Cinema of Alain Resnais,* p. 94.
10. Ward, *Resnais* p. 63.
11. Ward, *Resnais* pp. 63–64.
12. See Gustav Hartlaub, "Zur Einfuhrung," *Neur Schlichkeit,* (Städtische Kunsthalle, Mannheim, 1925).
13. Ward, *Resnais* p. 65.
14. Alain Resnais interview with Win Sharples, Jr., *Filmmaker's Newsletter* (December 1974), pp. 31–34.

15. If we do not require that the reader understand a book at the first reading, why should we require that a film be made so that the viewer totally grasps it at the first viewing?
16. Some of *Muriel* is epic, some is dramatic. On the whole, I think Brecht would accept it as a serious step towards his concept of an epic film.
17. There are four types of metonymy: the one Resnais prefers to use is that of substituting the effect for the cause.
18. I am indebted to Marie-Claire Ropars for inspiring this analysis.
19. Marie-Claire Ropars, from a handout at a seminar on *Muriel* at Harvard University, November 9, 1977.
20. Jean-Luc Godard in Richard Round, *Godard on Godart* (Doubleday, Garden City N.Y. 1968), p. 118.
21. Michel Vianey, *En Attendant Godard,* (B. Grasset, Paris, 1967) p. 118.
22. Jacques Rivetter in "Les Malheurs du Muriel" seminar, *Cahiers du Cinéma* No. 149 (Nov, 1963), p. 27.
23. *loc. cit.*
24. Susan Sontag, "Resnais' *Muriel*" *Film Quarterly* Vol. XVII, No. 2 (*Winter* 1963–1964), p. 23. See also pp. 24–27.
25. From the published script of *Muriel* by Jean Cayrol, (Walter-Verlag, Olten, Germany, 1965). p. 108. My translation.

Chapter Six

1. Marie Claire Ropars, from a handout at a seminar on *Muriel* at Harvard University, November 9, 1977.
2. Cayrol, *Muriel,* p. 36. My translation.
3. Chaim Calev, "Descriptive Comments on *Providence,*" *1000 Eyes* (March 1977), p.3.
4. Jean-Jacques Servan-Schreiber, *Lieutenant in Algeria,* (New York: Alfred Knopf, 1957), pp. 199–200.
5. Pierre Kast, "Les Malheurs du *Muriel,*" *Cahiers du Cinéma* No. 149 (November 1963), p. 20.
6. Daniel Yakir, interview with Alain Resnais, *1000 Eyes* (March 1977), pp. 3-4.
7. The new German cinema, with its social rather than political or art-for-art's-sake interest, excels at precisely this kind of cinema. The successors to the heritage of *Muriel* should be looked for among the young BRD directors.
8. Franco Solinas, Gillo Pontecorvo's *The Battle of Algiers: The Complete Scenario* (New York: Scribner's Sons, 1973), p. 84.
9. Conversation with the author.
10. Alain Resnais as quoted in Wolfgang Gersch, *Film bei Brecht* (Carl Hanser Verlag, Munich, 1976), p. 307. My translation.
11. Bertolt Brecht Archives, *Mappe* 331, p. 128.

12. Alain Resnais, *L'Avant-Scene* Nos. 61-62 (special Resnais double issue) (July-September 1966), p. 46.
13. Marsha Kinder, *Close Up* (New York; Harcourt Brace Jovanovich) p. 336.
14. Robert Benayoun, review of *Muriel, Positif* No. 56 (November 1963), p. 4.
15. Yakir *1000 Eyes*, p. 3.
16. *Ibid.*
17. Bosley Crowther, in the *New York Times*, October 31, 1963 in *The New York Times Film Reviews* (New York, N.Y. Times, 1970), pp. 373–374.
18. *Ibid.*

Chapter Seven

1. Alain Resnais interviewed by Win Sharples, Jr., *Filmmaker's Newsletter* (December 1974), p. 34.
2. Susan Sontag, "Resnais' *Muriel*," *Film Quarterly*, Vol. XVII No. 2 pp. 23-27.
3. Resnais, interviewed by Sharples, p. 34.
4. *loc. cit.*, p. 33.
5. *loc. cit.*, p. 31.
6. *loc. cit.*, p. 31.
7. Bosley Crowther, *The New York Times*, September 2, 1966.
8. Joseph Losey, "Speak, Think, Stand Up," *Film Culture* No. 50-51 (Fall and Winter, 1970), p. 58.
9. Leo Braudy, *Film in a Frame* (Doubleday, Garden City, 1977), p. 94.
10. See François Truffaut interviewed in *Cahiers du Cinéma* No. 138 (December, 1962), p. 41–59.
11. Jacques Rivette, "Les Malheurs du *Muriel*," *Cahiers du Cinéma* No. 149 (Nov., 1963), p. 27.
12. Alain Resnais interviewed by Sharples, *op. cit.*, p. 33.
13. See Jean Luc Godard interview, *Cahiers du Cinéma* No. 138, (December, 1962).
14. Armes, *The Cinema of Alain Resnais*, p. 134.
15. Michel Caen, *La Guerre Est Finie* reviewed, *Cahiers du Cinéma* No. 182 (October 1966), pp. 75–76.
16. Alain Resnais interview in *Positif* (October 1966), p. 33.
17. Annie Goldmann, *Cinema et societe moderne*, (Editions Anthropos, Paris, 1971), p. 217.
18. Ward, *Resnais*, p. 95.
19. *Ibid.*
20. See Screenplay to *Masculine-Feminine* by Jean-Luc Godard (New York: Grove Press, 1966). Godard states this in voice-over narration.
21. Michel Caen, review of *La Guerre Est Finie, Caheirs du Cinéma* No. 182 (October 1966), p. 75–76.

22. Interview with Jorge Semprun by Jean-Louis Pays, *Positif,* No. 79 (October 1966), p. 45.
23. *Ibid.*, p. 46.
24. *Ibid.*, p. 41.
25. *Ibid.*, p. 49.
26. *Ibid.*, p. 49.
27. Ward, *Resnais*, p. 109.
28. Semprun, *Positif, op. cit.*, p. 50.
29. *Ibid.*, p. 30.
30. *Ibid.*
31. Bosley Crowther, *The New York Times* (September 2, 1966).

Chapter Eight

1. See Jacques Sternberg, screenplay for *Je T'Aime, Je T'Aime*, published in French in *L'Avant-Scene* No. 91 (April, 1969).
2. Sontag, "Resnais, Muriel," *Film Quarterly*, pp. 23–27.
3. Jean-Luc Godard, quoted in translation by James Monaco, *The New Wave* (Oxford U.P. NYC, 1976), pp. 182–183.
4. A.D. Fokker, *Time and Space, Weight, and Inertia*, (Pergamon Press, Oxford, 1965), pp. xii–xiii.
5. Roger Greenspun, *The New York Times* (September 15, 1970).

Chapter Nine

1. Alain Resnais, post card sent to Jorge Semprun, quoted in "De Lovecraft a *Stavisky*." *Le Stavisky D'Alain Resnais* (Gallimard, Paris, 1974), p. 10.
2. Frederic Vitoux, *Positif* No. 161 (September 1974), p. 66
3. Alain Resnais, quoted in Bounoure, p. 187.
4. Alain Resnais, quoted in Armes, *The Cinema of Alain Resnais*, p. 23
5. Alain Resnais, interviewed by Win Sharples, Jr., *Filmmakers' Newsletter* (December 1974), p. 33.
6. Alain Resnais, interviewed by Max Egly, *Imageet Son* No. 128 (Feb. 1960), as quoted in Armes, p. 23.
7. *loc. cit.*
8. *loc. cit.*
9. Francis Lacassin, "Dick Tracy Meets Muriel," *Sight and Sound* (Spring 1967), p. 212.
10. *Ibid.*, p. 213.
11. *Ibid.*, p. 214.
12. *Ibid.*, p. 213.
13. Jim Steranko in conversation with the author.
14. Michelangelo Antonioni in conversation with the author.

Chapter Ten

1. François Truffaut, "Une certain tendence du cinéma français," *Cahiers du Cinéma* No. 31 (January, 1954), p. *15–29*.

2. Alain Resnais, interviewed by Daniel Yakir, *1000 Eyes*, pp. 3–4.
3. Unsigned review of *Providence* in *Continental* (November 1976), pp. 8–9.
4. *loc. cit.*
5. Marsha Kinder, "The Art of Dreaming in *Three Women* and *Providence:* Structures of the Self," *Film Quarterly* (Fall 1977). p. 11.
6. Alain Resnais, Interviewed by Daniel Yakir, *1000 Eyes*, pp. 3–4.
7. Bertolt Brecht, quoted by Wolfgang Gersch, *Film bei Brecht*, p. 328.
8. Claude Ollier, "Dr. Jerry and Mr. Hyde," *Cahiers du Cinéma* No. 155 (May, 1964), p. 40. It would be interesting to ask whether either Ollier or Resnais had ever read Bergson's book on laughter, *Rire* (1900).
9. *Ibid.*
10. *Ibid.*
11. Alain Resnais interviewed by Marc Terasse, *Les nouvelles littéraires* No. 2571, (February 10-17, 1977), p. 11.
12. Molly Haskell, "Mental Mayhem at This Year's Marienbad," *The Village Voice* (February 1977), p. 45.
13. Elizabeth Bowen, Introduction to *Katherine Mansfield: Stories* (New York: Vintage, 1956), p. xi.
14. Michelangelo Antonioni, in a conversation with the author.

Chapter Eleven

1. Eric Rohmer, quoted by Melton S. Davis, "Rohmer's Formula: Boy Talks with Girl, Boy Argues with Girl, Boy Says. . ." *The New York Times Magazine* November 21, 1971.
2. It has been suggested by several film critics that Truffaut's *La Peau Douce* has borrowed from *Muriel*. These borrowings are thematic, however, and not structural.
3. Resnais, in articles and essays by critics during the time of the New Wave was highly praised, but Truffaut, when interviewed in *Cahiers du Cinéma* No. 138, said that Resnais should have alerted people to how difficult it was to make successfully a Resnais film.
4. *Ibid.*
5. Resnais to Marc Terrasse, *Les nouvelles littéraires* No. 257 (February 10-17, 1977), p. 11.
6. The seminar on "Les Malheurs du Muriel" in *Cahiers* suggested among other things that Resnais' fate was that he was too French, too singular; for he worked in opposition to the trend of being part of a vast national cinema as in the U.S.A. and the U.S.S.R. This singularity, however, somewhat mysteriously made Resnais a part of a "cinema of pessimism," of retreat, to use Jacques Rivette's words. Somehow, Resnais' role as head of a movement revising narrative in cinema was forgotten in a rather vanglorious attempt to locate Resnais socioculturally.
7. Hilton Kramer, in the Preface to *The Age of the Avantegarde: 1956-1972* (New York: Farrar, Straus and Giroux, the Noonday Press, 1972).

8. Alain Resnais in an interview with Daniel Yakir, *1000 Eyes*, (March 1977), p. iii.

9. Andres Sarris, *The Village Voice* (August 1, 1977), p. 88.

10. Thomas Elsaesser, "Editorial: The Cinema of Irony," *Monogram* No. 5 (1971), p. 1.

11. Sarris, *op. cit.*, p. 37.

12. Elsaesser, *op. cit.*, p. 1.

13. Alain Resnais, interview with Marc Terrasse, *Les nouvelles littéraires* No. 2571 (February 10-17, 1977), p. 11.

14. Terry Fox, "Wenders Crosses The Border," *The Village Voice* (October 3, 1977), p. 43.

Selected Bibliography

Primary Sources

Interviews with Alain Resnais

The following interviews are divided into those dealing with general topics and those dealing with specific films. The latter are included under the title of the film under discussion.

BERETTA, VINICIO. "Le due anime di Alain Resnais." *Settimo Giorno* XIV, No. 37, (September 12, 1961). About the schizoid quality in Resnais' cinema.

BURCH, NOEL. "A Conversation with Alain Resnais." *Film Quarterly* (Spring 1960). Resnais talks about his last four short films.

CARTA, JEAN AND MICHEL MESNIL, *Esprit* No. 6 (June 1960). Resnais says he is unconcerned who the author of a film really is.

EGLY, MAX. *Image et Son* No. 128 (February 1960). Resnais talks about his predilection for comics. "The rules of the shooting script and of editing are the same in comics as in the cinema." An indispensible interview for the serious student of Resnais.

FILM KRITIK (unsigned) Issue 10 (1964). Resnais talks about why he thinks Brechtian devices should be put into a film.

GRAHAM, PETER. *Granta* (Cambridge University) (December 1961). Resnais discusses acting in his films. "I rely on instinctive acting although not as much as the followers of the Method."

HILLERET, GEORGES. *Sept Jours* (August 11, 1960). On Resnais' early life and film career.

JEUNE CINEMA 16 (unsigned) (June–July 1966). Resnais talks about censorship.

PHILLIPE, ANNE. *Les Lettres françaises,* March 12–18, 1959). Resnais describes the first feature film he made, Ouverte pour cause d'Inventaire (1946), which has been lost. He says it was shot in "camera-stylo style," as a sort of diary with Daniele Delorme searching for an old raincoat.

PINGAUD, BERNARD. *L'Arc* No. 31 (1967). Interviews with Resnais' collaborators: Cayrol on scripting *Muriel;* Semprun on scripting *La Guerre Est Fini;* deTowarnicki on scripting "The Adventures of Harry Dickson"; Sternberg on scripting *Je T'Aime, Je T'Aime*; and with Baudrot on being Resnais' continuity girl.

ROUMETTE, SYLVAIN. *Clarté* No. 33 (February 1961). A major, indispensible interview. Covers most of the significant comments Resnais made about why he is not an "author" but is only, literally, a "director." Resnais also stresses the fragmentation of modern life and how his films replicate this.

TRUFFAUT, FRANÇOIS. *Arts* (February 20, 1956). Resnais admits how much he is indebted to the documentary style of Italian filmmaker Luciano Emmer.

UYTTERHOEVEN, PIERRE. *Image et Son* No. 148 (February 1962). Resnais talks about why he gave up on "A suivre, a n'en plus finir," the film he abandoned in favor of *Muriel.*

LE CHANT DU STRYENÉ

GRAHAM, PETER. *Varsity,* Cambridge University (May 19, 1962). Resnais discusses *Le Chant du Styrené* and says it is "far less an industrial documentary than a synthesis of verbal abstraction and lyricism.

GUERNICA

PREMIER PLAN, unsigned (1956). Resnais discusses his short film, *Guernica,* and talks about man's pleasure in destruction, and of making experiments on human material.

LA GUERRE EST FINIE

BABY, YVONNE. *Le Monde* (May 11, 1966).

CINEMA 66, unsigned No. 106 (May 1966).

CINEMA 66, unsigned No. 109 (September–October 1966).

GAUTHIER, GUY. *Image et Son* No. 196 (July 1966).

MABEN, ADRIAN. *Films & Filming* (October 1966).

STAFF OF *POSITIF* (October 1966). An important interview as the Marxist critics of *Positif* are enthusiastic about *La Guerre Est Fini* as a political film and do not find it too aestheticized.

HIROSHIMA MON AMOUR

DELAHAYE, MICHEL. *Cinema 59* No. 58 (July 1959). Resnais describes how, for him, a script gives the basic algebraic concept of the film he is making.

LES LETTRES FRANÇAIS, unsigned (May 14–20, 1959). "*Hiroshima mon amour*, film scandaleux?"

QUIGLEY, ISOBEL. *The Spectator* (January 15, 1960). Resnais tells that the woman's cry, "Oh how I was young once," in *Hiroshima* represents a "longing for the state of innocence that regards love as, if not eternal, at least eternally important."

RAVAR, RAYMOND. "*Tu n'as rien vu à Hiroshima.*" Free University of Brussels. 1962. An interview-critique published as a pamphlet.

LAST YEAR AT MARIENBAD

ARCHER, EUGENE. *The New York Times* (March 18, 1962). On *Marienbad* and Resnais' awareness of the Algerian war.

BABY, YVONNE. *Le Monde* (August 29, 1961).

BRUNIUS, JACQUES. *Sight and Sound* (Winter 1961–62). Brunius says *Marienbad* is the greatest film ever made.

BAKER, PETER. *Films & Filming* (November 1961).

HOUSTON, PENELOPE. *Sight and Sound* (Winter 1961–62).

JUIN, HUBERT. "Introduction à la methode d'Alain Resnais et d'Alain Robbe-Grillet." *Les Lettres françaises* No. 888 (August 10–18, 1961).

LABARTHE, ANDRE AND JACQUES RIVETTE. *Cahiers du Cinema* No. 123 (September 1961). A major interview with Alain Resnais and Alain Robbe-Grillet but one which should now be read with some skepticism in light of Robbe-Grillet's recent revelations that he was really somewhat at cross-purposes with Resnais on the conception of *Marienbad.* (In English in *Films and Filming*, March 1962)

STANBROOK, ALAN. *Isis,* Oxford University (May 16, 1962). Resnais says that the shot of "A" looking at the photos is "not a real image but an evocative one, implying the existence of multiple realities."

MURIEL

BENAYOUN, ROBERT. *Positif* 50–52 (Marach 1963)

PROVIDENCE

TERRASSE, MARC. *Les nouvelles litterares* No. 2571 (February 10–17, 1977). Resnais says he is not yet clear about what the film means.

YAKIR, DANIEL. *1,000 Eyes Magazine* (March 1977).

STAVISKY

SHARPLES, JR., WIN. *Filmmaker's Newsletter*, (December 1974). Important interview on *Stavisky,* on Resnais' career, his love of associationism and his borrowing from the comics.

TOUTE LA MEMOIRE DU MONDE

BABY, YVONNE. *Les lettres françaises* No. 118 (April 1957).

VAN GOGH

CINE-CLUB No. 3 (December 1948). "Une Experience." Resnais describes his tactic in filming *Van Gogh.* This interview is as close as Resnais has ever come to writing an essay on the formal strategy behind his cinema.

Secondary Sources

Books

ARMES, ROY. *The Cinema of Alain Resnais.* London: A. Zwemmer Ltd. and New York: A.S. Barnes & Co., 1968. An important and useful analysis of Resnais' art.

BOURNOURE, GASTON. *Alain Resnais.* Paris: Edition Seghers, 1962.

SEMPRUN, JORGE. *Reperages: Photographies de Alain Resnais.* Paris: Editions du Chene, 1974. Semprun, a long-time associate of Resnais, sheds light on Resnais' methods in this discussion of the still photos that Resnais takes to research locations.

WARD, JOHN. *Alain Resnais, or the Cinema of Time.* Garden City, New York: Doubleday & Co., 1968. This is a Bergsonian "reading" of Resnais' cinema as a whole, and each of his films through *La Guerre Est Fini* and *Loin du Vietnam.* While interesting in its discussion of the problems of narrative and of the relation of Bergson to Resnais, its greatest value is Ward's reading of *La Guerre Est Fini.*

Part of a Book

COWIE, PETER. *Antonioni, Bergman, Resanis.* London: Tantivy Press; New York: A.S. Barnes & Co. 1963. Only thirty-five pages are devoted to Resnais and the book only covers the documentaries, and *Hiroshima* and *Marienbad.* It is useful for the comments on *Hiroshima* and *Marienbad* and for the numerious extracts (seventy-five) from other reviewers on Resnais' early work.

Magazine and Newspaper Articles

BORY, JEAN-LOUIS. "Muriel," *Arts et loisirs,* September 25–October 1. 1963. Bory praises the collaboration between Cayrol and Resnais in making *Muriel.* In the following issue of *Arts et loisirs,* Bory, in praising Rozier's Adieu Phillipine, calls it a "breath of fresh air" and in the best of the tradition of Truffaut-Godard-Resnais."

BURCH, NOEL. "Four Documentaries," *Film Quarterly,* Fall, 1959. Burch predicts great things for Resnais on the basis of *Night and Fog.*

CAEN, MICHEL. "La Guerre Est Fini," *Cahiers du Cinema* No. 183, October, 1966. Caen relates *La Guerre Est Fini* to Godard's *Masculine-Feminine*.

CAHIERS DU CINEMA. "Les Malheurs du *Muriel*," *Cahiers du Cinema* No. 149, Oct. 1963; pp. 20–34. A seminar on Resnais' *Muriel*. The most important socio-cultural discussion of Resnais' work in any language. Participants included Pierre Kast, Claude Ollier, Andre Labarthe, Jacques Rivette, Jean-Louis Comolli, François Weyergans, Jean Domarchi and Jean Fieschi. Resnais did not participate.

CASHIERS DU CINEMA. "Hiroshima, notre amours." *Cahiers du Cinema* No. 97 July 1959. Resnais' *Hiroshima* is discussed by Domarchi, Donoil-Valcroze, Godard, Kast, Rivette and Rohmer. The critiques are nouvelle and a bit vague.

CALEV, CHAIM. "Observations on *Providence*," *1000 Eyes* Magazine, March, 1977. The author claims Resnais' work has successively moved away from realism.

COLPI, HENRI. "Editing Hiroshima mon amour," *Sight and Sound*, Vol. 29, No. 1, Winter 1959–60. *Hiroshima*'s editor describes the editing strategy of this film.

———. "Musique d'Hiroshima," *Cahiers du Cinema* No. 103, January 1960. The music structure of *Hiroshima* elucidated by its editor.

CROWTHER, BOSLEY. "*Last Year at Marienbad*," *The New York Times* March 8, 1962, reprinted in *New York Times Film Reviews*, pp. 354–355. Crowther likes *Marienbad because* he can see it as a dream.

———. "*Muriel*," *The New York Times* Oct. 31, 1963, reprinted in *The New York Times Film Reviews* pp. 373–374. Crowther does not like *Muriel* because he finds it unnecessarily fragmented and he says the film is a waste of Resnais' talent.

———. "La Guerre Est Fini," *The New York Times* September 2, 1966, reprinted in *The New York Times Film Reviews*, p. 403. Crowther likes the film. He reviews it again in *The New York Times* Feb. 2, 1967.

DELAIN, MICHEL. "Resnais et le Limousin," *L'Express*, Edition International No. 1300, June 7–13, 1976. On the making of *Providence*. Resnais says he chooses actors because of the quality of their voices.

GODARD, JEAN-LUC. "Chacun son tour," *Cahiers du Cinema* No. 92, February, 1959. Godard praises Resnais' *Chant du Styrené* and comments on how Resnais uses montage to animate inanimate material in a singular way.

GREENSPUN, ROGER. "*Je T'Aime, Je T'Aime*," *The New York Times* September 15, 1970. Greenspun intelligently tells why he doesn't like the film.

HASKELL, MOLLY. "Mental Mayhem at This Year's *Marienbad*," *The Village Voice*, February 7, 1977, p. 45. Haskell, an ante-bellum romanticist, is most struck by how *Providence* strikes her sensibilities without her knowing why.

KAEL, PAULINE. "Fantasies of the Art House Audience," *Sight and Sound*, Winter 1961–62. Kael asks: "Who is selling virtue?" "Is *Hiroshima* an elaborate masochistic fantasy for intellectuals?" She answers "yes."

KINDER, MARSHA. "The Art of Dreaming in *Three Women* and *Providence:* Structures of the Self," *Film Quarterly*, Fall, 1977. This article largely attempts to impose a dream structural reading of *Providence*. It is very important as it corroborates how people fail to see Resnais for what he is and how they must invent a context with which to deal with the associative style.

LACASSIN, FRANCIS. "Dick Tracy Meets *Muriel*," *Sight and Sound*, Spring, 1967. An important article on why the comics are important to Resnais.

LACASSIN, FRANCIS, "Alain Resnais: The Quest for Harry Dickson," *Sight and Sound*, Summer, 1967. The definitive article on Resnais' strange interest in making a film about the fictitious detective, Harry Dickson.

NOGUERA, RUI. "Interview with Delphine Seyrig," *Sight and Sound*, Fall, 1969. A revealing interview on Resnais' work with film actors by his "leading lady."

SADOUL, GEORGES. "Un Grand film, un grand homme," *Les Lettres Françaises*, May 14–20, 1959. A leading French film historian praises *Hiroshima*.

SONTAG, SUSAN, "Resnais' *Muriel*," *Film Quarterly*, Vol. XVII, No. 2. A serious clear and logical critique on why *Muriel* tries to do too much at once and consequently fails. Sontag says *Muriel* does not, like great art, drive home its point to completion. The article, however, fails to deal with the associative style of the narrative and put this into the interpretation.

WEILER, A.H., "Hiroshima," *The New York Times*, May 17, 1960, reprinted in *The New York Times Film Reviews*, pp. 336–338. Weiler praises *Hiroshima*. An important review which helped Resnais establish a foothold in the U.S.A.

Filmography

Short Films

Resnais' earliest short films, *Fantomas* to *Malfray* are no longer available; they are listed below in chronological order with as much information as now exists.

FANTOMAS (1936) 8mm
Script: Alain Resnais

L' AVENTURE DE GUY (date unknown) 16mm

SCHEMA D'UNE IDENTIFICATION (1946) 16mm silent
Cast: Gerard Phillipe and François Chaumette

VISITE À LUCIEN COUTAUD (1947) 16mm

VISITE À FELIX LABISSE (1947) 16mm

VISITE À HANS HARTUNG (1947) 16mm

VISITE À CESAR DOMELA (1947) 16mm

PORTRAIT DE HENRI GOETZ (1947) 16mm

VISITE À MAX ERNST (1947) 16mm
(also known as JOUNREE NATURELLE)

LA BAGUE (1947) 16mm
Cast: Marcel Marceau

L' ALCOOL TUE (Les Films de la Roue, 1947) 16mm
Producers: Christiane and Paul Renty
Director: Alain Resnais under the pseudonym Alzin Rezarail
Script: Remo Forlani Roland Dubillard

LE LAIT NESTLÈ (L'Agence ABC, 1947) 16mm
Directors: Remo Forlani, Fernand Marzelle, Alain Resnais
Running time: one minute (This was a commercial for Nestlé)

CHATEAUX DE FRANCE (Cine-Gimm, 1948) 16mm color

VAN GOGH (1948) 16mm and 35 mm
Script: Robert Hessens, Gaston Diehl
Cinematography: Henri Ferrand
Running time: 20 minutes; an 18 minute version was distributed in the U.S.
U.S. premiere: January 1950

MALFRAY (1948) 16mm

GAUGUIN (Pantheon 1950) 35mm
Producer: Pierre Braunberger
Script: Gaston Diehl
Cinematography: Henri Ferraud
Music: Darius Milhaud
Running time: 11 minutes

GUERNICA (Pantheon, 1950) 35mm
Producer: Pierre Braunberger
Script: Robert Hesseus
Text: Paul Eluard
Cinematography: Henri Ferraud
Running Time: 12 minutes

LES STATUES MEURENT AUSSI (Presence Africaine/Tadie-Cinema, 1950-1953) 35mm
Directors: Alain Resnais, Chris Marker
Cinematography: Ghislain Cloquet
Running time: 30 minutes

NUIT ET BROUILLARD (Night and Fog) (Argos Films/Como Films, 1955) black and white and Eastmancolor
Cinematography: Ghislain Cloquet, Sacha Vierny
Editors: Enri Colpi, Jasmine Chasney
Music: Hanns Eisler
Commentary: Jean Cayrol
Running time: 31 minutes

TOUTE LA MÉMOIRE DU MONDE (Les Films de la Pleiade, 1956) 35mm, black and white

Script: Remo Forlani
Cinematography: Ghislain Cloquet
Music: Maurice Jarre
Music Director: Georges Delerue
Running time: 22 minutes

LE CHANT DU STYRÉNE (La Societé Pechiney, 1958) 35mm Dyaliscope (1:2:17 "CinemaScope") and Eastmancolor
Producer: Pierre Braunberger
Cinematography: Sacha Vierny
Editor: Alain Resnais
Music: Pierre Barbaud
Music Director: Georges Delarue
Commentary: Raymond Queneau
Running time: 19 minutes

LOIN DU VIETNAM (Slon, 1967) 35mm, black and white
Directors: Chris Marker, Alain Resnais, William Klein, Joris Ivens, Claude Lelouch, Jean-Luc Godard.
Resnais' segment features Bernard Fresson as actor
Running time: 120 minutes
New York premiere: June 14, 1968

Feature Films

OUVERTE POUR CAUSE D'INVENTAIRE (1946) 16mm
Cast: Danièle Delorme, Nadine Alari, Pierre Trabaud
All prints of this film are lost

HIROSHIMA MON AMOUR (1959) Argos Films/Como Films/Daiei Motion Pictures/Pathé Overseas
Producer: Samy Halfon
Screenplay: Marguerite Duras
Cinematography: Sacha Vierny (France), Michio Takahashi (Japan)
Set Design: Esaka, Mayo, Petri
Music: Giovanni Fusco, Georges Delerue
Editing: Henri Colpi, Jasmine Chasney, Anne Sarraute
Cast: Emmanuelle Riva (Elle), Eiji Okada (Lui), Bernard Fresson (L'Allemand), Stella Dassas (La Mère), Pierre Barbaud (Le Père).
Time: 91 minutes
New York premiere: January 7, 1960
16mm rental: Audio Brandon

LAST YEAR AT MARIENBAD (1961) Terra Film/Société Nouvelle des Films Comoron/Precitel/Como Films/Argos Films/Les Films Tamara/Cinetel/Silver Films/Cineriz
Producers: Pierre Courau and Raymond Froment
Screenplay: Alain Robbe-Grillet
Cinematography: Sacha Vierny
Camera: Phillipe Brun
Set Design: Jacques Saulnier
Music: Francis Seyrig
Editing: Henri Colpi, Jasmine Chasney
Cast: Delphine Seyrig (A), Giorgio Albertazzi (X), Sacha Pitoeff (M).
Time: 93 minutes
New York premiere: March 7, 1962
16 rental: Audio Brandon

MURIEL OR THE TIME OF A RETURN (1963) Argos Films/Alpha Productions/Eclair/Les Films de Pleiade/Dear Films
Producer: Anatole Dauman
Screenplay: Jean Cayrol
Cinematography: Sacha Vierny
Camera: Phillipe Brun
Set design: Jacques Saulnier
Music: Hans Werner Henze
Editing: Kenout Peltier and Eric Pluet
Cast: Delphine Seyrig (Helene), Jean-Pierre Kerien (Alphonse). Jean-Baptiste Thieree (Bernard), Nita Klein (Francoise), Laurence Badie (Claudie), Martine Vatel (Marie-Do).
Time: 115 minutes
New York premiere: Sept. 18, 1963
16mm rental: Contemporary/McGraw-Hill

LA GUERRE EST FINIE (1966) Sofracima/Europa Film
Producer: Alain Queffelean
Screenplay: Jorge Semprun
Cinematography: Sacha Vierny
Set design: Jacques Saulnier
Music: Giovanni Fusco
Editing: Eric Pluet
Cast: Yves Montand (Diego), Ingrid Thulin (Marianne), Genevieve Bujold (Nadine), Michel Piccoli (Customs Officer), Annie Farge (Agnes), Jean Bouise (Ramon), Gerard Lartigau (Student leader), Bernard Fresson (Sarlat)
Time: 122 minutes
New York premiere: Sept. 22, 1966
16mm rental: Audio Brandon

JE T'AIME, JE T'AIME (1968) Parc Film
Producer: Mag Bodard
Screenplay: Jacques Sternberg
Cinematography: Jean Boffety
Set design: Jacques Dugied
Sound: Antoine Nonfanti
Cast: Claude Rich (Claude Ridder), Olga Georges-Picot (Catrine), Anouk Ferjak (Wiana)
Time: 95 minutes
New York premiere: Sept. 14, 1970
16mm rental: New Yorker Films

STAVISKY (1974) Ariane Films/Cerito Films/Euro International
Producers: Alexandre Mnouchkine and Georges Dancigers
Screenplay: Jorge Semprun
Cinematography: Sacha Vierny
Camera: Phillipe Brun
Set Decoration: Jacques Saulnier
Music: Stephen Sondheim
Cast: Jean-Paul Belmondo (Stavisky), Annie Duperey (Arlette Stavisky), Charles Boyer (Baron Raoul), François Perier (Albert Borelli), Claude Rich (Inspector Bonny), Michael Lonsdale (Dr. Mezy), Silvia Badesco (Erna Wolfgang), Yves Peneau (Trotsky).
Time: 95 min.
New York premiere: New York Film Festival, Oct., 1974
16mm rental: Cinema 5, New York

PROVIDENCE (1977) Action Films/SFP Production
Producers: Kalaus Hellwig, Yves Gasser, Yves Peyrot
Screenplay: David Mercer
Cinematography: Ricardo Aronovitch (Eastmancolor-Panavision)
Set design: Jacques Saulnier
Music: Miklos Rosza
Editing: Albert Hurgenson
Cast: Sir John Gielgud (Clive Langham), Dirk Bogarde (Claude), David Warner (Kevin), Ellen Burstyn (Sonia), Elaine Stritch (Helen), Denis Lawson (Dave).
Time: 110 min
New York premiere
16mm rental (English language version): Cinema 5, New York

Appendix

Unrealized Projects

1. "Les Adventures d'Harry Dickson," script by Frederic de Towarnicki, 1951.
2. "Les Mauvais Coups," from Roger Vailland's novel, 1951.
3. "Pierrot Mon Ami," from Raymond Queneau's novel, 1951.
4. "Un Dimanche Tous ensemble," script by Remo Forlani, 1956.
5. "L'Ile Noire," script by Remo Forlani, 1957. This was an adventure story based on Tintin.
6. "La Tête contre les Murs," from Hervé Bazin's novel, 1957
7. "Vie de Louis Feuillade," In 1964 Resnais wrote an hommage-like introduction to a book on Feuillade. No script for this project existed.
8. "La Dermission," from Daniel Anselme's novel, 1960.
9. "A Suivre, a n'en plus finir," from Annie-Marie de Villaine's novel, scripted by her in 1960. Resnais filmed *Muriel* instead of this story about the Algerian War.
10. "Red Ryder," a project based on the American comic strip character, 1964.
11. "Deliverez Nous du Bien" (Deliver Us From Good), a project based on the life of the Marquis de Sade with the collaboration of Richard Seaver, 1970.
12. "The Inmates," a project devised with Stan Lee of Marvel Comics, 1971.
13. "Arkham" based on the world of H. P. Lovecraft. Work on this project was interrupted by the *Stavisky* project. Lack of funds may have been a problem. A few ideas from this project went into *Providence*.

Index